WEIGHT WATCHERS®
MEALS IN MINUTES
C·O·O·K·B·O·O·K

WEIGHT WATCHERS®
MEALS IN MINUTES
C·O·O·K·B·O·O·K

Photography by Gus Francisco

NAL BOOKS

NEW AMERICAN LIBRARY

A DIVISION OF PENGUIN BOOKS USA INC., NEW YORK
PUBLISHED IN CANADA BY
PENGUIN BOOKS CANADA LIMITED, MARKHAM, ONTARIO

*WEIGHT WATCHERS is a registered trademark of
Weight Watchers International, Inc.*

Copyright © 1989 by Weight Watchers International, Inc.

All rights reserved. For information address
New American Library.

Published simultaneously in Canada by
Penguin Books Canada Limited.

Designed by Julian Hamer

Food stylist: Nina Procaccini

Prop stylist: Linda Cheverton

Illustrations by Robbii Wesson

Nutrition analysis by Hill Nutrition Associates, Inc.

Weight Watchers is a registered trademark of
Weight Watchers International, Inc.

 NAL BOOKS TRADEMARK REG. U.S. PAT. OFF. AND FOREIGN COUNTRIES
REGISTERED TRADEMARK—MARCA REGISTRADA
HECHO EN FAIRFIELD, PA

SIGNET, SIGNET CLASSIC, MENTOR, ONYX, PLUME,
MERIDIAN and NAL BOOKS are published *in the United
States* by New American Library, a division of Penguin Books
USA, Inc., 1633 Broadway, New York, New York 10019, *in
Canada* by Penguin Books Canada Limited, 2801 John Street,
Markham, Ontario L3R 1B4.

LIBRARY OF CONGRESS CATALOGING-IN-PUBLICATION DATA
Weight Watchers meals in minutes cookbook / photography
     by Gus Francisco.
          p.   cm.
     ISBN 0-525-94021-9
          1. Reducing diets — Recipes.   I. Francisco, Gus.
II. Weight Watchers International.   III. Title: Meals
in minutes cookbook.
RM222.2.W3214   1989
641.5′635 — dc20   89-12718
                                                     CIP

First Printing, January, 1990
1 2 3 4 5
PRINTED IN THE UNITED STATES OF AMERICA

Acknowledgments

Super-fast and super-easy are great ways to do things when you're cooking. Just the opposite is true, however, when it comes to writing a cookbook. In fact, putting a cookbook together requires painstaking attention to detail, loads of patience, and many, many hours of hard work by a dedicated staff of professionals. We would like to thank our own staff for their patience and hard work, beginning with Eileen Pregosin, under whose leadership the Publications Management Department has produced another outstanding cookbook.

Thanks go to our talented chefs, Nina Procaccini, Susan Astre, Christy Foley-McHale, and Judi Rettmer. They developed and tested more than 300 recipes for this book, and also did the food styling for our beautiful photographs. We are also grateful to Jackie Hines for her assistance in the test kitchen.

We would like to extend our gratitude to the five individuals who comprise our editorial staff: Patricia Barnett, Isabel Fleisher, Anne Neiwirth, Elizabeth Resnick-Healy, and April Rozea. They handled the arduous task of researching, writing, editing, and proofreading the manuscript. And thanks, too, to Melonie Rothman for her fine secretarial skills.

And to Barbara Warmflash, many thanks for managing all of the additional areas so necessary to the publication of this book.

WEIGHT WATCHERS INTERNATIONAL

Contents

Introduction

You're up early to pack lunches and get the kids off to school...then you rush to get ready for work. There's no time for a leisurely breakfast. What to eat? It has to be quick, nutritious, and satisfying.

You're planning to go for a brisk walk after work...but first you have to take the kids to soccer practice and ballet lessons...and there's a PTA meeting at eight o'clock. You just don't have the time to fuss over supper. What to cook? It has to be tasty and easy to fix.

You've had a busy day at work...company's coming tonight and you still have a few errands to run. There's no way you can prepare a complicated and time-consuming dinner. What to serve? It has to be fast, festive, and utterly delicious.

Fast, delicious, satisfying, nutritious...and supportive of your weight-loss efforts. That's a tall order for any kind of recipe. Oh, how you'd love a collection of super-fast, super-easy recipes that would fit your busy life-style *and* help you achieve your weight-loss goals. Just wishful thinking? Not at all, because the cookbook you've been wishing for is here!

Weight Watchers Meals in Minutes Cookbook is brimming with fast, delicious, satisfying dishes you and your family will love. It contains over 300 recipes that can be prepared in 30 minutes or less, including 100 microwave recipes; so when you want a meal or a snack in a hurry, there's no need to look any further than the pages of this book for inspiration. And because the recipes are from Weight Watchers, you know that they are both nutritious and helpful to your weight-loss efforts.

What kinds of recipes can taste so good and be so easy to prepare? Just take a look at a few examples: entrées such as Mediterranean-Style Shrimp, Chicken and Mushrooms in Parmesan Cream, Veal Chops Italiana, and Pork Medallions with Cran-Orange Sauce. Lunch or brunch dishes like Western Eggs in Potato Shells and Scrambled Huevos Rancheros. Side dishes that include Sausage and Apple "Stuffing," Linguine with Vegetables, Broccoli and Walnut Sauté, Fruited Rice with Cinnamon, and much, much more.

Of course, we haven't forgotten about desserts. Just wait until you try them—you won't believe how scrumptious they are. Best of all, like every one of our recipes, these desserts were developed with your weight-loss efforts in mind, so you can go ahead and enjoy them. Mint-Chocolate Pudding, Peach and Almond Cream, Pineapple-Orange Cake, Oatmeal-Raisin Cookies, and Banana-Yogurt Orleans are but a few of our marvelous selections. Your sweet tooth never had it so good!

Besides offering scores of wonderful recipes, this cookbook shows you how to get out of the kitchen *fast*. That's because it's overflowing with ideas to help you speed shopping, cooking, and cleanup. You'll learn how to make your kitchen — and your life — more organized and efficient.

And when it comes to efficiency, nothing beats the microwave oven. That's why we have included 100 microwave recipes throughout the book, plus a special microwave section on page 14. This handy section is a fact-filled guide to making the most of your microwave, and it's packed with all the information you need for successful microwave cooking. It also includes more than a dozen "mini-recipes" for the most commonly prepared foods. If you own a microwave oven, you'll refer to this section time and time again for great microwave tips.

Super-fast, super-easy are the watchwords of life in the '90s. At Weight Watchers, we understand this — which is why none of the recipes in this book takes more than 30 minutes to prepare. We know you've got better things to do than to spend all your time in the kitchen.

We hope you enjoy the delicious recipes in this book, and we wish you much success in achieving your weight-loss goals.

The Express Lane

Time is one of our most precious commodities today. It seems we always have more and more things to do and less and less time in which to do them. And let's face it — not many of us want to spend a lot of time on cooking, cleanup, grocery shopping, meal planning, and other food-related chores. In this chapter, you'll find dozens of ideas to help you make these tasks faster, easier, and much more pleasant.

Shopping Shortcuts

Do you whisk into the supermarket each day to buy a few items, or do you stock up during one major weekly shopping trip? Frequent trips to the market, coupled with slow service and long lines at the checkout counter, can chip away at your valuable free time — time you would probably rather spend doing something you enjoy.

You can cut down on the amount of time you spend doing the grocery shopping if you plan all your meals in advance, make a shopping list, and shop only once a week. You may still have to stop off once during the week for perishable items, but all in all, you should spend less time at the supermarket.

Planning a week of meals isn't easy, but it's worth the effort and it eliminates last-minute confusion over what to prepare. Write down menu items for each day on a sheet of paper or in a weekly diary. If you need some inspiration, go through your favorite cookbooks or your own recipe collection and select dishes you might want to serve. Be sure to save these menus to use again another time.

In addition to planning meals ahead, you might want to attach a list of frequently used staples to your pantry or refrigerator door. As you begin to run low on an item, circle it on your list, and add new items when necessary.

To help speed your grocery shopping, organize your weekly shopping list by categories that correspond to the setup of the aisles at your favorite super-market. If you would rather not make a specific list, try writing a general list that is broken down into categories and quantities (for example: fruit—5 varieties; cheeses—2 hard, 1 soft; vegetables—3 fresh, 1 frozen). And if you're a coupon clipper, this is the time to sort through and organize your coupons, not when you're at the checkout counter.

Now, with list in hand, you're ready for your weekly trip to the supermarket. Once you're there, remember to purchase frozen foods last and ask the cashier to pack them together in one bag. This will keep them colder longer. If there is still room in the bag, add refrigerated items; the frozen foods will help keep them cold. Some people keep an insulated cooler in the trunk of the car for transporting frozen foods, particularly in hot weather.

To save time and energy when you return home, unpack all the groceries at the same time and arrange them on your counter. Then you'll only need to open the refrigerator and freezer doors once to put items away. (Be sure to put frozen items away first to avoid partial thawing of foods.)

When you put groceries away in your pantry, group similar items together so they will be easier to find when you need them. For example, keep canned fruits in one area, canned vegetables in another, baking needs in still another, and so on. If you're organized when putting things away, you'll save yourself a great deal of time when you need to find an ingredient. And if children are helping you put away the groceries, label the shelves with a general description of what goes there. A picture of the food will aid small children, who love to help when they can.

Meals in a Jiffy

If you're looking to cut the amount of time you spend preparing meals, begin by thinking about the types of meals you usually serve. A quick meal is usually a simple meal. If you do want to prepare a special dessert or a hearty, homemade soup, then the other components of the meal should be simple foods such as broiled chicken, a steamed vegetable, and a tossed salad with bottled dressing.

Before beginning to prepare a recipe, read it over carefully, get out all the ingredients, and do all the necessary preparation. When you're ready to begin, you'll have everything you need right at your fingertips. To help you keep track of ingredients, keep them to your right and as you use each item, move it to the left. This is especially helpful when baking, since it's easy to add an ingredient twice if you're not paying close attention. Also, try to plan preparation so the utensils can be reused without washing (for example, use measuring spoons to measure dry ingredients before liquid ones).

If you have time between steps in a recipe, use it to do other tasks, such as setting the table or packing a brown-bag lunch.

You can shorten midweek cooking time by using some extra weekend time for food preparation. Here's how. Let's say your family likes chicken or turkey. You can roast and serve the bird on the weekend, then freeze leftovers in individual containers for use in weekday meals or brown-bag lunches. Remember to label what you freeze with the date, contents, and quantity.

You'll save time in the long run if you prepare ingredients for several days' recipes at one time. Blanch, slice, or chop vegetables or shred cheese and then store these items in resealable plastic bags or plastic containers. Label each with the date, contents, and quantity.

Although it is usually a little more costly to purchase ingredients in the form called for in a recipe, it's a great timesaver. Shredded cheese, chicken cutlets, peeled and deveined shrimp, and salad-bar vegetables may be worth the higher price to you if your time is at a premium.

Clean as You Cook

You'll get out of the kitchen faster if you clean up as you cook, rather than waiting for a major KP operation at the end of the meal. Wipe up counter spills as they occur. Leave your dishwasher open so you can easily dispose of dirty utensils and cookware. Set cooled saucepans and skillets in a sink filled with soapy water to loosen food residues before washing and they will be easier to clean. Fill pots that contained cereal, egg, or milk with cold water rather than hot, and let them stand in the sink until you're ready to wash them. They'll come clean quickly.

To minimize cleanup, sift flour over a sheet of wax paper or a paper plate rather than a bowl. Line your counter with a sheet of aluminum foil to keep it clean while you cook.

Organizing Kitchen Clutter

Do you spend more time in the kitchen than you really need to? One reason may be poor organization. While the design of your kitchen may be far from ideal, there are things you can do to make your time there more efficient and pleasant.

If you're the lucky person with a large and spacious kitchen, you may find that you spend a good deal of time walking from appliance to work center and back again. Solve this predicament by keeping cookware, utensils, and small appliances close to where they are used. Keep the coffee pot near the sink, baking pans near the oven, saucepans and skillets near the range, microwavable cookware near the microwave, and rarely used appliances out of sight.

If your problem is a small kitchen, you will want to make the most of minimal storage space by being as inventive as possible. Set up shelves where space permits, and invest in a spice rack (be sure to hang it in a cool, dark place—not near the stove). Attach hooks to the back of cabinet doors for pot holders and dish towels. Purchase small kitchen appliances that can be suspended from the bottom of cabinets.

Try to avoid buying too many kitchen gadgets. A few basic pieces of equipment, such as high-quality knives, can do the job of several gadgets and take up much less space.

Convenience Equipment

The Blender

If you own a blender, use it to make a satisfying milkshake. Whenever ½ cup of skim milk is included in one of our Menu Planners, you may combine it in the blender with 1 cup of cold diet soda to make a frothy shake. Raspberry, chocolate, and black cherry are a few of the delicious flavors you might try. Or blend milk with chocolate syrup or a reduced-calorie spread.

Here are some more blender ideas:
- Use the blender to make graham cracker crumbs for dessert recipes.

■ For a real timesaver, measure right in the blender container; most are marked in cups and ounces.

■ When processing liquids, never fill the blender to the top; always start on low speed and gradually increase to the desired speed.

The Food Processor

When it comes to saving time, you just can't beat the food processor. This handy appliance can blend, chop, grate, shred, mix, slice, and make crumbs. Food processors are available in large-capacity models as well as in compact models that are great for smaller processing jobs, such as mincing garlic.

Here are some additional hints to help you get the most from your food processor:

■ Slice or chop vegetables in quantity to use in salads. Store these prepared vegetables in covered containers or plastic bags for use during the week.

■ Process dry foods before moist ones, even if the dry ingredients are needed last. You won't have to wash the work bowl as often.

■ Rinse the work bowl and blades immediately after use for easy cleanup.

■ If you accidentally overprocess a food, don't discard it—try to find another use for it. Fruits can be used in sauces; vegetables can be seasoned, cooked, and served as purees.

The Freezer

Your freezer can be a key to speedier meals if you prepare foods in advance and freeze them for later use. The following are some pointers for freezer use:

■ Wrap foods (such as meats) for the freezer in moisture- and vapor-resistant wrap that molds easily to the shape of the food, or in resealable plastic freezer bags, first removing as much air as possible.

■ When freezing soups or stews, fill the plastic containers close to the top to keep air out, but remember to leave room for the expansion that occurs as the liquid freezes. A layer of plastic wrap placed directly on the food surface will help prevent ice crystals from forming.

■ When freezing chops or patties, place a double sheet of wax paper between each one and they will separate more easily.

■ Freeze leftovers in serving-size portions; use the microwave for quick thawing and heating.

■ Keep the freezer temperature at 0°F or lower and check the temperature periodically with a refrigerator-freezer thermometer.

■ Use the microwave oven on the defrost setting to thaw frozen meats, fish, and poultry quickly, or allow enough time to thaw in the refrigerator. Never thaw food at room temperature—bacteria can multiply rapidly and cause spoilage.

- Label all packages with the date and contents.

Here are some more time-saving freezer tips:

- For a good breakfast in a hurry, prepare and freeze muffins, pancakes, or French toast in advance, then just pop them into the toaster-oven or microwave on busy mornings.
- Casseroles and stews containing meat, fish, or poultry with vegetables or pasta freeze well because they are usually coated with sauce. Avoid freezing mixtures that contain cooked potatoes, as they tend to lose their shape and texture.
- Cakes, cookies, fruit pies, and cobblers all freeze well, as do pastry and cookie doughs.
- Keep flour and coffee (beans, ground, instant, or freeze-dried) in the freezer. They will stay fresh for months.
- Freeze fresh herbs from your garden or from the supermarket when in season. Snip off the leaves, rinse well, blot dry with paper towels, and freeze in plastic freezer bags. When a recipe calls for fresh herbs, just break off the amount you need, add to your recipe, and return the rest to the freezer. Don't use frozen herbs as a garnish, though, since the freezing process will leave them looking wilted and less attractive.

The Food File

It's a good idea to familiarize yourself with the wealth of information in this section before you begin to cook. When you know exactly what to shop for, you will save time and avoid costly mistakes, such as buying the wrong ingredient. The tips on the best preparation and cooking methods to use, as well as important nutrition information, will also help you.

About Ingredients

- The weights of fruits and vegetables given in the recipes are the weights you should purchase; that is, they are the weights before peeling, cutting, or any other procedure has been done. For example, if a recipe calls for 1 pound of pears, cored, pared, and diced, you should purchase 1 pound of pears, then proceed according to recipe directions.

- Recipes that serve two can be doubled or tripled; however, be cautious with seasonings—they cannot automatically be doubled or tripled. Increase seasonings gradually to taste.

- Canned and frozen fruit and juice should not contain added sugars, although artificial sweetener is permitted. Canned fruit may be packed in its own juice or in another fruit juice, a juice blend, or water.

- We have used fresh vegetables in our recipes unless otherwise indicated. If you substitute frozen or canned vegetables, you will have to adjust the cooking times accordingly.

- The herbs used in these recipes are dried unless otherwise indicated. If you are substituting fresh herbs, use approximately four times the amount of dried (for example, 1 teaspoon chopped fresh parsley instead of ¼ teaspoon dried parsley leaves). If fresh herbs are indicated and you wish to substitute dried, use approximately ¼ the amount of fresh (for example, ¼ teaspoon dried basil instead of 1 teaspoon chopped fresh basil). If you are substituting ground (powdered) herbs for dried leaves, use approximately half the amount of dried (¼ teaspoon ground thyme instead of ½ teaspoon dried thyme leaves).

- If you are substituting fresh spices for ground, use approximately eight times the amount of ground (for example, 1 teaspoon minced pared gingerroot instead of ⅛ teaspoon ground ginger).

- The many varieties of vegetable oils have certain characteristics that make them appropriate for specific uses, but very often one can easily be substituted for another. If no particular type is specified, you can use safflower, sunflower, soybean, corn, cottonseed, or any combination of these. Since olive oil, Chinese sesame oil, walnut oil, and peanut oil have distinctive flavors, they have been specifically called for. There are two types of sesame oil: light and dark. The light oil is relatively flavorless and may be used as a substitute for any other vegetable oil. When sesame oil is specified, use the dark variety. This product, made from toasted sesame seed, has a rich amber color and a characteristic sesame flavor.

- If you store nut and seed oils (such as walnut, hazelnut, peanut, almond, and sesame) in the refrigerator after opening, they won't become rancid or develop odors. These oils are generally more expensive, too, so buy them in small quantities and store them properly once they are opened.

- Recipes calling for lettuce leaves assume the use of either iceberg or romaine; 4 lettuce leaves provide 1 Vegetable Exchange. If any other type of lettuce is used (for example, Boston or Bibb), 8 lettuce leaves provide 1 Vegetable Exchange.

- If a recipe calls for butter or whipped butter, use lightly salted butter unless otherwise specified.

- Some of our recipes make use of unusual ingredients such as wild mushrooms, sun-dried tomatoes, or radicchio (red chicory). Don't be afraid to explore and experiment with foods like these—they'll add exciting new flavors to your cooking. If you can't get them, use the substitutions we frequently suggest in the recipes.
- To make our recipes more interesting, we have called for a variety of vinegars, such as balsamic, raspberry, and seasoned rice. If you are unable to find them, red wine vinegar may be substituted.
- If a liqueur specified in a recipe is unavailable, you may substitute one of your favorites.
- Fresh mussels and clams should be purchased live and should have shells that are tightly closed. Give any slightly open shells a hard tap; they should snap shut, but if they don't, do not use them. Remember that shells will open during cooking; any that remain closed should be discarded. It's a good idea to buy more shellfish than you need for the recipe in case you have to discard some. That way, you will avoid last-minute dashes to the store for more.
- Hot chili peppers contain volatile oils that can make your skin and eyes burn. When you work with these peppers, be sure to wear rubber gloves and don't touch your face or eyes. Before continuing with the recipe, wash hands, knife, and cutting board thoroughly to remove all traces of the pepper.
- Get in the habit of reading product labels—it's a good way to make sure the item you are using is what the recipe calls for. Labels contain a great deal of nutrition information that will help you succeed on the Food Plan.

Gourmet Garnishes

Think a garnish takes too much time and effort? Here are a few that are a cinch to make.
- Sprinkle chopped scallion over a bowl of dip.
- Dip lemon or lime slices or wedges in chopped parsley or paprika for a good accompaniment for fish.
- Sprinkle grated carrot over a salad or soup.
- As a lovely touch for a fish dish, make lemon or lime twists. Just cut into a citrus slice from the edge to the center, then twist in opposite directions.
- Decorate a salad with tomato slices dipped in chopped parsley.
- Garnish a salad with radish roses or carrot curls.
- Dip lettuce leaves in paprika.
- Garnish fruit salad with strips of orange peel, mint leaves, or shredded toasted coconut. (Remember, for every teaspoon of shredded coconut add 10 Optional Calories to the Exchange Information.)

- Use a hollowed-out green, red, or yellow bell pepper as a serving bowl for a dip or for tuna or egg salad.
- A pickle fan adds a nice touch to a sandwich platter. Start from the top of the pickle and make several lengthwise slashes to about ¼ inch from the stem end. Spread the slices out to form a fan.

Sometimes you don't need much of a garnish at all, especially if you arrange the food creatively in a pretty dish. Be sure to leave a portion of the plate showing. Don't overgarnish.

Getting Good Results from the Recipes

You can ensure good results and eliminate a lot of time-wasting mistakes by using the correct procedures and utensils. Read these tips before you start to cook.

- Read through a recipe completely before you begin. Make sure you understand the method and have all of the ingredients and utensils on hand. Gather all ingredients and any special utensils needed in one place.
- Use nonstick cookware so that you can cook without fat. If you don't own cookware with a nonstick surface, spray an ordinary pan with nonstick cooking spray.
- Do not marinate foods in aluminum containers. Because certain foods react with aluminum, it's a good idea to use only glass or stainless-steel containers. You can also marinate in plastic bags. Place marinade and items to be marinated in a leakproof plastic bag, close the bag securely, and let the ingredients marinate according to recipe directions.
- If you don't have a meat mallet, use a skillet or saucepan to pound meat. Place a sheet of plastic wrap over the meat and pound with the bottom of the skillet (or saucepan) until meat reaches the desired thickness.
- When using eggs, it's a good idea to break each one into a cup or bowl before combining with other ingredients or additional eggs. You'll avoid wasting other items should an egg happen to be spoiled or should a piece of shell fall into the egg.
- When dissolving flour, cornstarch, or arrowroot in liquid, add the dry ingredient to the liquid, not vice versa. This helps prevent lumps.
- When a recipe calls for the use of custard cups, select items made of heatproof glass or heavy ceramic.
- If a food is to be chilled or frozen after cooking, always allow it to cool slightly before refrigerating or freezing. Placing a very hot item in the refrigerator or freezer can adversely affect the functioning of the appliance. If a large quantity of food is to be refrigerated or frozen, divide it into smaller portions after cooking

so that it will cool faster and reduce the chances of spoilage. Cover all items to be refrigerated; cover or properly wrap all items to be frozen to prevent freezer-burn.

■ Some recipes call for blanched ingredients. Blanching is really very easy to do; just plunge the ingredient into boiling water for one to two minutes, then rinse with or plunge into cold water to stop the cooking process. Blanched vegetables are great for snacks and crudités.

■ It's important to check the accuracy of your oven thermostat occasionally since a discrepancy can affect the quality of your baking. To determine if the thermostat of your oven is registering correctly, place an oven thermometer on a rack centered in the oven. Set the oven temperature, wait 10 to 15 minutes, and then check the thermometer. If the actual oven temperature does not match the temperature setting, you will have to adjust the setting higher or lower to compensate for the difference until the oven can be repaired.

■ To prevent heat loss, close the oven door promptly after inserting food and do not open it during the cooking time.

■ Some recipes include instructions to preheat the oven. If you decide not to preheat, add an extra 5 to 10 minutes to the cooking time.

■ The cooking times on most recipes are approximate and should be used as a guide. Remember, not all ovens are alike, so be sure to check for doneness as directed.

■ When baking, place the pan in the middle of the center oven rack so that air circulates freely and food bakes evenly. It's best to use one oven rack at a time. If you are using two racks, place them so that the oven is divided into thirds, then stagger the pans so that one is not directly above the other.

■ When using only some of the cups in a muffin pan, it's a good idea to partially fill the empty cups with water. This will prevent the pan from warping or burning. When ready to remove the muffins from the pan, drain off the water very carefully; remember, it will be boiling hot.

■ When broiling, 4 inches is the standard distance from the heat source and should be used with any recipes that do not specify otherwise. If it is necessary to broil closer to or farther away from the heat, the appropriate distance will be indicated.

■ All the recipes in this book can be prepared in 30 minutes or less, but this does not include chilling or marinating time. So if you've finished preparing a recipe that must chill for 30 minutes or an hour, you are free to leave the house knowing the food will be ready when you need it. If, on the other hand, you need to marinate a portion of the recipe before you can move on to the next step, use this time to prepare another portion of the recipe, do a little cleanup, or plan tomorrow's menu.

Using the Exchange and Nutrition Information

Each recipe in this book is followed by an Exchange Information statement which tells you how one serving of the item prepared from that recipe fits into the Food Plan. You will find this statement useful when preparing your menus as it will help you keep track of your Exchanges. If you make any changes in the recipes, be sure to adjust the Exchange Information accordingly.

If you don't want to use all the Exchanges indicated in the Exchange Information on a recipe, you have two choices. Once a day you may count one Exchange from the Protein, Fruit, Bread, or Milk Exchange as a Floating Exchange. Or you can convert these Exchanges, as well as the Fat Exchange, into Optional Calories. For example, if a recipe provides 3 Protein Exchanges, you might want to count 2 Protein Exchanges toward your Daily Totals and count 1 Protein Exchange as Optional Calories. To help you convert Food Exchanges to Optional Calories, use the following caloric values:

Food Exchange	Optional Calories per Exchange
Fruit	60
Fat	40
Protein	70
Bread	80
Milk	90

Since many people are concerned about nutrition, on each recipe we have also included the per serving nutrition analysis for calories, protein, fat, carbohydrate, calcium, sodium, cholesterol, and dietary fiber. These figures were calculated using the most up-to-date data available; they will change if the recipe is altered, even if the substitution in ingredients does not affect the Exchange Information. The nutrition information for recipes containing cooked items, such as rice, pasta, or vegetables, has been calculated on the assumption that no extra salt or fat has been added during cooking.

Notes on Nutrition

No matter how important time is to you, don't cut corners on nutrition. Remember, a variety of nutritious foods, eaten in moderation, is the key to safe weight loss.

The objective of daily menu planning is to provide yourself with basic nutrients while staying within your caloric limit. Remember that no single food supplies all the essential nutrients in the amounts needed; *variety* is the key to success. The greater the variety of food, the less likely you are to develop a deficiency or an excess of any nutrient, and your diet will be interesting.

Our bodies require about 40 different nutrients to stay healthy, including proteins, fats, carbohydrates, fiber, vitamins, minerals, and water. Some of the ways we use these nutrients are for energy, growth, repair of body tissue, and regulation and control of body processes. It is the amount of proteins, fats, and carbohydrates in foods that determines their caloric content.

- Proteins are necessary for building and maintaining body tissue and are excellent sources of iron and B vitamins. The best sources of protein are poultry, lean meat, fish, eggs, milk, cheese, legumes, and peanut butter.

- Carbohydrates are the body's primary source of energy, and provide fiber and B vitamins as well. Fruits, vegetables, cereals, breads, legumes, and whole grains are excellent sources of carbohydrates.

- Fats are the most concentrated source of energy and provide essential fatty acids. Fats also carry fat-soluble vitamins to body cells. Margarine, mayonnaise, and vegetable oils are pure sources of fat; lean meat, fish, poultry, cheese, eggs, and milk also contain fat.

- Fiber is an important element in the diet as it helps maintain regularity, may help lower blood cholesterol levels, and may control levels of blood sugar. Bran products, whole grains, legumes, fruits, and vegetables are good sources of fiber.

- Vitamins and minerals are also essential in order for the body to function properly. For example, the B vitamins help cells convert carbohydrates into energy; vitamin C helps give strength to body tissues; vitamin A is important for good vision.

- Iron, one of the most difficult minerals to get in ample supply (especially for women), is a vital mineral because it is essential to the formation of red blood cells. Good sources are lean meat, poultry, shellfish, liver, legumes, and enriched grains.

- Sodium is a significant factor in weight control; it affects the body's water balance and causes some people to retain water, thereby adding to weight. Sodium occurs naturally in some foods, and additional amounts are often added in processing prepared foods. It is recommended that your daily sodium intake not exceed 3 grams (3,000 milligrams). Keep in mind that just ¼ teaspoon of salt contains 533 milligrams of sodium!

- Calcium builds and maintains strong bones and teeth and is essential in order to prevent osteoporosis in later years. The best sources of calcium are, of course, milk and other dairy products. However, calcium is also found in sardines and salmon (canned with bones), tofu and cooked soybeans, and in certain vegetables and fruits, such as cooked collard, turnip, and mustard greens, broccoli, spinach, and oranges.

■ Cholesterol is an essential part of all body tissue and is found in foods of animal origin. Because high blood cholesterol has been associated with increased risk of heart disease, it is recommended that your cholesterol intake be limited to an average of 300 milligrams per day, based on your weekly cholesterol intake. To lower your cholesterol intake, choose low-fat dairy products, cut down on eggs, red meat, and organ meats, trim all visible fat from meats, cook meats on a rack (bake, roast, or broil), and, whenever possible, select poultry or fish in place of meats.

Microwave Magic

The number one convenience appliance on the market today, the microwave oven is an all-around timesaver that's energy efficient as well. It's not just for reheating leftovers, either. Microwave cooking is actually the very best cooking method for certain foods. Here are a few ways the microwave oven can work its magic for you.

■ Preheating isn't necessary for microwave cooking—a big timesaver! Just place the food in the oven and start cooking.

■ Frozen foods defrost in minutes in the microwave instead of in hours or days in the refrigerator.

■ The microwave cooks food in less time than a conventional oven, so it uses less energy.

■ Foods can be served in the same utensils in which they are cooked. Heat soup in a microwavable mug or soup bowl rather than a saucepan; leftovers can be heated on a microwavable dinner plate.

■ Cooking is safer than in conventional ovens because there are no hot surfaces either inside or outside the oven on which to burn yourself. That means school-age children can safely prepare their own after-school snacks in the microwave. However, remember to use pot holders as the cookware can become hot.

■ The microwave oven cavity remains cool, which means there are no baked-on spills or spatters. The oven interior can be wiped clean with a damp cloth or sponge.

■ Because microwave cooking time is short and uses little or no added water, the amount of vitamins and minerals that leak into the cooking liquid and are therefore discarded is minimal. Sauces, soups, and other liquids, most vegetables, fish, and fruits are at their best when cooked in the microwave oven.

▪ Microwave cooking requires less margarine, butter, and oil—you will need only enough for flavoring.

Microwave Power Levels

The recipes in this book were tested in 650- to 700-watt microwave ovens with variable power levels. If you own a lower-wattage oven, you can still count on terrific results if you increase the cooking time of the recipe, check it, and then add more cooking time if necessary. If you are using a higher wattage oven, you'll need to decrease the cooking time slightly.

A microwave oven's power levels control the percentage of power introduced into the oven cavity and automatically cycle the power on and off. Lower power levels cook food more slowly; higher power levels cook food faster. Of course, power levels can vary, depending on the brand of oven. The power levels in the ovens we used follow. If the levels in your oven are different from these, the recipe may need to be adjusted.

High (100%)
Medium-High (60–70%)
Medium (50%)
Medium-Low (30%)
Low (10–20%)

Microwave Cooking Techniques

The following techniques will help you get the best results.

Piercing—It is important to pierce the skin or outer membrane of foods such as winter squash, potatoes, frankfurters, and chicken livers in order to keep them from bursting in the microwave. You can pierce food with a sharp paring knife or the tines of a fork. When microwaving eggs that have been removed from their shells, pierce the membrane of the yolk with a toothpick before cooking. And remember, *never* microwave eggs in the shell; they will burst and you'll have a real mess to clean up.

Rotating or Turning—Cakes, pies, muffins, and some casseroles require rotating during cooking. This must be done when a food cannot be stirred or rearranged, and involves moving the cooking utensil by a half or quarter turn.

Stirring—Stirring food partway through the cooking process redistributes the heat and shortens the cooking time.

Rearranging—The corners or sides of a cooking utensil receive more energy than the center, making it necessary to rearrange foods that can't be stirred. Chicken parts, potatoes, and corn on the cob are some of the foods that need to be rearranged during cooking.

Standing Time—Some of our recipes call for standing time, which can take place in or out of the microwave oven. This method allows for complete cooking of the center and thicker areas of the food without overcooking the edges or thin sections. It works because foods that have been microwaved continue to cook even after the cooking time is completed.

Microwave Cookware

There is no need to buy a whole new set of cookware—chances are that some of the cookware you already own can be used in the microwave oven. Today there are utensils that can be used in both conventional and microwave ovens. In general, ovenproof glass, ceramic, and pottery dishes that have no metallic trim are microwavable, and some types of cookware can even go from freezer to microwave to table. However, plastic margarine containers and similar types of plastic storage containers are not intended to withstand the high temperatures of the microwave and should not be used. In fact, plastic containers should not be used at all unless recommended by the manufacturer.

It's a good idea to test the cookware you already own to see if it is safe to use in the microwave. To do this, place the utensil in the oven along with—but not touching—a 1-cup glass measure filled with ½ cup of cool water. (The water absorbs microwaves and prevents damage to your oven.) Microwave on High (100%) for 1 minute. The utensil should be cool or slightly warm to the touch. If it is hot, it is not safe for use in the microwave.

Microwave Accessories

While the microwave oven can do many wonderful things for food, it cannot sear, brown, or crisp unless you use a *browning tray*. This specially coated tray is first placed in the microwave oven without the food, where it absorbs microwave energy and becomes very hot. Browning occurs when the food is placed on the preheated dish and microwaved.

Some microwave ovens come equipped with *rotating turntables*. If yours does not, you can purchase a battery-operated or spring-wound turntable to place on the floor of your microwave. With a turntable, food cooks more evenly and there is no need to stop the cooking process and manually rotate the food or dish.

Many microwave ovens are equipped with a built-in probe that is used to determine doneness. If your oven does not have this built-in probe, you may want to invest in a *microwave thermometer;* conventional thermometers cannot be used in the microwave oven.

The Use of Metal in the Microwave

With the exception of aluminum foil, metal should not be used in the microwave oven. This is because metal reflects microwaves away from the food rather than allowing them to pass through. Aluminum foil, however, is helpful because it can be used to shield areas that might get overcooked.

When thawing frozen foods, you can use small pieces of foil to protect already thawed outer edges which may begin to cook before the center of the food is fully thawed. It is important not to allow the foil to come in contact with the oven walls as this can cause damage to the microwave.

Microwave Covers

Paper can be used in the microwave for short cooking times and is often used as a cover. Wax paper, paper towels, and plastic wrap are all common microwave covers. Of course, some microwave cookware comes with its own matching covers.

Plastic Wrap — Plastic wrap forms a tight cover that keeps in moisture. Use only those wraps labeled "for microwave use" since other brands may become distorted from the heat that develops in the food during cooking. Remember to fold back a corner of the plastic wrap when covering the dish to allow excess steam to escape, a technique we refer to as venting. If a recipe requires that you cover a dish tightly with plastic wrap, however, you will need to pierce the plastic with a knife before removing it. Then carefully remove the plastic in a direction away from you to avoid a steam burn.

Paper Towels — Microwavable paper towels absorb moisture, allow steam to escape, and reduce spattering. Avoid printed and recycled paper because it may contain impurities; in addition, dyes and inks may leak into the food.

Wax Paper — Covering a dish with wax paper holds in heat, speeds the cooking process, and prevents the food from spattering onto the oven walls.

Microwave Oven Cleanup

Be sure to wipe up spills from the interior surface of the oven as soon as possible or the food particles will become spoiled and rancid, causing unpleasant odors. Cabbage and other highly seasoned foods can also cause odors. You can remove such odors by boiling a combination of ½ cup of lemon juice or white vinegar and 1 cup of water in a large microwavable glass for several minutes. Let stand for 5 to 6 minutes and remove.

Microwave Miracles

It's miraculous! The microwave oven lets you prepare all kinds of foods in a fraction of the time they would take using conventional methods. Here is a sampling of some of the things it does best.

Vegetables

For crisp, brightly colored, and highly nutritious vegetables, the microwave method is unparalleled. Cooking time is brief and very little water is needed. You'll get the best results if you follow these pointers.

- Cut vegetables into uniform size and thickness.
- Pierce the skins on whole vegetables (such as potatoes) with a fork before microwaving to permit steam to escape and to prevent the vegetables from bursting.
- Arrange whole or halved vegetables in a circle on a dish or on the oven floor, leaving space between each. Rotate the vegetables during cooking and they will cook more evenly.
- Because asparagus tips and broccoli florets are more tender than the stalks and require less energy to cook, arrange them so that the tips or florets are in the center of the dish and the stalks are at the outer edge.

Here's how to microwave vegetables.

1. Arrange vegetables in a microwavable container, add a few tablespoons of water, and cover with a lid or vented plastic wrap. The water will provide steam, resulting in quick and even cooking.
2. Microwave on High (100%) for the amount of time recommended in either the recipe or the owner's manual for your oven.
3. Halfway through cooking, stir, rearrange, or turn the vegetables over.
4. Instructions often specify standing time, since the vegetables will continue cooking after microwaving is completed. This important step helps to avoid overcooking and permits vegetables to become tender without losing their texture.

Baked Potatoes — Whole potatoes bake in just minutes in the microwave. In fact, a whole potato cooks in less time than potato slices because the skin helps to hold in steam and heat. To cook, pierce a 6-ounce potato with a fork, then place the potato on a sheet of paper towel on the floor of the oven. Microwave for 4 to 6 minutes, turning the potato over halfway through the cooking process. Let stand to soften.

Acorn Squash — To cook a 1-pound acorn squash, cut it in half crosswise, then remove and discard the seeds. Place squash halves, cut-side down, in a microwavable 8 x 8 x 2-inch baking dish. Cover with vented plastic wrap and cook on High (100%) for 5 minutes until squash is fork-tender, rotating dish ½ turn halfway through cooking.

Corn on the Cob — Corn on the cob can be microwaved in the husk or with the husk removed. To cook 2 small ears of corn on the cob in the husk, place corn on the floor of the oven, leaving a space between each ear. Microwave for 4 to 5 minutes, turning corn halfway through the cooking process. To remove the husk, wrap the base end of the corn with a paper towel and, holding the towel-covered base, gently fold back the leaves of the husk, being careful of hot steam. Pull out corn silk and remove the husk.

There are two ways to microwave husked corn. The first method involves placing both ears of corn in a microwavable 8 x 8 x 2-inch baking dish along with ¼ cup of water, leaving space between each ear. Cover the baking dish with vented plastic wrap and cook for 5 to 6 minutes, until the corn is cooked through, rotating the dish ¼ turn every 2 minutes.

The second method for cooking husked corn will save you from having to wash a baking dish. Wrap each ear of corn individually in plastic wrap or wax paper and place on the floor of the oven. Microwave for 5 to 6 minutes, turning corn over halfway through the cooking process.

Other Foods

Toasted Coconut — Spread 1 tablespoon of coconut evenly on a microwavable glass plate and microwave on High (100%) for 40 to 50 seconds, checking and stirring every 20 seconds. Toasted, shredded coconut is delicious sprinkled over fresh fruit salad, reduced-calorie gelatin, pudding, or ice cream.

Bacon — Why pan-fry bacon when it's so much simpler to microwave it? Arrange 2 slices of bacon in a single layer on a microwavable roasting rack or on a microwavable plate lined with three layers of paper towel. Cover with paper towel to prevent spattering and cook on High (100%) for 1 to 2 minutes. For crisper bacon, let stand for 1 to 2 minutes.

Pasta and Rice—To give new life to yesterday's rice or pasta, in a 1-quart microwavable bowl arrange 1 cup of cooked pasta or rice. Cover with wax paper and microwave on High (100%) for 1 to 2 minutes for that just-cooked taste.

Instant rice is ideal for the microwave oven. Measure 4 ounces of instant rice and set in a 1½-quart microwavable bowl; stir in 1 cup of hot tap water. Cover with vented plastic wrap and microwave on High (100%) for 10 minutes. Drain and serve.

Although pasta can be cooked in the microwave oven with satisfactory results, you won't save any time using this method. However, you can save time by using *both* range and microwave. While the pasta is cooking on the range, use your microwave for preparing the other steps in the recipe.

Scrambled Egg in a Bowl—In a small microwavable bowl, microwave ½ teaspoon of margarine on High (100%) for 10 seconds, until melted. Add egg and 2 tablespoons of skim, low-fat, or whole milk (or water) and beat with a fork until combined. Microwave partially covered for 1 minute on Medium-High (70%); stir and continue to cook on Medium-High, partially covered, until almost set, ½ to 1 minute. Let stand ½ to 1 minute before serving.

Melting by Microwave—The microwave is great for melting chocolate, margarine, and butter. You don't even need to wait until the item is completely melted—just stir the last small pieces into the already melted mixture until it is completely smooth.

Put the "Pop" Back in Popcorn—Did you know that you can reheat cold popcorn? For each cup of prepared popcorn, microwave on High (100%) for 15 to 20 seconds to bring back that delicious just-popped flavor.

Just-Right Gelatin—Here's the simplest way we know to make gelatin dessert, using just one bowl. In a small microwavable bowl measure the water as directed on the package and microwave on High (100%), 2 to 3 minutes, until boiling. Add the gelatin and stir until dissolved. Stir in cold water or ice cubes. If the gelatin has set before you've added the other ingredients (fruit, vegetables, or nuts), soften it in the microwave (make sure it's in a microwavable container) on Medium (50%) for 1 to 1½ minutes for a 3-ounce package of prepared gelatin, 1 to 2 minutes for a 6-ounce package. Stir in the additional ingredients and pop the gelatin mixture back into the refrigerator until it is firm.

Divine Dried Fruit—To plump dried fruit, arrange it in a 6-ounce microwavable custard cup, sprinkle with a small amount of water, and microwave on High (100%) for 15 to 30 seconds.

Succulent Citrus—Want to get more juice out of lemons, limes, and oranges? Microwave on High (100%) for 15 to 30 seconds before squeezing.

Barbecued Chicken—Tired of the long wait for that family favorite, barbecued chicken? While the grill is heating, partially cook the chicken in the microwave. Finish it on the grill, basting with your favorite sauce. The chicken will be done in half the time.

Softening Ice Cream—To soften a solid block of ice cream or ice milk, put the container in the microwave on Low (20%) for about 45 seconds. Scooping will be much easier.

A Note on the Recipe Symbols

Ⓜ The microwave symbol appears on recipes that can be prepared in the *microwave oven*.

Ⓒ The penny appears on *budget* recipes.

Since *all recipes* can be prepared in 30 minutes or less, we are not using the clock symbol.

Eggs and Cheese

Whether it's breakfast, brunch, lunch, or a quick dinner, you're only minutes away from a marvelous meal with the wonderful recipes in this chapter. Sample Baked Eggs Florentine, Prosciutto-Cheese Omelet, or Potato–Sausage Frittata. Check out cheese with our Microwave Mozzarella Sandwich or Ham and Cheese Corn Bread Rolls. Speedy and delicious, egg and cheese dishes are often elegant enough for company meals. Try one next time you entertain.

Baked Eggs Florentine ⊙

1 teaspoon margarine
1 cup thawed and well-drained
    frozen chopped spinach
¼ cup part-skim ricotta cheese
1 tablespoon grated Parmesan
    cheese, divided
¼ teaspoon salt
⅛ teaspoon *each* pepper and
    ground nutmeg
2 eggs
2 teaspoons half-and-half (blend
    of milk and cream)

Preheat oven to 350°F. In 9-inch nonstick skillet melt margarine; add spinach and cook over high heat, stirring frequently, until spinach is heated through, 2 to 3 minutes. Transfer to medium mixing bowl; add ricotta cheese, 2 teaspoons Parmesan cheese, the salt, pepper, and nutmeg and mix well.

Spray two 10-ounce custard cups with nonstick cooking spray; spoon half of the spinach mixture into each cup. Using the back of a spoon, make an indentation in center of each portion. Being careful not to break yolk, break 1 egg into a small dish, then slide into 1 indentation; repeat with remaining egg. Pour 1 teaspoon half-and-half over each egg and then sprinkle each with remaining ½ teaspoon Parmesan cheese. Bake until eggs are set, 8 to 10 minutes.

MAKES 2 SERVINGS

Each serving provides: 1½ Protein Exchanges;
    1 Vegetable Exchange; ½ Fat Exchange;
    25 Optional Calories
Per serving: 183 calories; 14 g protein; 12 g fat;
    7 g carbohydrate; 273 mg calcium; 528 mg sodium;
    287 mg cholesterol; 2 g dietary fiber

Use your microwave oven to thaw frozen vegetables in minutes, or plan ahead and let them thaw in your refrigerator overnight or while you're at the office.

Microwave Buttery Scrambled Eggs Ⓒ Ⓜ

1 tablespoon whipped butter
4 eggs
1 tablespoon *each* chopped
  chives *or* scallion (green onion)
  and grated Romano *or*
  Parmesan cheese
2 teaspoons chopped fresh
  parsley
Dash pepper

In 2½-cup microwavable mixing bowl micro-wave butter on High (100%) for 30 seconds, until melted. Using a wire whisk, in separate small mixing bowl beat together remaining ingredients; add to butter in mixing bowl. Cover with vented plastic wrap and micro-wave on Medium-High (70%) for 2½ min-utes, stirring halfway through cooking. Microwave on Low (30%) for 30 seconds. Let stand for 1 minute.

MAKES 2 SERVINGS

Each serving provides: 2 Protein Exchanges;
    40 Optional Calories
Per serving: 194 calories; 13 g protein; 15 g fat;
    1 g carbohydrate; 87 mg calcium; 198 mg sodium;
    558 mg cholesterol; 0.1 g dietary fiber

Variation: Microwave Scrambled Eggs —
Substitute 1 tablespoon margarine for the butter. Add 1½ Fat Exchanges to Exchange Information and decrease Optional Calories to 15.

Per serving: 220 calories; 13 g protein; 18 g fat;
    2 g carbohydrate; 88 mg calcium; 235 mg sodium;
    551 mg cholesterol; 0.1 g dietary fiber

Prosciutto-Cheese Omelet

For a decorative touch, garnish the serving platter with tomato slices and fresh basil leaves.

½ ounce prosciutto (Italian-style ham), chopped
2 tablespoons *each* chopped fresh basil and part-skim ricotta cheese
3 eggs
1 tablespoon water
Dash *each* salt and pepper
1 tablespoon *each* whipped butter, divided, and grated Parmesan cheese

In small mixing bowl combine prosciutto, basil, and ricotta cheese and stir to combine; set aside. Using a fork, in separate small mixing bowl combine eggs, water, salt, and pepper and beat until combined.

In 9-inch nonstick skillet melt 2 teaspoons butter; add egg mixture and cook over medium-high heat until bottom of omelet is set and lightly browned, 1 to 2 minutes. Spoon prosciutto mixture over half of the omelet. Using a spatula, loosen omelet around edges; then, using a pancake turner, fold omelet in half and slide onto flameproof plate. Melt remaining teaspoon butter; using pastry brush, brush omelet with butter and sprinkle with Parmesan cheese. Broil until cheese is melted, 30 seconds.

MAKES 2 SERVINGS

Each serving provides: 2 Protein Exchanges;
 40 Optional Calories
Per serving: 195 calories; 14 g protein; 14 g fat;
 3 g carbohydrate; 152 mg calcium; 368 mg sodium;
 430 mg cholesterol; 0 g dietary fiber

Fresh basil can be frozen and used year-round. Just remove leaves from stems, rinse and dry with paper towels, and freeze in a plastic container or freezer bag.

BLT Egg Muffin Ⓜ

2 eggs
¼ cup skim *or* nonfat milk
Dash pepper
4 sun-dried tomato halves (not
    packed in oil), chopped
2 slices crisp bacon, crumbled
1 English muffin (2 ounces), split
    in half and toasted
2 lettuce leaves

Using a fork, in small microwavable bowl combine eggs, milk, and pepper and beat until combined; stir in tomatoes. Microwave on High (100%) for 2 minutes, stirring twice during cooking. Stir in bacon and microwave on High for 1 minute.

To serve, top each muffin half with a lettuce leaf and half of the egg mixture.

MAKES 2 SERVINGS

Each serving provides: 1 Protein Exchange;
    1 Bread Exchange; 1¼ Vegetable Exchanges;
    55 Optional Calories
Per serving: 210 calories; 12 g protein; 9 g fat;
    19 g carbohydrate; 78 mg calcium; 340 mg sodium;
    280 mg cholesterol; 1 g dietary fiber (this figure does
    not include English muffin; nutrition analysis not
    available)

Scramble and microwave eggs in the same bowl and you'll have no messy skillet to wash. What a time-saver on busy mornings!

Vegetables, Ham, and Eggs

2 teaspoons olive *or* vegetable oil
1 cup sliced onions
½ cup *each* sliced red and
   green bell pepper
1 small garlic clove, minced
1 medium tomato, diced
3 eggs
1 tablespoon whole milk
Dash *each* salt and pepper
1 ounce diced boiled ham

In 9-inch nonstick skillet heat oil; add onions, bell peppers, and garlic and cook over high heat, stirring frequently, until tender-crisp, about 2 minutes. Add tomato and cook, stirring occasionally, until heated through, about 1 minute. Transfer to serving platter; set aside and keep warm.

Using a fork, in small mixing bowl combine eggs, milk, salt, and pepper and beat until combined; stir in ham. To same skillet add egg mixture and cook over medium-high heat, stirring frequently, until eggs are set, 3 to 4 minutes.

To serve, spoon egg mixture over vegetable mixture.

MAKES 2 SERVINGS

Each serving provides: 2 Protein Exchanges;
   3 Vegetable Exchanges; 1 Fat Exchange;
   5 Optional Calories
Per serving: 237 calories; 14 g protein; 14 g fat;
   13 g carbohydrate; 82 mg calcium; 352 mg sodium;
   420 mg cholesterol; 2 g dietary fiber

Rinse cookware containing raw egg residue in cold water prior to washing in hot water for an easier cleanup.

Scrambled Huevos Rancheros ⊙

2 teaspoons olive *or* vegetable oil,
   divided
2 flour tortillas (6-inch diameter
   each)
3 eggs
1 tablespoon sour cream
4 drops hot sauce
Dash *each* salt and pepper
¼ cup *each* diced red bell pepper
   and scallions (green onions)
1 tablespoon seeded and minced
   jalapeño pepper
½ medium tomato, diced
1 ounce Monterey Jack cheese,
   shredded

Preheat oven to 350° F. Using a pastry brush, brush half of the oil over both sides of each tortilla. On nonstick baking sheet arrange tortillas in a single layer and bake until warm, about 1 minute.

Into each of two 10-ounce custard cups carefully fit 1 tortilla; return to oven and bake until crisp, 3 to 4 minutes longer.

Using a fork, in small mixing bowl combine eggs, sour cream, hot sauce, salt, and pepper and beat until combined. In 9-inch skillet heat remaining teaspoon oil; add bell pepper, scallions, and jalapeño pepper and cook over high heat, stirring frequently, until tender-crisp, about 30 seconds. Pour egg mixture over vegetables in skillet and cook, stirring frequently, just until eggs are set, about 2 minutes. Stir in tomato and cook until heated through, 30 seconds to 1 minute. Divide egg mixture into each tortilla-lined custard cup and sprinkle each portion with half of the cheese.

MAKES 2 SERVINGS

Each serving provides: 2 Protein Exchanges;
   1 Bread Exchange; 1 Vegetable Exchange;
   1 Fat Exchange; 15 Optional Calories
Per serving: 311 calories; 15 g protein; 21 g fat;
   16 g carbohydrate; 208 mg calcium; 398 mg sodium;
   427 mg cholesterol; 1 g dietary fiber

Mexican Eggs in Potato Shells ⒸⓂ

1 baking potato (9 ounces), baked
2 tablespoons sour cream, divided
1 teaspoon margarine
2 tablespoons *each* minced onion
  and green bell pepper
1 tablespoon seeded and minced
  jalapeño pepper
1 medium tomato, blanched,
  peeled, seeded, and diced
2 eggs
½ ounce Cheddar cheese,
  shredded

Cut potato in half lengthwise and, using a spoon, scoop out pulp from halves, leaving ¼-inch-thick shells; reserve shells. In small mixing bowl combine potato pulp and 1 tablespoon sour cream; mash and set aside.

In small nonstick skillet melt margarine; add onion and peppers and sauté over medium-high heat, stirring frequently, until vegetables are tender-crisp, 2 to 3 minutes. Add tomato and continue cooking, stirring frequently, until heated through and flavors blend, 2 to 3 minutes. Add half of the sautéed vegetables to pulp mixture and stir to thoroughly combine. Spoon half of pulp mixture into each reserved potato shell.

Set potato shells in 1-quart microwavable shallow casserole. Using the back of a spoon, make a deep indentation in center of each potato. Break 1 egg into a small dish, then slide into 1 indentation; repeat with remaining egg. Using a toothpick, lightly pierce membrane of yolks in several places, being careful not to pierce yolks. Tightly cover casserole with plastic wrap and microwave on Medium (50%) for 3 minutes, until egg whites are opaque. Sprinkle half of the cheese over each egg; re-cover with plastic wrap and microwave on Medium for 1 minute, until cheese is melted. Top each portion with half of the remaining vegetable mixture and sour cream.

MAKES 2 SERVINGS

Each serving provides: 1¼ Protein Exchanges;
  1½ Bread Exchanges; 1¼ Vegetable Exchanges;
  ½ Fat Exchange; 35 Optional Calories
Per serving: 268 calories; 12 g protein; 13 g fat;
  27 g carbohydrate; 121 mg calcium; 157 mg sodium;
  288 mg cholesterol; 1 g dietary fiber

Western Eggs in Potato Shells Ⓜ

Bake the potato in the microwave oven or in the conventional oven the night before.

1 baking potato (9 ounces), baked
2 tablespoons sour cream
1 teaspoon margarine
1 ounce Canadian-style bacon, diced
2 tablespoons *each* minced onion and green bell pepper
2 eggs

Cut potato in half lengthwise and, using a spoon, scoop out pulp from halves, leaving ¼-inch-thick shells; reserve shells. In small mixing bowl combine potato pulp and sour cream; mash and set aside.

In small nonstick skillet melt margarine; add bacon, onion, and bell pepper and sauté over medium-high heat, stirring frequently, until vegetables are tender-crisp, 2 to 3 minutes. Add to pulp mixture and stir to thoroughly combine. Spoon half of pulp mixture into each reserved potato shell.

Set potato shells in 1-quart microwavable shallow casserole. Using the back of a spoon, make a deep indentation in center of each potato. Break 1 egg into a small dish, then slide into 1 indentation; repeat with remaining egg. Using a toothpick, lightly pierce membrane of yolks in several places, being careful not to pierce yolks. Tightly cover casserole with plastic wrap and microwave on Medium (50%) for 3 minutes, until egg whites are opaque.

MAKES 2 SERVINGS

Each serving provides: 1½ Protein Exchanges; 1½ Bread Exchanges; ¼ Vegetable Exchange; ½ Fat Exchange; 35 Optional Calories
Per serving: 248 calories; 12 g protein; 12 g fat; 24 g carbohydrate; 66 mg calcium; 308 mg sodium; 287 mg cholesterol; 0.1 g dietary fiber

Cheese-Filled Cucumber Slices

A pretty hors d'oeuvre for your next party.

1 large cucumber (about
   9½ ounces)
½ ounce Swiss *or* Gruyère cheese,
   shredded
2 tablespoons part-skim ricotta
   cheese
1 tablespoon *each* chopped
   scallion (green onion), chopped
   fresh dill *or* ¼ teaspoon dillweed, and whipped cream
   cheese
Dash *each* salt and white pepper

Cut off ends of cucumber. Using tines of a fork, score peel of cucumber. Cut cucumber in half crosswise and, using a melon baller or small spoon, remove and discard seeds from both halves; set aside.

In small mixing bowl thoroughly combine remaining ingredients. Spoon half of the cheese mixture into cored section of each cucumber half. Wrap each half in plastic wrap and refrigerate until chilled, about 1 hour.

To serve, remove plastic wrap and carefully slice each cucumber half into 6 equal slices.

MAKES 2 SERVINGS, 6 SLICES EACH

Each serving provides: ½ Protein Exchange;
   1⅛ Vegetable Exchanges; 15 Optional Calories
Per serving with Swiss cheese: 83 calories; 5 g protein;
   5 g fat; 5 g carbohydrate; 137 mg calcium;
   124 mg sodium; 16 mg cholesterol; 1 g dietary fiber
With Gruyère cheese: 85 calories; 5 g protein; 5 g fat;
   5 g carbohydrate; 140 mg calcium; 130 mg sodium;
   17 mg cholesterol; 1 g dietary fiber

Goat Cheese Toasts with Olivada

Olivada, which is a chopped olive mixture, tops this unique hors d'oeuvre.

1 ounce chèvre (French goat
   cheese), at room temperature
¼ cup part-skim ricotta cheese
1 tablespoon *each* chopped
   chives and fresh basil *or*
   ½ teaspoon basil leaves
12 large pitted black olives,
   minced
1 teaspoon *each* rinsed drained
   capers and red wine vinegar
2 teaspoons olive oil
1 large garlic clove, minced
2 ounces French bread, diagonally
   cut into 12 equal slices

In small mixing bowl combine cheeses, chives, and basil; stir well and set aside.

In separate small bowl combine olives, capers, and vinegar; stir and set aside.

In small nonstick saucepan combine oil and garlic and cook over medium heat, swirling oil in pan occasionally to prevent garlic from burning, until garlic is golden, 1 to 2 minutes. Remove from heat and set aside.

On baking sheet arrange bread slices in a single layer and broil 5 to 6 inches from heat source until golden brown. Turn bread slices over and, using a pastry brush, lightly brush each slice of bread with an equal amount of the garlic-oil mixture, being sure to use all of mixture. Spread an equal amount of cheese mixture over each slice of bread (about 1 tablespoon). Broil until cheese is melted, 1 to 2 minutes. Top each slice of bread with an equal amount of the olive mixture (about 1 teaspoon).

MAKES 2 SERVINGS

Each serving provides: 1 Protein Exchange;
   1 Bread Exchange; 2 Fat Exchanges
Per serving: 266 calories; 9 g protein; 17 g fat;
   20 g carbohydrate; 156 mg calcium; 512 mg sodium;
   23 mg cholesterol; 2 g dietary fiber

Ham and Cheese Corn Bread Rolls ⓒ

1½ ounces (¼ cup) uncooked
    yellow cornmeal
3 tablespoons all-purpose flour
1 tablespoon granulated sugar
1 teaspoon double-acting baking
    powder
3 egg whites
⅛ teaspoon cream of tartar
2 tablespoons vegetable oil
5 ounces Cheddar cheese,
    shredded, divided
2 tablespoons plain low-fat yogurt
1 tablespoon pickle relish
1 teaspoon mustard
6 ounces thinly sliced boiled ham

Preheat oven to 400°F. Line 15 x 10½ x 1-inch nonstick jelly-roll pan with wax paper; spray paper with nonstick cooking spray and set aside.

In small mixing bowl combine cornmeal, flour, sugar, and baking powder; set aside. Using electric mixer on medium speed, in large mixing bowl beat egg whites with cream of tartar until stiff but not dry. Alternately fold in cornmeal mixture and oil; fold in 2 ounces cheese. Spread batter evenly in prepared pan and bake for 5 to 6 minutes (top should spring back when lightly touched with finger; *do not overbake*). Remove from oven and turn bread onto a towel; remove and discard wax paper. Starting at wide end, roll bread with towel; set on wire rack and let cool for 5 minutes.

In small mixing bowl combine yogurt, relish, and mustard; set aside. Unroll bread, remove towel and top with ham slices; spread yogurt mixture over ham and sprinkle with remaining 3 ounces cheese. Reroll bread and place, seam-side down, in nonstick jelly-roll pan and bake at 400°F until cheese is melted, about 5 minutes.

To serve, cut into 12 equal slices.

MAKES 6 SERVINGS, 2 SLICES EACH

Each serving provides: 2 Protein Exchanges;
    ½ Bread Exchange; 1 Fat Exchange;
    20 Optional Calories
Per serving: 240 calories; 15 g protein; 14 g fat;
    13 g carbohydrate; 221 mg calcium; 616 mg sodium;
    40 mg cholesterol; 0.1 g dietary fiber (this figure does
    not include cornmeal; nutrition analysis not available)

Why is some cornmeal yellow rather than white? It's the variety of corn that's dried and ground into meal that determines the color. Except for the fact that white cornmeal has a trace of vitamin A, there is no difference between the two.

Mushrooms Stuffed with Herb Cheese ⊙

16 medium mushrooms
3 tablespoons whipped cream
cheese
1 tablespoon *each* chopped fresh
parsley and fresh basil *or*
½ teaspoon basil leaves
2 teaspoons grated Parmesan
cheese
1 small garlic clove, minced
2 teaspoons plain dried bread
crumbs

Preheat oven to 450°F. Remove and chop stems of mushrooms, reserving caps. Using a fork, in small mixing bowl combine chopped mushrooms, cream cheese, parsley, basil, Parmesan cheese, and garlic and mix well.

Fill each reserved mushroom cap with an equal amount of cream cheese mixture (about 1 teaspoon) and arrange in 8 x 8 x 2-inch nonstick baking pan. Sprinkle an equal amount of bread crumbs over stuffing portion of each mushroom. Pour ¼ cup water into bottom of pan and bake until mushrooms are fork-tender and lightly browned, 8 to 10 minutes.

MAKES 4 SERVINGS, 4 MUSHROOMS EACH

Each serving provides: 1 Vegetable Exchange;
    35 Optional Calories
Per serving: 46 calories; 2 g protein; 3 g fat;
    4 g carbohydrate; 26 mg calcium; 52 mg sodium;
    8 mg cholesterol; 1 g dietary fiber

Mushrooms tend to absorb the water they are washed in, so rather than washing, wipe them clean with paper towels.

Roulades of Fruit, Cheese, and Ham

1 small pear (about 5 ounces),
    cored, pared, and cut into
    6 equal wedges
2 tablespoons lemon juice
¼ cup part-skim ricotta cheese
1 ounce Stilton *or* Gorgonzola
    cheese, crumbled
1 tablespoon *each* chopped
    chives and sour cream
2 ounces thinly sliced prosciutto
    (Italian-style ham), cut into
    6 slices

In small bowl combine pear wedges and lemon juice; set aside. In small mixing bowl combine cheeses, chives, and sour cream; set aside.

On work surface arrange one slice of prosciutto; spread ⅙ of the cheese mixture over surface of prosciutto and top with a pear wedge. Starting from narrow end, roll prosciutto up jelly-roll fashion and arrange seam-side down on serving platter. Repeat procedure 5 more times, making 5 more rolls.

MAKES 2 SERVINGS, 3 ROLLS EACH

Each serving provides: 2 Protein Exchanges;
    ½ Fruit Exchange; 15 Optional Calories
Per serving: 200 calories; 12 g protein; 11 g fat;
    14 g carbohydrate; 179 mg calcium; 617 mg sodium;
    39 mg cholesterol; 2 g dietary fiber

Kidney Bean Quesadillas ⊙

2 ounces rinsed drained canned
    red kidney beans
1 small garlic clove, minced
1 teaspoon chopped fresh cilantro
    (Chinese parsley) *or* Italian
    (flat-leaf) parsley
2 flour tortillas (6-inch diameter
    each)
2 tablespoons *each* chopped
    tomato and green bell pepper,
    divided
2 ounces Cheddar cheese,
    shredded, divided
2 teaspoons vegetable oil

Using a fork, in small mixing bowl combine beans, garlic, and cilantro (or parsley) and mash until combined; set aside.

In 9-inch nonstick skillet cook 1 tortilla over medium-high heat, turning once, until heated through and flexible, 1 to 2 minutes on each side. Transfer to plate; spread half of the bean mixture over half of tortilla. Top bean mixture with half of the tomato and bell pepper, and then with half of the cheese. Fold tortilla in half to cover filling; repeat procedure with remaining tortilla, vegetables, and cheese.

In same skillet heat oil; add filled tortillas and cook, turning once, until cheese is melted, 2 to 3 minutes on each side. Remove from skillet and cut each tortilla in half.

MAKES 2 SERVINGS

Each serving provides: 1½ Protein Exchanges;
    1 Bread Exchange; ¼ Vegetable Exchange;
    1 Fat Exchange
Per serving: 265 calories; 12 g protein; 16 g fat;
    20 g carbohydrate; 263 mg calcium; 415 mg sodium
    (estimated); 30 mg cholesterol; 2 g dietary fiber

Potato-Sausage Frittata

1 teaspoon *each* vegetable oil and
  margarine
6 ounces pared all-purpose
  potatoes, thinly sliced
2 tablespoons minced onion *or*
  scallion (green onion)
3 eggs
2 tablespoons water
2 ounces cooked veal sausage
  links, thinly sliced

Preheat oven to 425°F. In 10-inch nonstick skillet that has an oven-safe or removable handle combine oil and margarine and heat until margarine is melted; arrange potato slices in a single layer in bottom of skillet and top with onion (or scallion). Cover and cook over medium-high heat, turning once, until potatoes are crisp and browned, 3 to 4 minutes.

In small mixing bowl beat together eggs and water; add egg mixture to skillet and cook until bottom is set, 1 to 2 minutes. Arrange sausage slices over eggs. Transfer skillet to oven and bake until eggs are set and golden brown, 8 to 10 minutes.

MAKES 2 SERVINGS

Each serving provides: 2½ Protein Exchanges;
    1 Bread Exchange; ⅛ Vegetable Exchange;
    1 Fat Exchange
Per serving: 293 calories; 19 g protein; 16 g fat;
    17 g carbohydrate; 55 mg calcium; 498 mg sodium
    (estimated); 440 mg cholesterol; 2 g dietary fiber

Parmesan and Mixed Green Salad

To give this recipe a stronger cheese taste, rather than using grated Parmesan cheese, purchase a chunk of Parmesan cheese and shave it with a vegetable peeler. Grate any remaining cheese in a food processor and store in a resealable container in the refrigerator.

1 cup *each* torn radicchio (red chicory), Bibb, Boston, and red leaf lettuce*
2 ounces grated Parmesan cheese
1 tablespoon *each* minced shallot *or* onion, balsamic *or* red wine vinegar, and lemon juice
2 teaspoons *each* olive *or* vegetable oil and water
¼ teaspoon granulated sugar
Dash *each* salt and pepper

In large salad bowl combine lettuce and cheese. Using a wire whisk, in cup or small bowl combine remaining ingredients and beat until blended. Pour dressing over salad and toss to coat. Serve immediately.

MAKES 2 SERVINGS

Each serving provides: 1 Protein Exchange; 4 Vegetable Exchanges; 1 Fat Exchange; 3 Optional Calories
Per serving: 179 calories; 12 g protein; 12 g fat; 7 g carbohydrate; 414 mg calcium; 532 mg sodium; 19 mg cholesterol; 2 g dietary fiber

*Any lettuce may be substituted for the radicchio, Bibb, Boston, and red leaf lettuce.

Spinach Salad with Blue Cheese-Bacon Dressing

3 cups spinach leaves, thoroughly washed, drained, and torn into pieces
½ cup shredded carrot
2 ounces rinsed drained canned red kidney beans
¼ cup *each* diced red bell pepper and shredded red cabbage
1 tablespoon thinly sliced red onion
¼ cup plain low-fat yogurt
½ ounce blue cheese, crumbled
1 slice crisp bacon, crumbled
2 teaspoons reduced-calorie mayonnaise
1 teaspoon white wine vinegar
1½ ounces Cheddar cheese, shredded
2 eggs, hard-cooked and cut into halves

In salad bowl combine spinach, carrot, beans, bell pepper, cabbage, and onion and toss to combine.

In small mixing bowl combine yogurt, blue cheese, bacon, mayonnaise, and vinegar and stir to combine. Pour dressing over salad; top with Cheddar cheese and egg halves.

MAKES 2 SERVINGS

Each serving provides: 2 Protein Exchanges;
½ Bread Exchange; 4 Vegetable Exchanges;
½ Fat Exchange; ¼ Milk Exchange;
20 Optional Calories
Per serving: 309 calories; 21 g protein; 18 g fat;
16 g carbohydrate; 382 mg calcium; 582 mg sodium
(estimated); 308 mg cholesterol; 4 g dietary fiber

Warm Caesar Salad

Make a special dinner even more special with this variation on a classic salad.

2 eggs
1 tablespoon lemon juice
2 drained canned anchovy fillets, mashed
Dash *each* salt and pepper
4 cups torn romaine lettuce*
2 teaspoons olive *or* vegetable oil
1 small garlic clove, mashed
1 ounce onion- and garlic-flavored croutons
½ ounce grated Parmesan cheese

Using a fork, in large mixing bowl combine eggs, lemon juice, anchovies, salt, and pepper and beat until combined; add lettuce and toss to coat. Set aside.

In 10-inch nonstick skillet heat oil; add garlic and cook over medium heat, stirring frequently, until golden, about 30 seconds. Add lettuce mixture and cook, stirring constantly, until moisture has evaporated, 2 to 3 minutes. Add croutons and cheese; stir to combine and serve immediately.

MAKES 2 SERVINGS

Each serving provides: 1¼ Protein Exchanges;
1 Bread Exchange; 1 Vegetable Exchange;
1 Fat Exchange; 5 Optional Calories
Per serving: 189 calories; 12 g protein;
13 g fat; 6 g carbohydrate; 165 mg calcium;
449 mg sodium; 281 mg cholesterol; 2 g dietary fiber

*Four cups torn romaine lettuce yield about 1 cup cooked lettuce.

Goat Cheese Pita Pizza

Use your microwave to thaw the broccoli, or in the morning put it in the refrigerator and it will thaw in time for dinner.

¼ cup part-skim ricotta cheese
2 ounces chèvre (French goat cheese), at room temperature
1 tablespoon *each* grated Parmesan cheese, divided, chopped fresh parsley, and fresh basil *or* ½ teaspoon basil leaves
2 teaspoons olive *or* vegetable oil
1 garlic clove, minced
4 sun-dried tomato halves (not packed in oil)
¼ cup water
½ cup thawed and well-drained frozen chopped broccoli
2 pitas (2 ounces each)

Using a fork, in small mixing bowl combine ricotta cheese, chèvre, 2 teaspoons Parmesan cheese, the parsley, and the basil and mix well; set aside.

In 9-inch nonstick skillet heat oil; add garlic and sauté over medium-high heat, stirring frequently, for 1 minute. Add tomatoes and water and cook until tomatoes are softened, 1 to 2 minutes. Using a slotted spoon, remove tomatoes from liquid and cut each in half. Return to skillet; add broccoli and cook, stirring frequently, until liquid has evaporated, 2 to 3 minutes.

On baking sheet arrange pitas in a single layer and broil, turning once, until lightly browned, 1 to 2 minutes on each side.

Onto each pita spread ⅓ of the cheese mixture (about 2 tablespoons); top each with half of the broccoli mixture. Top each pizza with half of the remaining cheese mixture (about 1 tablespoon) and then sprinkle each with ½ teaspoon of the remaining Parmesan cheese. Broil until cheese mixture is melted and pizzas are heated through, 3 to 4 minutes.

MAKES 2 SERVINGS, 1 PIZZA EACH

Each serving provides: 1½ Protein Exchanges; 2 Bread Exchanges; 1½ Vegetable Exchanges; 1 Fat Exchange; 15 Optional Calories
Per serving: 412 calories; 18 g protein; 17 g fat; 49 g carbohydrate; 224 mg calcium; 872 mg sodium (estimated); 38 mg cholesterol; 3 g dietary fiber

Avocado Grilled Cheese Sandwich

2 slices pumpernickel bread
  (1 ounce each)
1½ ounces thinly sliced Monterey
  Jack cheese with jalapeño
  peppers
3 tomato slices
⅛ medium avocado (about
  1 ounce), pared and thinly sliced
¼ cup alfalfa sprouts

Onto 1 slice of bread arrange cheese, tomato, avocado, and sprouts; top with remaining slice of bread.

Spray small nonstick skillet with nonstick cooking spray; set sandwich in skillet, cover, and cook over medium-low heat until bottom is lightly browned, about 3 minutes. Carefully turn sandwich over and cook until other side is lightly browned and cheese is melted, about 3 minutes longer.

MAKES 1 SERVING

Each serving provides: 1½ Protein Exchanges;
    2 Bread Exchanges; 1½ Vegetable Exchanges;
    1 Fat Exchange
Per serving: 345 calories; 17 g protein; 17 g fat;
    35 g carbohydrate; 355 mg calcium; 613 mg sodium;
    46 mg cholesterol; 4 g dietary fiber

To store the unused portion of an avocado, brush the cut surface with lemon juice, leaving the pit in place. Wrap in plastic wrap and refrigerate until needed.

Microwave Mozzarella Sandwich © Ⓜ

2 slices whole wheat bread,
   toasted
1 teaspoon olive *or* vegetable oil
1 large plum tomato, sliced
2 ounces mozzarella cheese,
   shredded
1 tablespoon chopped fresh basil
Dash pepper

Onto 1 side of each slice of bread drizzle ½ teaspoon oil; top each slice of bread with half of the tomato slices and 1 ounce cheese. Sprinkle each sandwich with 1½ teaspoons basil and pepper. Set sandwiches on microwavable plate or large paper plate; cover with wax paper and microwave on Medium-High (70%) for 2 minutes, until cheese is melted.

MAKES 2 SERVINGS

Each serving provides: 1 Protein Exchange;
   1 Bread Exchange; ½ Vegetable Exchange;
   ½ Fat Exchange
Per serving: 162 calories; 8 g protein; 9 g fat;
   13 g carbohydrate; 183 mg calcium; 229 mg sodium;
   23 mg cholesterol; 2 g dietary fiber

Fish and Shellfish

Practically nothing beats fish for ease of preparation, versatility, and top-notch nutrition. Now that people everywhere are eating more fish as part of the trend toward a more healthful diet, you'll certainly want to check out this chapter. You'll find dozens of marvelous ways to serve your favorites. Enjoy tropical-style Mango Shrimp, spicy Orange-Gingered Sea Bass, or traditional Fish Amandine. For a new way to prepare a French classic, try Microwave Coquilles St. Jacques. And if you're bored with plain old tuna, wait until you taste Tuna Steaks with Mustard Butter, Tuna Provençal, and Tuna Teriyaki.

Smoked Salmon Pinwheel Appetizers

¼ **cup part-skim ricotta cheese**
1 ounce chèvre (French goat cheese)
1 tablespoon *each* **diced tomato and chopped fresh basil** *or* **½ teaspoon basil leaves**
Dash pepper
1 ounce smoked salmon (lox), cut into 4 strips (5 inches x ½ inch each)
1 cup chopped lettuce
4 cherry tomatoes, cut into quarters
2 tablespoons chopped red onion
2 teaspoons olive oil
1 teaspoon rinsed drained capers

Using a fork, in small mixing bowl combine cheeses, diced tomato, basil, and pepper and stir well to thoroughly combine. On narrow side of 1 strip of salmon spoon ¼ of cheese mixture (about 2 tablespoons); roll salmon strip jelly-roll fashion to enclose cheese mixture, making a pinwheel. Repeat procedure with remaining salmon strips and cheese mixture, making 3 more pinwheels.

To serve, line each of 2 individual serving plates with ½ cup lettuce. Onto each portion of lettuce decoratively arrange 2 pinwheels, surrounded by 8 tomato quarters and sprinkled with 1 tablespoon onion. Drizzle 1 teaspoon oil over pinwheels on each plate and then sprinkle with ½ teaspoon capers.

MAKES 2 SERVINGS, 2 PINWHEELS EACH

Each serving provides: 1½ Protein Exchanges;
    1½ Vegetable Exchanges; 1 Fat Exchange
Per serving: 165 calories; 9 g protein; 12 g fat;
    6 g carbohydrate; 138 mg calcium; 279 mg sodium;
    26 mg cholesterol; 1 g dietary fiber

Italian Clam Soup Ⓜ

To thoroughly remove sand from clams, refer to Clams Casino recipe (page 53).

9 cherrystone clams*
¼ cup bottled clam juice
Water
**½ cup drained canned Italian
  tomatoes, finely chopped**
2 tablespoons dry white table wine
**1 tablespoon chopped fresh
  parsley**
1 teaspoon olive *or* vegetable oil
**⅛ teaspoon *each* thyme leaves,
  oregano leaves, and basil leaves**
Dash red pepper flakes
**½ cup cooked small shell
  macaroni (hot)**

In 2-quart microwavable casserole combine clams, clam juice, and ¼ cup water; cover with vented plastic wrap and microwave on High (100%) for 3 minutes, until clam shells open. Set aside and let cool.

In separate 2-quart microwavable casserole combine 1¼ cups water, the tomatoes, wine, parsley, oil, thyme, oregano, basil, and pepper flakes; microwave on High, uncovered, for 1 minute.

Remove clams from shells, reserving cooking liquid, and discarding shells; chop clams and add to tomato mixture. Line sieve with cheesecloth and pour reserved cooking liquid through sieve into tomato mixture, discarding solids. Stir to combine and microwave, uncovered, on High for 4 minutes, until soup is heated through. Add macaroni.

MAKES 2 SERVINGS, ABOUT ¾ CUP EACH

Each serving provides: 1½ Protein Exchanges;
  ½ Bread Exchange; ½ Vegetable Exchange;
  ½ Fat Exchange; 20 Optional Calories
Per serving: 146 calories; 13 g protein;
  3 g fat; 13 g carbohydrate; 70 mg calcium;
  212 mg sodium; 28 mg cholesterol; 1 g dietary fiber

*Nine cherrystone clams will yield about 3 ounces cooked seafood.

Microwave Swordfish Chowder Ⓜ

Bacon gives this hearty chowder an added boost. Make cleanup easier by cooking the bacon between sheets of paper towel in the microwave.

3 ounces diced pared all-purpose
   potato
¼ cup *each* thinly sliced celery,
   diced green bell pepper, diced
   onion, and diced carrot
1 teaspoon vegetable oil
1 cup canned ready-to-serve
   chicken broth
½ cup canned Italian tomatoes
   (with liquid); drain, seed, and
   dice tomatoes, reserving liquid
1 teaspoon chopped fresh parsley
¼ teaspoon basil leaves
⅛ teaspoon *each* thyme leaves
   and salt
Dash pepper
3 ounces cubed swordfish (½-inch
   cubes)
1 slice crisp bacon, crumbled

In 1-quart microwavable casserole combine potato, celery, bell pepper, onion, carrot, and oil and stir to thoroughly coat; cover with vented plastic wrap and microwave on High (100%) for 3 minutes, stirring halfway through cooking. Add broth, tomatoes with liquid, parsley, basil, thyme, salt, and pepper; microwave on High, uncovered, for 2 minutes. Add fish and stir to combine; microwave on High, uncovered, for 2 minutes, until fish is cooked through and flakes easily when tested with a fork. Let stand for 1 minute. Sprinkle soup with bacon.

MAKES 2 SERVINGS, ABOUT 1¼ CUPS EACH

Each serving provides: 1 Protein Exchange;
   ½ Bread Exchange; 1½ Vegetable Exchanges;
   ½ Fat Exchange; 40 Optional Calories
Per serving: 171 calories; 12 g protein; 7 g fat;
   16 g carbohydrate; 43 mg calcium; 849 mg sodium;
   19 mg cholesterol; 2 g dietary fiber

Quick Clam Chowder Ⓜ

To thoroughly remove sand from clams, refer to Clams Casino recipe (page 53).

6 ounces diced pared all-purpose potato
1 cup thoroughly washed sliced leeks (white portion only) *or* **diced onions**
½ cup *each* **sliced celery and carrot**
2 teaspoons margarine
2 cups canned Italian tomatoes (with liquid); drain and chop tomatoes, reserving liquid
2 slices crisp bacon, crumbled
¼ teaspoon thyme leaves, crushed
1 dozen littleneck clams,* scrubbed

In 4-quart microwavable casserole combine potato, leeks (or onions), celery, carrot, and margarine; cover with vented plastic wrap and microwave on High (100%) for 6 minutes, until potato is softened. Add tomatoes with liquid, bacon, and thyme; re-cover with vented plastic wrap and microwave on High for 5 minutes, until potato is soft and mixture is thoroughly heated. Arrange clams around edge of casserole with hinged side of each clam toward edge of casserole, leaving a space between each. Re-cover with vented plastic wrap and microwave on High for 5 minutes, rotating casserole ½ turn after 3 minutes. Stir chowder, re-cover, and let stand for 5 minutes.

MAKES 2 SERVINGS, ABOUT 2 CUPS EACH

Each serving provides: 1 Protein Exchange;
    1 Bread Exchange; 4 Vegetable Exchanges;
    1 Fat Exchange; 45 Optional Calories
Per serving: 276 calories; 14 g protein;
    8 g fat; 38 g carbohydrate; 149 mg calcium;
    620 mg sodium; 24 mg cholesterol; 5 g dietary fiber

*One dozen littleneck clams will yield about 2 ounces cooked seafood.

Clams Casino Ⓜ

Purchase clams the day before you plan to cook them so you can give them a thorough cleaning. To be sure that clams are free of sand, place them in a large bowl and cover with uncooked cornmeal and some water; refrigerate overnight. Before preparing, discard the cornmeal mixture and thoroughly scrub the clams, rinsing them under cold running water.

2 tablespoons *each* minced onion
  and red *or* green bell pepper
1 tablespoon whipped butter
1 small garlic clove, minced
3 tablespoons seasoned dried
  bread crumbs
2 slices crisp bacon, crumbled
1 dozen cherrystone clams*
2 tablespoons freshly squeezed
  lemon juice

In small microwavable mixing bowl combine vegetables, butter, and garlic and microwave on High (100%) for 2 minutes, until vegetables are softened. Add bread crumbs and bacon and stir to combine.

Remove and discard top shell from each clam. Loosen meat in remaining shell halves and arrange around edge of microwavable rack, leaving a space between each. Spoon an equal amount of vegetable-bacon mixture over each clam and microwave on High (100%) for 3 minutes, rotating rack ½ turn halfway through cooking. Drizzle clams with lemon juice.

MAKES 2 SERVINGS

Each serving provides: 2 Protein Exchanges;
  ½ Bread Exchange; ¼ Vegetable Exchange;
  70 Optional Calories
Per serving: 196 calories; 18 g protein; 7 g fat;
  13 g carbohydrate; 69 mg calcium; 493 mg sodium;
  52 mg cholesterol; 1 g dietary fiber

*One dozen cherrystone clams will yield about ¼ pound cooked seafood.

Clams and Mussels with Vegetable Sauce Ⓜ

To thoroughly remove sand from clams, refer to Clams Casino recipe (page 53).

½ cup *each* diced carrot, celery, and thoroughly washed leeks (white portion only)
2 tablespoons dry white table wine *or* dry vermouth
1 tablespoon whipped butter
¼ teaspoon *each* thyme leaves, salt, and pepper
6 *each* small littleneck clams and medium mussels,* scrubbed
2 large plum tomatoes, chopped
1 tablespoon chopped fresh Italian (flat-leaf) parsley

In 9-inch microwavable pie plate combine vegetables, wine (or vermouth), butter, thyme, salt, and pepper. Cover with vented plastic wrap and microwave on High (100%) for 4 minutes, until vegetables are softened, stirring once halfway through cooking. Stir vegetables and move to center of plate. Arrange clams around outer edge of plate with hinged side of each clam toward rim of plate, leaving a space between each clam.

Cover pie plate loosely with plastic wrap and microwave on High for 3 minutes, until clam shells begin to open and turn white, rotating plate ½ turn after 1 minute. Arrange mussels between clams on plate with hinged side of each mussel toward rim of plate; top vegetable mixture with tomatoes and parsley. Cover pie plate loosely with plastic wrap and microwave on High for 2 minutes, until mussel and clam shells open, rotating plate ½ turn halfway through cooking.

MAKES 2 SERVINGS

Each serving provides: 1½ Protein Exchanges; 2½ Vegetable Exchanges; 40 Optional Calories
Per serving with white wine: 150 calories; 12 g protein; 5 g fat; 13 g carbohydrate; 69 mg calcium; 467 mg sodium; 33 mg cholesterol; 1 g dietary fiber
With vermouth: Increase calories to 155

*Six littleneck clams will yield about 1 ounce cooked seafood and 6 medium mussels will yield about 2 ounces cooked seafood.

Mussels in Vegetable Vinaigrette Ⓜ

½ cup chopped scallions (green
   onions)
¼ cup *each* diced red and green
   bell pepper
4 sun-dried tomato halves (not
   packed in oil), diced
1 teaspoon olive *or* vegetable oil
1 dozen medium mussels,*
   scrubbed
2 teaspoons apple cider vinegar
⅛ teaspoon thyme leaves,
   crushed
Dash pepper

In 9-inch microwavable pie plate combine scallions, bell peppers, tomatoes, and oil and stir to thoroughly coat; microwave on High (100%) for 1½ minutes, until softened. Arrange mussels around edge of pie plate with hinged side of each mussel toward edge of plate, leaving a space between each. Cover with vented plastic wrap and microwave on High for 3 minutes. Add remaining ingredients and stir to combine; re-cover with vented plastic wrap and microwave on High for 30 seconds. Let stand for 1 minute.

MAKES 2 SERVINGS

Each serving provides: 2 Protein Exchanges;
   2 Vegetable Exchanges; ½ Fat Exchange
Per serving: 148 calories; 15 g protein; 5 g fat;
   11 g carbohydrate; 44 mg calcium; 218 mg sodium;
   32 mg cholesterol; 2 g dietary fiber

*One dozen medium mussels will yield about ¼ pound cooked seafood.

So many recipes call for sliced, diced, or chopped vegetables. To save time, slice and dice a few days' worth of frequently used vegetables and store them in plastic bags in the refrigerator.

Crabby Corn Cakes

Grate lime peel before squeezing the lime, otherwise it will be difficult to grate.

2 tablespoons *each* chopped red bell pepper and onion
5 ounces thawed frozen crabmeat
1 day-old corn muffin (2 ounces), made into crumbs
1 egg, separated
1 tablespoon freshly squeezed lime juice, divided
½ teaspoon hot sauce
2 teaspoons vegetable oil, divided
3 tablespoons sour cream
1 tablespoon Dijon-style mustard
¼ teaspoon grated lime peel

Spray 10-inch nonstick skillet with nonstick cooking spray; add bell pepper and onion and sauté over medium-high heat, stirring frequently, until softened, 1 to 2 minutes. Transfer to medium mixing bowl; add crabmeat, corn muffin crumbs, egg yolk, 2 teaspoons lime juice, and the hot sauce and stir to thoroughly combine. Set aside.

Using electric mixer on high speed, in small mixing bowl beat egg white until stiff but not dry; gently fold into crabmeat mixture.

In same skillet heat 1 teaspoon oil; using half of crabmeat mixture and making 4 cakes, drop mixture into skillet. Cook over medium-high heat, turning once, until cakes are lightly browned, 2 to 3 minutes on each side. Transfer cakes to serving platter; set aside and keep warm. Repeat procedure using remaining oil and crabmeat mixture and making 4 more cakes.

While crab cakes are cooking prepare sauce. In small mixing bowl combine sour cream, mustard, remaining teaspoon lime juice, and the lime peel and stir well to combine.

To serve, top each portion of crab cakes with half of the sour cream mixture.

MAKES 2 SERVINGS, 4 CAKES EACH

Each serving provides: 3 Protein Exchanges; 1 Bread Exchange; ¼ Vegetable Exchange; 1½ Fat Exchanges; 50 Optional Calories
Per serving: 333 calories; 26 g protein; 17 g fat; 18 g carbohydrate; 176 mg calcium; 717 mg sodium; 260 mg cholesterol; 1 g dietary fiber

When a recipe calls for you to make crumbs — graham cracker, bread, or the more unusual corn muffin — look to your food processor to do it in a jiffy.

Crustless Seafood Quiche Ⓜ

¼ cup chopped red bell pepper
2 tablespoons chopped onion
1 teaspoon olive *or* vegetable oil
4 ounces thawed frozen imitation
   fish
1 cup whole milk
2 eggs
3 tablespoons instant nonfat dry
   milk powder
⅛ teaspoon white pepper
Dash ground nutmeg
2 ounces Muenster cheese,
   shredded, divided
4 tomato slices

Spray 8-inch microwavable pie plate with nonstick cooking spray; add bell pepper, onion, and oil and stir to thoroughly coat. Microwave on High (100%) for 1 minute, until vegetables are tender. Add imitation fish and stir to combine; spread mixture over bottom of pie plate.

Using a wire whisk, in small mixing bowl beat together whole milk, eggs, milk powder, pepper, and nutmeg; stir in 1 ounce cheese. Pour milk mixture over fish mixture in pie plate; microwave on Medium-High (70%) for 13 minutes, rotating pie plate ½ turn every 5 minutes, until quiche is set. Decoratively arrange tomato slices on quiche, sprinkle with remaining 1 ounce cheese, and micro-wave on Medium-High for 2 minutes, until cheese is melted. Let stand for 5 minutes.

MAKES 4 SERVINGS

Each serving provides: 2 Protein Exchanges;
   ½ Vegetable Exchange; ¼ Fat Exchange;
   ¼ Milk Exchange; 30 Optional Calories
Per serving: 184 calories; 14 g protein; 11 g fat;
   8 g carbohydrate; 233 mg calcium; 213 mg sodium;
   168 mg cholesterol; 0.3 g dietary fiber

Sweet and Sour Seafood

A summertime recipe that combines fresh nectarines and seafood.

¼ cup rice vinegar
2 tablespoons teriyaki sauce
2 teaspoons cornstarch
½ teaspoon Chinese sesame oil
1½ teaspoons peanut *or* vegetable oil
1 cup sliced shiitake *or* white mushrooms
½ cup *each* red bell pepper strips and diagonally sliced scallions (green onions)
1 small garlic clove, minced
1 teaspoon grated pared gingerroot
5 ounces shelled and deveined medium shrimp
10 ounces nectarines, blanched, pared, pitted, and sliced
2 ounces thawed frozen imitation fish, sliced
Dash pepper (optional)

In 1-cup liquid measure combine vinegar, teriyaki sauce, cornstarch, and Chinese sesame oil and stir to dissolve cornstarch; set aside.

In 10-inch skillet heat peanut (or vegetable) oil; add vegetables, garlic, and gingerroot and cook over medium-high heat, stirring frequently, until tender-crisp, about 3 minutes. Add shrimp and stir quickly to combine. Add vinegar mixture and cook, stirring constantly, until mixture thickens. Reduce heat to low; stir in nectarines, imitation fish, and, if desired, pepper. Cook until thoroughly heated, 1 to 2 minutes.

MAKES 2 SERVINGS

Each serving provides: 3 Protein Exchanges;
   2 Vegetable Exchanges; 1 Fat Exchange;
   1 Fruit Exchange; 10 Optional Calories
Per serving: 259 calories; 22 g protein; 7 g fat;
   29 g carbohydrate; 71 mg calcium; 844 mg sodium;
   116 mg cholesterol; 2 g dietary fiber

Blanching fruit or vegetables means you'll need boiling water. Why not use your microwave to do the boiling and keep your kitchen cool.

Citrus Scallops

½ pound bay scallops *or* sea
   scallops (cut into 1-inch pieces)
1 tablespoon *each* chopped
   chives, freshly squeezed lemon
   and lime juice, and whipped
   butter, melted
⅛ teaspoon paprika

Preheat broiler. In 1-quart flameproof shallow
casserole combine all ingredients. Broil until
scallops are golden brown, about 3 minutes.

MAKES 2 SERVINGS

Each serving provides: 3 Protein Exchanges;
   25 Optional Calories
Per serving: 130 calories; 19 g protein; 4 g fat;
   4 g carbohydrate; 31 mg calcium; 212 mg sodium;
   45 mg cholesterol; trace dietary fiber

*Butter and margarine melt in
seconds in the microwave.*

Microwave Coquilles St. Jacques Ⓜ

While the scallop mixture cooks in the microwave, use the time to shred the cheese.

½ pound bay scallops *or* sea
    scallops, cut into 1-inch pieces
2 tablespoons dry white table wine
1 tablespoon minced shallot
    (or onion)
1 small bay leaf
¼ cup evaporated skimmed milk
1 tablespoon all-purpose flour
¼ cup sliced mushrooms
½ ounce Gruyère *or* Swiss
    cheese, shredded
2 tablespoons plain dried bread
    crumbs

In 1-quart microwavable shallow casserole combine scallops, wine, shallot (or onion), and bay leaf; cover with vented plastic wrap and microwave on High (100%) for 2 minutes, until scallops are opaque and cooked through. Using a slotted spoon, transfer scallops to 1-quart flameproof casserole, reserving wine mixture. Remove and discard bay leaf.

Using a fork or small wire whisk, in 1-cup liquid measure combine milk and flour and stir well to dissolve flour. Stir flour mixture into wine mixture; add mushrooms and microwave, uncovered, on Medium (50%) for 3 minutes, until mixture thickens. Add to scallops in flameproof casserole and stir to combine.

Preheat broiler. In small bowl combine cheese and bread crumbs; sprinkle evenly over scallop mixture. Broil 5 to 6 inches from heat source until topping is lightly browned, 1 to 2 minutes.

MAKES 2 SERVINGS

Each serving provides: 3¼ Protein Exchanges;
    ½ Bread Exchange; ¼ Vegetable Exchange;
    ¼ Milk Exchange; 15 Optional Calories
Per serving with Gruyère cheese: 210 calories;
    25 g protein; 4 g fat; 15 g carbohydrate; 206 mg calcium;
    291 mg sodium; 47 mg cholesterol; 0.4 g dietary fiber
With Swiss cheese: 207 calories; 25 g protein; 3 g fat;
    16 g carbohydrate; 203 mg calcium; 286 mg sodium;
    46 mg cholesterol; 0.4 g dietary fiber

Mediterranean-Style Shrimp

1 teaspoon olive oil
½ cup *each* diagonally sliced
    scallions (green onions), sliced
    zucchini, and green bell pepper
    strips
½ ounce pignolias (pine nuts),
    toasted
1 small garlic clove, minced
⅔ cup water
1 packet instant chicken broth
    and seasoning mix
5 ounces shelled and deveined
    medium shrimp
6 dried apricot halves
1 tablespoon golden raisins
2 ounces rinsed drained canned
    chick-peas
1 medium tomato, cored and
    diced
1 cup cooked couscous
    (semolina), hot
Garnish: Italian (flat-leaf) parsley
    sprig

In 9-inch nonstick skillet heat oil; add vegetables, pignolias, and garlic and cook over medium heat, stirring constantly, until vegetables are tender-crisp, about 2 minutes. Add water and broth mix and stir to combine; cook over high heat until mixture comes to a boil. Add shrimp, apricot halves, and raisins and stir to combine. Reduce heat to medium, cover, and cook until shrimp just turn pink, 3 to 4 minutes. Add chick-peas and tomato and stir to combine; cook until heated through, about 1 minute.

To serve, on serving platter arrange couscous and top with shrimp mixture; garnish with parsley.

MAKES 2 SERVINGS

Each serving provides: 3 Protein Exchanges;
    1 Bread Exchange; 2½ Vegetable Exchanges;
    1 Fat Exchange; 1 Fruit Exchange; 5 Optional Calories
Per serving: 341 calories; 29 g protein; 8 g fat;
    40 g carbohydrate; 98 mg calcium; 752 mg sodium
    (estimated); 151 mg cholesterol; 4 g dietary fiber
    (this figure does not include pignolias and couscous;
    nutrition analyses not available)

Bacon-Shrimp Broil

Your microwave oven can crisp the bacon for this recipe in just a few minutes.

½ **pound large shrimp**
2 tablespoons *each* **chopped**
   scallion (green onion) and water
1 tablespoon *each* **dry sherry,**
   teriyaki sauce, and freshly
   squeezed lemon juice
2 slices crisp bacon, crumbled

Shell and devein shrimp, leaving last segment and tail in place. Using a sharp knife, butterfly shrimp by splitting each along back, down to tail, cutting as deep as possible without going through to the other side.

In small mixing bowl (not aluminum*) combine scallion, water, sherry, teriyaki sauce, and lemon juice and stir to combine; add shrimp and bacon and toss to coat with marinade. Cover with plastic wrap and refrigerate for 15 minutes.

Preheat broiler. In flameproof 9 x 9 x 2-inch baking pan arrange shrimp in a single layer, tail feathers up. Pour marinade mixture evenly over shrimp and broil 5 to 6 inches from heat source until shrimp turn pink, 3 to 4 minutes.

MAKES 2 SERVINGS

Each serving provides: 3 Protein Exchanges;
   ⅛ Vegetable Exchange; 50 Optional Calories
Per serving: 143 calories; 20 g protein; 4 g fat;
   3 g carbohydrate; 41 mg calcium; 637 mg sodium;
   171 mg cholesterol; 0.2 g dietary fiber

*It's best to marinate in glass or stainless-steel containers; acidic ingredients such as sherry and lemon juice may react with aluminum, causing color and flavor changes in food.

Mango Shrimp

2 tablespoons reduced-calorie
   apricot spread (16 calories per
   2 teaspoons)
1 tablespoon plus 2 teaspoons
   freshly squeezed lime juice,
   divided
1 tablespoon plus 1 teaspoon
   hoisin sauce
1 teaspoon grated pared
   gingerroot
½ pound shelled and deveined
   large shrimp
¼ small mango (about 3¼ ounces
   with rind, without pit), pared
   and cubed
2 tablespoons plus 2 teaspoons
   apricot nectar
2 teaspoons olive *or* vegetable oil
1 small jalapeño pepper, seeded
   and sliced

In small mixing bowl (not aluminum*) combine apricot spread, 2 teaspoons lime juice, the hoisin sauce, and the gingerroot and stir well to combine; add shrimp and turn to coat with marinade. Cover and refrigerate at least 30 minutes.

In blender container combine mango, nectar, and remaining tablespoon lime juice and process until smooth; transfer to small saucepan. Using slotted spoon, transfer shrimp to plate and set aside. Add marinade mixture to mango mixture in saucepan and cook over medium heat, stirring occasionally, until heated through, 3 to 4 minutes. Reduce heat to low and keep warm.

In 10-inch nonstick skillet heat oil; add pepper and sauté over medium heat until pepper is lightly browned, about 1 minute. Remove and discard pepper slices. Add shrimp to skillet and sauté over high heat, turning once, until browned, 3 to 4 minutes on each side.

To serve, pour any pan juices into mango mixture and stir to combine. Spread half of the mango mixture on serving platter; top with shrimp and remaining mango mixture.

MAKES 2 SERVINGS

Each serving provides: 3 Protein Exchanges;
   1 Fat Exchange; ½ Fruit Exchange;
   45 Optional Calories
Per serving: 236 calories; 24 g protein; 7 g fat;
   20 g carbohydrate; 68 mg calcium; 509 mg sodium;
   173 mg cholesterol; 0.5 g dietary fiber

*It's best to marinate in glass or stainless-steel containers; acidic ingredients such as lime juice may react with aluminum, causing color and flavor changes in food.

Pasta with Spinach and Shrimp

½ cup canned ready-to-serve chicken broth
¼ teaspoon oregano leaves
⅛ teaspoon *each* crushed red pepper and garlic powder
2 cups thoroughly washed and drained spinach,* chopped
2 teaspoons olive *or* vegetable oil
½ pound shelled and deveined medium shrimp
1 tablespoon minced shallot *or* onion
1½ cups cooked linguine (hot)
2 teaspoons grated Parmesan cheese

In 2-quart saucepan combine broth, oregano, red pepper, and garlic and bring to a boil. Reduce heat to low; add spinach and cook, stirring occasionally, until spinach is wilted and bright green, about 2 minutes; set aside.

In 9-inch nonstick skillet heat oil; add shrimp and shallot (or onion) and cook over high heat, stirring occasionally, until shrimp turn pink. Transfer shrimp to saucepan with spinach; add linguine and cook over medium heat, tossing to combine, until mixture is heated through, about 1 minute.

To serve, transfer spinach mixture to serving bowl and sprinkle with Parmesan cheese.

MAKES 2 SERVINGS

Each serving provides: 3 Protein Exchanges;
 1½ Bread Exchanges; ½ Vegetable Exchange;
 1 Fat Exchange; 20 Optional Calories
Per serving: 310 calories; 30 g protein; 8 g fat;
 29 g carbohydrate; 151 mg calcium; 496 mg sodium;
 174 mg cholesterol; 3 g dietary fiber

*Two cups fresh spinach yield about ½ cup cooked spinach.

Pickled Shrimp

½ cup thinly sliced onion
¼ cup rice vinegar
1 tablespoon lemon juice
½ garlic clove, sliced
½ pound shelled and deveined
   medium shrimp
1 tablespoon chopped fresh
   Italian (flat-leaf) parsley
2 teaspoons olive *or* vegetable oil

In small saucepan combine onion, vinegar, lemon juice, and garlic and cook over high heat until mixture comes to a boil. Add shrimp and stir to combine; cook until shrimp just turn pink, about 1 minute. Remove from heat and stir in remaining ingredients. Let cool slightly. Transfer to container (not aluminum*), cover, and refrigerate until chilled, at least 4 hours or overnight.

MAKES 2 SERVINGS

Each serving provides: 3 Protein Exchanges;
   ½ Vegetable Exchange; 1 Fat Exchange
Per serving: 181 calories; 24 g protein; 7 g fat;
   6 g carbohydrate; 72 mg calcium; 176 mg sodium;
   173 mg cholesterol; 0.3 g dietary fiber

*It's best to marinate in glass or stainless-steel containers; acidic ingredients such as vinegar and lemon juice may react with aluminum, causing color and flavor changes in food.

Puffy Shrimp Toasts

5 ounces shelled and deveined
  shrimp, lightly chopped
2 tablespoons chopped scallion
  (green onion)
1 tablespoon *each* teriyaki sauce
  and dry sherry
1¾ teaspoons peanut *or*
  vegetable oil
¼ teaspoon *each* Chinese sesame
  oil and grated pared gingerroot
1 egg white
2 slices white bread (1 ounce
  each), each lightly toasted and
  cut into 4 triangles

In work bowl of food processor process shrimp, using on-off motion, until shrimp are minced *(do not overprocess).* Transfer to small mixing bowl; add scallion, teriyaki sauce, sherry, oils, and gingerroot and mix well. Set aside.

Preheat oven to 350°F. Using electric mixer on high speed, in separate small mixing bowl beat egg white until stiff but not dry. Onto each bread triangle spread ⅛ of the shrimp mixture. Spread ⅛ of the beaten white over shrimp mixture on each bread triangle, being sure to cover all of the shrimp mixture. Arrange bread triangles on nonstick baking sheet and bake until shrimp mixture is cooked through and topping is lightly browned, 10 to 15 minutes.

MAKES 4 SERVINGS, 2 TOASTS EACH

Each serving provides: 1 Protein Exchange;
  ½ Bread Exchange; ½ Fat Exchange;
  10 Optional Calories
Per serving: 110 calories; 10 g protein; 3 g fat;
  9 g carbohydrate; 35 mg calcium; 310 mg sodium;
  54 mg cholesterol; 0.3 g dietary fiber

Shrimp Gruyère Ⓜ

To add a golden color to this recipe, transfer cooked shrimp to a nonstick baking sheet and broil until lightly browned.

7 ounces large shrimp
1 tablespoon *each* freshly squeezed lemon juice and dry sherry
1 garlic clove, minced
3 tablespoons plain dried bread crumbs
1 ounce Gruyère cheese, shredded
1 tablespoon *each* chopped fresh Italian (flat-leaf) parsley and whipped butter, melted
⅛ teaspoon salt
Dash white pepper
Garnish: 2 *each* lemon slices, lime slices, and watercress sprigs

Shell and devein shrimp, leaving last segment and tail in place. Using a sharp knife, butterfly shrimp by splitting each along back, down to tail, cutting as deep as possible without going through to the other side; spread shrimp open so they lie flat.

In small glass or stainless-steel mixing bowl combine lemon juice, sherry, and garlic; add shrimp and toss to coat with marinade. Cover with plastic wrap and refrigerate for 15 minutes.

In separate small mixing bowl combine bread crumbs, cheese, parsley, butter, salt, and pepper; add 1 tablespoon marinade mixture, discarding remaining marinade, and stir until mixture is thoroughly combined and moistened.

Onto center of each shrimp spoon an equal amount of cheese mixture and press mixture firmly so it adheres to shrimp. In 1-quart microwavable shallow casserole arrange shrimp in a circle, stuffing-side up, with tails facing toward center of casserole and leaving a space between each shrimp. Cover with wax paper and microwave on Medium (50%) for 3 minutes. Rotate casserole ½ turn and microwave on Medium for 3 minutes, until shrimp turn pink.

MAKES 2 SERVINGS

Each serving provides: 3 Protein Exchanges; ½ Bread Exchange; 35 Optional Calories
Per serving: 207 calories; 20 g protein; 9 g fat; 9 g carbohydrate; 191 mg calcium; 445 mg sodium; 162 mg cholesterol; 0.5 g dietary fiber

Stir-Fry Chili Shrimp

2 teaspoons olive *or* vegetable oil
¼ cup seeded and thinly sliced
   mild *or* hot chili pepper
½ cup *each* diced onion and red
   bell pepper
1 small garlic clove, minced
½ pound shelled and deveined
   medium shrimp
2 tablespoons *each* chopped
   fresh cilantro (Chinese parsley)
   or Italian (flat-leaf) parsley and
   freshly squeezed lime juice
Dash *each* salt and crushed red
   pepper
1 cup cooked long-grain rice (hot)

In 9-inch skillet heat oil; add chili pepper and cook over medium heat, stirring constantly, until tender, about 30 seconds. Add onion, bell pepper, and garlic and cook, stirring frequently, until tender-crisp, about 1 minute longer. Add shrimp and cook, stirring quickly and frequently, until shrimp are just turning pink, about 2 minutes. Add remaining ingredients except rice, stir to combine, and cook until flavors blend, about 1 minute.

To serve, on serving platter arrange rice and top with shrimp mixture.

MAKES 2 SERVINGS

Each serving provides: 3 Protein Exchanges;
   1 Bread Exchange; 1¼ Vegetable Exchanges;
   1 Fat Exchange
Per serving: 305 calories; 26 g protein; 7 g fat;
   34 g carbohydrate; 89 mg calcium; 237 mg sodium;
   173 mg cholesterol; 2 g dietary fiber

Fillets and Vegetables Ⓜ

½ cup *each* sliced celery and
　　diced onion
2 teaspoons margarine
2 fish fillets (flounder, sole, *or*
　　scrod), ¼ pound each
2 large plum tomatoes, sliced
Dash *each* salt, white pepper, and
　　lemon juice

In 8-inch microwavable pie plate combine celery, onion, and margarine and microwave on High (100%) for 2 minutes, until vegetables are softened. Stir vegetables to coat with margarine; arrange fish fillets over vegetables. Arrange tomato slices over fish and then sprinkle with salt, pepper, and lemon juice. Microwave on Medium-High (70%) for 3 minutes, rotating pie plate ½ turn halfway through cooking, until fish is cooked through and flakes easily when tested with a fork.

MAKES 2 SERVINGS

Each serving provides: 3 Protein Exchanges;
　　2 Vegetable Exchanges; 1 Fat Exchange
Per serving with flounder *or* sole: 165 calories;
　　23 g protein; 5 g fat; 6 g carbohydrate; 47 mg calcium;
　　234 mg sodium; 54 mg cholesterol; 2 g dietary fiber
With scrod: 155 calories; 21 g protein; 5 g fat;
　　6 g carbohydrate; 44 mg calcium; 203 mg sodium;
　　49 mg cholesterol; 2 g dietary fiber

A microwavable pie plate is a handy and versatile utensil. Besides its obvious use for pies, it's great for microwaving foods that should be arranged in a circle with longer-cooking areas toward the rim of the plate (such as broccoli florets and chicken legs).

Fish Amandine

2 sole *or* flounder fillets (¼ pound each)
1 tablespoon plus 1 teaspoon all-purpose flour
2 teaspoons olive *or* vegetable oil
1 tablespoon whipped butter
½ ounce sliced almonds
¼ cup dry white table wine
1 tablespoon freshly squeezed lemon juice
⅛ teaspoon *each* salt and white pepper
1 teaspoon chopped fresh Italian (flat-leaf) parsley
Garnish: 3 lemon slices, halved Italian (flat-leaf) parsley sprigs

On sheet of wax paper or a paper plate dredge fillets in flour, lightly coating both sides and reserving remaining flour. Spray 10-inch nonstick skillet with nonstick cooking spray; add oil and heat. Add fillets to skillet and cook over medium-high heat, turning once, until fish is lightly browned and flakes easily when tested with a fork, 2 to 3 minutes on each side. Transfer fillets to serving platter; set aside and keep warm.

In same skillet melt butter; add almonds and sauté over medium-low heat, stirring frequently, until lightly browned, 1 to 2 minutes. Add remaining reserved flour and stir quickly to combine; stir in wine, lemon juice, salt, and pepper. Cook, stirring occasionally, until mixture is reduced by ⅓ and slightly thickened, 1 to 2 minutes. Pour almond mixture over fillets; sprinkle with chopped parsley and garnish with lemon slices and parsley sprigs.

MAKES 2 SERVINGS

Each serving provides: 3½ Protein Exchanges;
  1½ Fat Exchanges; 75 Optional Calories
Per serving: 252 calories; 23 g protein; 12 g fat;
  6 g carbohydrate; 46 mg calcium; 262 mg sodium;
  62 mg cholesterol; 0.5 g dietary fiber

Fisherman's Sausage Ⓒ Ⓜ

½ pound haddock fillets
20 oyster crackers, made into fine
   crumbs
2 tablespoons *each* chopped
   scallion (green onion), diced
   pimiento, and chopped fresh
   dill
1 tablespoon *each* lemon juice
   and white wine Worcestershire
   sauce
1 egg white
Water
Garnish: lemon slice and
   dill sprigs

In work bowl of food processor process fish into a paste; add crumbs and process until combined. Transfer to medium mixing bowl; add scallion, pimiento, dill, lemon juice, and Worcestershire sauce and stir to combine. Using electric mixer on medium-high speed, in small mixing bowl beat egg white until stiff peaks form; fold into fish mixture.

In 13 x 9 x 2-inch microwavable baking dish microwave 3 cups water on High (100%) for 6 minutes, until boiling. While water is boiling, shape fish mixture. Line work surface with 18-inch long sheet of plastic wrap; transfer fish mixture to center of plastic wrap and shape into a 12-inch-long sausage. Wrap sausage in plastic wrap, twisting ends of wrap tightly and tying each into a knot. Place sausage in boiling water and microwave on High, until firm, for 6 minutes, turning sausage over halfway through cooking. Fill large mixing bowl with ice water; immediately transfer sausage to bowl and let cool. Drain sausage and refrigerate at least 4 hours or overnight.

To serve, remove and discard plastic wrap and thinly slice sausage. Decoratively arrange slices on serving platter and garnish with lemon slice and dill sprigs.

MAKES 2 SERVINGS

Each serving provides: 3 Protein Exchanges;
   ½ Bread Exchange; ¼ Vegetable Exchange;
   10 Optional Calories
Per serving: 152 calories; 24 g protein; 2 g fat;
   9 g carbohydrate; 60 mg calcium; 254 mg sodium;
   65 mg cholesterol; 0.2 g dietary fiber (this figure does
   not include oyster crackers; nutrition analysis not
   available)

Microwave "Fried" Fish ⓜ

The microwave oven gives you crispy fish fillets in a flash.

1 tablespoon plus 1½ teaspoons
   plain dried bread crumbs
½ teaspoon grated Parmesan
   cheese
⅛ teaspoon basil leaves
Dash pepper
2 teaspoons margarine
2 lemon *or* gray sole fillets
   (3 ounces each)

On sheet of wax paper or a paper plate combine bread crumbs, cheese, basil, and pepper and stir to thoroughly combine; set aside. In microwavable cup microwave margarine on High (100%) for 30 seconds, until melted. Brush both sides of each fillet with melted margarine, using all of the margarine, and then dredge each fillet in bread crumb mixture, lightly coating both sides. Place each fillet on a sheet of paper towel; fold sides of each towel over each fillet to enclose, and arrange folded-sides down on microwavable plate. Microwave on Medium-High (70%) for 2 minutes. Let stand for 2 minutes, until fish is cooked through and flakes easily when tested with a fork. Remove and discard paper towels.

MAKES 2 SERVINGS

Each serving provides: 2 Protein Exchanges;
   ¼ Bread Exchange; 1 Fat Exchange; 3 Optional Calories
Per serving: 132 calories; 17 g protein; 5 g fat;
   4 g carbohydrate; 30 mg calcium; 156 mg sodium;
   41 mg cholesterol; 0.2 g dietary fiber

Parmesan Fillets ☻

**2 teaspoons *each* olive oil
and freshly squeezed lemon
juice
1 scrod *or* flounder fillet
(7 ounces), cut in half crosswise
½ ounce grated Parmesan
cheese, divided**

Preheat broiler. In cup or small bowl combine oil and lemon juice. On nonstick baking sheet arrange fillets in a single layer and, using pastry brush, brush both sides of each fillet with ¼ of the oil mixture. Sprinkle top of each fillet with half of the cheese. Broil until golden brown and fish flakes easily when tested with a fork, 3 to 4 minutes.

MAKES 2 SERVINGS

Each serving provides: 3 Protein Exchanges;
   1 Fat Exchange
Per serving with scrod: 162 calories; 23 g protein; 7 g fat;
   1 g carbohydrate; 102 mg calcium; 175 mg sodium;
   54 mg cholesterol; dietary fiber data not available
With flounder: 172 calories; 24 g protein; 8 g fat;
   1 g carbohydrate; 105 mg calcium; 206 mg sodium;
   59 mg cholesterol; dietary fiber data not available

Poached Fillets Vinaigrette Ⓜ

¼ cup seeded and diced tomato
1 teaspoon *each* chopped fresh
   parsley and olive oil
¼ teaspoon rosemary leaves,
   crushed
2 fish fillets (grouper, flounder,
   or sole), ¼ pound each
2 tablespoons *each* dry white
   table wine, water, and balsamic
   or red wine vinegar

In small mixing bowl combine tomato,
parsley, oil, and rosemary; set aside.

In 1-quart microwavable shallow casserole
arrange fish fillets; set aside. In cup or small
bowl combine wine, water, and vinegar and
pour half of mixture over each fillet. Cover
with vented plastic wrap and microwave on
Medium-High (70%) for 4 minutes, rotating
casserole ½ turn halfway through cooking,
until fish is cooked through and flakes easily
when tested with a fork.

To serve, transfer fillets to serving platter;
top each fillet with half of the tomato mixture
and then with half of the cooking liquid.

MAKES 2 SERVINGS

Each serving provides: 3 Protein Exchanges;
   ¼ Vegetable Exchange; ½ Fat Exchange;
   15 Optional Calories
Per serving with grouper: 141 calories; 22 g protein;
   3 g fat; 2 g carbohydrate; 36 mg calcium; 63 mg sodium;
   42 mg cholesterol; 0.3 g dietary fiber
With flounder *or* sole: 141 calories; 22 g protein; 4 g fat;
   2 g carbohydrate; 26 mg calcium; 95 mg sodium;
   54 mg cholesterol; 0.3 g dietary fiber

*Check out the variety of micro-
wavable cookware available today.
Some is so attractive that you can
use it to bring food from the microwave to the table without having to
transfer it to a serving platter.*

Fluke with Lemon Sauce

2 fluke fillets (¼ pound each),
   each cut in half lengthwise
1 egg white
3 tablespoons seasoned dried
   bread crumbs
2 teaspoons olive *or* vegetable oil
1 garlic clove, minced
⅓ cup water
¼ cup dry white table wine
1 tablespoon *each* minced fresh
   parsley and freshly squeezed
   lemon juice
½ packet (½ teaspoon)
   instant chicken broth and
   seasoning mix

Dip 1 fish fillet in egg white, then into bread crumbs, coating both sides evenly; repeat procedure with remaining fillet, being sure to use all of the egg white and bread crumbs.

In 9-inch nonstick skillet heat oil; add fillets and cook over medium-high heat, turning once, until fish is cooked through and flakes easily when tested with a fork, about 3 minutes on each side. Transfer fish to serving platter; set aside and keep warm.

To same skillet add garlic and cook over medium heat until golden, about 15 seconds; stir in water, wine, parsley, lemon juice, and broth mix. Cook over high heat until mixture comes to a boil; continue cooking until mixture is reduced to about ¼ cup, about 4 minutes. Pour over fish fillets.

MAKES 2 SERVINGS

Each serving provides: 3 Protein Exchanges;
   ½ Bread Exchange; 1 Fat Exchange;
   45 Optional Calories
Per serving: 218 calories; 25 g protein; 6 g fat;
   10 g carbohydrate; 41 mg calcium; 665 mg sodium;
   55 mg cholesterol; 1 g dietary fiber

Variation: Halibut with Lemon Sauce — Substitute 2 halibut fillets (¼ pound each) for the fluke.

Per serving: 240 calories; 27 g protein; 7 g fat;
   10 g carbohydrate; 73 mg calcium; 635 mg sodium;
   37 mg cholesterol; 1 g dietary fiber

Fish fillets dredged in bread crumbs are so delicious — but what a mess to clean up! You can make your cleanup job easier by putting the bread crumbs on wax paper or a paper plate.

Red Snapper with Tomato Sauce

1 tablespoon all-purpose flour
Dash *each* salt and pepper
½ pound red snapper fillets
1 tablespoon olive *or* vegetable
   oil
½ cup diced red onion
1 small garlic clove, minced
½ cup tomato sauce

On sheet of wax paper or a paper plate combine flour, salt, and pepper; dredge fish in flour mixture, coating both sides.

In 9-inch nonstick skillet heat oil; add fish and cook over medium-high heat, turning once, until browned and fish flakes easily when tested with a fork, about 2 minutes on each side. Transfer fish to serving platter; set aside and keep warm.

In same skillet combine onion and garlic and cook over medium heat until onion is translucent, about 2 minutes. Stir in tomato sauce and cook, stirring frequently, until thoroughly heated, about 2 minutes.

To serve, top fish with tomato sauce.

MAKES 2 SERVINGS

Each serving provides: 3 Protein Exchanges;
   1 Vegetable Exchange; 1½ Fat Exchanges;
   15 Optional Calories
Per serving: 221 calories; 25 g protein; 8 g fat;
   11 g carbohydrate; 58 mg calcium; 509 mg sodium;
   42 mg cholesterol; 1 g dietary fiber

Orange-Gingered Sea Bass Ⓜ

¼ cup *each* julienne-cut red bell
   pepper, julienne-cut scallions
   (green onions), julienne-cut
   carrot, and diced red onion
2 tablespoons rice vinegar
1 tablespoon *each* thawed frozen
   concentrated orange juice
   (no sugar added) and orange
   zest*
1 teaspoon *each* grated pared
   gingerroot, vegetable oil, and
   Chinese sesame oil
2 sea bass fillets (¼ pound each)

In small mixing bowl combine all ingredients
except fillets and stir to thoroughly combine;
set aside. On microwavable serving platter
arrange fillets in a single layer; top each with
half of the vegetable mixture. Cover with
vented plastic wrap and microwave on
Medium-High (70%) for 3 minutes, rotating
platter ½ turn halfway through cooking.
Let stand for 1 minute, until fish is cooked
through and flakes easily when tested with
a fork.

MAKES 2 SERVINGS

Each serving provides: 3 Protein Exchanges;
   1 Vegetable Exchange; 1 Fat Exchange;
   ¼ Fruit Exchange
Per serving: 189 calories; 22 g protein; 7 g fat;
   9 g carbohydrate; 36 mg calcium; 86 mg sodium;
   47 mg cholesterol; 1 g dietary fiber

Variation: Orange-Gingered Halibut —
Substitute 2 halibut fillets (¼ pound each),
for the sea bass.

Per serving: 204 calories; 25 g protein; 7 g fat;
   9 g carbohydrate; 78 mg calcium; 70 mg sodium;
   36 mg cholesterol; 1 g dietary fiber

*The zest of the orange is the peel without any of the pith
   (white membrane). To remove zest from orange, use a
   zester or vegetable peeler; wrap orange in plastic wrap
   and refrigerate for use at another time.

Swordfish Mediterranean

2 teaspoons olive oil
½ cup chopped onion
2 garlic cloves, minced
1 cup canned Italian tomatoes
   (with liquid); drain, seed, and
   dice tomatoes, reserving liquid
¼ cup dry red table wine
6 Gaeta *or* black olives, pitted
1 tablespoon rinsed drained
   capers
9-ounce swordfish steak
⅛ teaspoon *each* salt and pepper

In 12-inch deep skillet heat oil; add onion and garlic and sauté over medium-high heat, stirring occasionally, until onion is softened, 1 to 2 minutes. Stir in remaining ingredients except fish, salt, and pepper. Reduce heat to low, cover, and cook, stirring occasionally, until flavors blend, 4 to 5 minutes. Add fish, salt, and pepper; cover and cook until fish is opaque and flakes easily when tested with a fork, 8 to 10 minutes.

MAKES 2 SERVINGS

Each serving provides: 3 Protein Exchanges;
    1½ Vegetable Exchanges; 1½ Fat Exchanges;
    30 Optional Calories
Per serving: 282 calories; 27 g protein; 13 g fat;
    10 g carbohydrate; 62 mg calcium; 798 mg sodium;
    50 mg cholesterol; 1 g dietary fiber

Squid Sauté

2 teaspoons olive *or* vegetable oil
½ cup *each* sliced onion, red bell
    pepper strips, and green bell
    pepper strips (3 x ½-inch strips)
1 small garlic clove, minced
2 tablespoons dry vermouth
1 tablespoon chopped fresh basil
    or ½ teaspoon basil leaves
2 teaspoons lemon juice
¼ teaspoon salt
Dash pepper
½ pound cleaned squid* (discard
    head and ink sac); cut body into
    rings and reserve tentacles

In 9-inch nonstick skillet heat oil; add vegetables and garlic and cook over high heat, stirring frequently, until vegetables are tender-crisp, 2 to 3 minutes. Add remaining ingredients except squid and bring mixture to a boil. Add squid rings and tentacles and stir to combine; cook just until squid turns white, 1 to 2 minutes (*do not overcook or squid will toughen*).

MAKES 2 SERVINGS

Each serving provides: 2 Protein Exchanges;
    1½ Vegetable Exchanges; 1 Fat Exchange;
    15 Optional Calories
Per serving: 143 calories; 12 g protein; 6 g fat;
    7 g carbohydrate; 47 mg calcium; 305 mg sodium;
    165 mg cholesterol; 1 g dietary fiber

*One-half pound cleaned squid will yield about ¼ pound
  cooked seafood.

Tuna Provençal

2 teaspoons olive oil
½ pound boneless tuna steaks, cut into cubes
½ cup *each* **sliced onion and red bell pepper strips**
1 tablespoon *each* **dry vermouth** *or* **dry white table wine and rinsed drained capers**
6 oil-cured black olives, halved and pitted
1 small garlic clove, minced
2 small plum tomatoes, cut lengthwise into quarters

In 9-inch skillet heat oil; add tuna and cook, stirring occasionally, until lightly browned on all sides, about 5 minutes. Add onion, bell pepper, vermouth (or wine), capers, olives, and garlic and stir to combine. Reduce heat to low, cover, and cook until vegetables are tender, about 3 minutes. Add tomatoes and stir to combine; cook until tomatoes are heated through, about 1 minute longer.

MAKES 2 SERVINGS

Each serving provides: 3 Protein Exchanges;
 1½ Vegetable Exchanges; 1½ Fat Exchanges;
 10 Optional Calories
Per serving with vermouth: 262 calories; 28 g protein;
 13 g fat; 7 g carbohydrate; 22 mg calcium;
 395 mg sodium; 43 mg cholesterol; 1 g dietary fiber
With white wine: Decrease calories to 260

Tuna Steaks with Mustard Butter

2 boneless tuna steaks (¼ pound each)
1 tablespoon *each* reduced-sodium soy sauce and rice vinegar
⅛ teaspoon ground ginger
1 tablespoon whipped butter, softened, divided
½ teaspoon powdered mustard

In container (not aluminum*) that is large enough to hold tuna in a single layer, arrange tuna. In cup or small bowl combine soy sauce, vinegar, and ginger; pour over tuna. Let stand for 5 minutes; turn tuna over and let stand 5 minutes longer. In cup or small bowl combine 2 teaspoons butter and the mustard and mix until combined; cover and refrigerate until ready to serve.

In 9-inch nonstick skillet melt remaining teaspoon butter; add tuna, reserving marinade, and cook over medium-high heat until bottom of tuna is browned, about 2 minutes; turn tuna over, drizzle with reserved marinade, and cook until browned, about 2 minutes longer.

To serve, transfer tuna steaks to serving platter and top each with half of the butter mixture.

MAKES 2 SERVINGS

Each serving provides: 3 Protein Exchanges; 25 Optional Calories
Per serving: 197 calories; 27 g protein; 9 g fat; 1 g carbohydrate; 4 mg calcium; 375 mg sodium; 51 mg cholesterol; dietary fiber data not available

*It's best to marinate in glass or stainless-steel containers; acidic ingredients such as rice vinegar may react with aluminum, causing color and flavor changes in food.

Tuna Teriyaki

Marinating is the secret to this tasty tuna. A minimum of 1 hour will be needed to flavor the tuna; but we suggest letting the tuna marinate overnight or while you're at the office.

2 tablespoons teriyaki sauce
1 tablespoon *each* rice vinegar and freshly squeezed lemon juice
1 teaspoon minced pared gingerroot
1 garlic clove, minced
2 boneless tuna steaks (¼ pound each)
1 teaspoon Chinese sesame oil

In shallow medium mixing bowl (not aluminum*) combine teriyaki sauce, vinegar, lemon juice, gingerroot, and garlic; add tuna and turn to coat. Cover with plastic wrap and refrigerate, turning occasionally, for at least 1 hour or overnight.

Preheat broiler. Remove tuna from marinade, reserving marinade. Brush each side of each tuna steak with ¼ of the oil; set tuna on nonstick baking sheet. Broil 5 inches from heat source, turning once, until tuna is cooked through and flakes easily when tested with a fork, 3 to 4 minutes on each side.

While tuna is cooking, cook marinade. Transfer reserved marinade to small saucepan and bring to a boil; boil until mixture is reduced to 2 tablespoons, about 4 minutes.

To serve, transfer tuna steaks to serving platter and top each with half of the marinade mixture.

MAKES 2 SERVINGS

Each serving provides: 3 Protein Exchanges;
 ½ Fat Exchange
Per serving: 204 calories; 28 g protein; 8 g fat;
 5 g carbohydrate; 8 mg calcium; 735 mg sodium;
 43 mg cholesterol; dietary fiber data not available

*It's best to marinate in glass or stainless-steel containers; ingredients such as vinegar and lemon juice may react with aluminum, causing color and flavor changes in food.

Mexican Lobster Salad

¼ pound shelled cooked lobster meat, cut into 1-inch pieces
¼ cup *each* diced green bell pepper and sliced celery
1 large plum tomato, cut into 8 equal wedges
1 tablespoon chopped fresh cilantro (Chinese parsley) *or* Italian (flat-leaf) parsley
1 tablespoon *each* seeded and minced jalapeño pepper and minced scallion (green onion)
½ small garlic clove, minced
1 tablespoon *each* sour cream and lime juice (no sugar added)
2 teaspoons olive *or* vegetable oil
Dash *each* salt and pepper
4 lettuce leaves

In medium mixing bowl combine lobster, bell pepper, celery, tomato, cilantro (or parsley), jalapeño pepper, scallion, and garlic; set aside. In small mixing bowl combine remaining ingredients except lettuce; pour over lobster mixture and toss to coat. Cover with plastic wrap and refrigerate until ready to serve.

To serve, line serving platter with lettuce; toss lobster mixture again and arrange on lettuce.

MAKES 2 SERVINGS

Each serving provides: 2 Protein Exchanges; 1½ Vegetable Exchanges; 1 Fat Exchange; 15 Optional Calories
Per serving: 129 calories; 13 g protein; 6 g fat; 5 g carbohydrate; 67 mg calcium; 304 mg sodium; 44 mg cholesterol; 1 g dietary fiber

Variation: Mexican Seafood Salad —Substitute ¼ pound thawed frozen imitation fish for the lobster.

Per serving: 130 calories; 10 g protein; 7 g fat; 8 g carbohydrate; 38 mg calcium; 170 mg sodium; 20 mg cholesterol; 1 g dietary fiber

Mixed Seafood Salad with Oriental Flavor

2 ounces *each* cooked bay *or* sea
  scallops (cut into 1-inch pieces),
  cooked shelled and deveined
  shrimp, and thawed frozen
  imitation fish, sliced
½ cup Chinese pea pods (snow
  peas), stem ends and strings
  removed, blanched
½ cup *each* drained canned straw
  or button mushrooms and
  drained canned baby corn ears
¼ cup *each* diagonally sliced
  scallions (green onions) and
  celery
2 tablespoons rice vinegar
1 tablespoon dry sherry
1½ teaspoons peanut *or*
  vegetable oil
1 small garlic clove, minced
½ teaspoon *each* grated pared
  gingerroot and Chinese sesame
  oil
8 lettuce leaves
1 teaspoon sesame seed, toasted

In large mixing bowl combine scallops, shrimp, imitation fish, pea pods, mushrooms, corn, scallions, and celery. In cup or small bowl combine remaining ingredients except lettuce and sesame seed; pour over seafood mixture and toss to coat. Cover and refrigerate until flavors blend, about 10 minutes.

To serve, line serving platter with lettuce leaves and top with seafood mixture; sprinkle with sesame seed.

MAKES 2 SERVINGS

Each serving provides: 3 Protein Exchanges;
  ¼ Bread Exchange; 2½ Vegetable Exchanges;
  1 Fat Exchange; 20 Optional Calories
Per serving: 205 calories; 20 g protein; 6 g fat;
  16 g carbohydrate; 90 mg calcium; 337 mg sodium;
  73 mg cholesterol; 3 g dietary fiber

When time is of the essence, use your microwave to cook scallops, shrimp, or other seafood when you need cooked seafood for a recipe.

Oriental Shrimp and Cucumber Salad

2 tablespoons teriyaki sauce
1 tablespoon *each* olive oil, rice
    vinegar, freshly squeezed
    lemon juice, and chopped fresh
    dill *or* ½ teaspoon dillweed
1 small garlic clove, minced
½ teaspoon minced pared
    gingerroot
¼ pound shelled and deveined
    cooked small shrimp, cut
    lengthwise into halves
½ cup seeded and thinly sliced
    cucumber
¼ cup thinly sliced red onion
8 lettuce leaves
6 cherry tomatoes, cut into halves

In medium mixing bowl (not aluminum*) combine teriyaki sauce, oil, vinegar, lemon juice, dill, garlic, and gingerroot; mix well. Add shrimp, cucumber, and onion and toss to coat. Cover with plastic wrap and refrigerate for at least 30 minutes.

To serve, line chilled serving platter with lettuce; top with shrimp mixture and tomato halves.

MAKES 2 SERVINGS

Each serving provides: 2 Protein Exchanges;
    2¼ Vegetable Exchanges; 1½ Fat Exchanges
Per serving: 158 calories; 14 g protein; 8 g fat;
    9 g carbohydrate; 66 mg calcium; 825 mg sodium;
    111 mg cholesterol; 1 g dietary fiber

*It's best to marinate in glass or stainless-steel containers; acidic ingredients such as rice vinegar and lemon juice may react with aluminum, causing color and flavor changes in food.

Sea Slaw Salad

6 ounces thawed frozen imitation
  fish, flaked
2 cups finely shredded green
  cabbage
1 cup grated carrots
¼ cup *each* diced onion, celery,
  green bell pepper, and plain
  low-fat yogurt
1 tablespoon plus 1 teaspoon
  reduced-calorie mayonnaise
1 tablespoon chopped fresh
  Italian (flat-leaf) parsley *or* fresh
  dill
2 teaspoons ketchup
1 teaspoon pickle relish
½ teaspoon *each* prepared
  horseradish, lemon juice,
  Dijon-style mustard, and
  Worcestershire sauce

In large salad bowl combine imitation fish and vegetables. In small mixing bowl combine remaining ingredients; pour over salad and toss to coat. Serve immediately or cover and refrigerate until ready to serve.

MAKES 2 SERVINGS

Each serving provides: 3 Protein Exchanges;
  3¾ Vegetable Exchanges; 1 Fat Exchange;
  ¼ Milk Exchange; 10 Optional Calories
Per serving: 195 calories; 16 g protein; 4 g fat;
  23 g carbohydrate; 123 mg calcium; 393 mg sodium;
  31 mg cholesterol; 2 g dietary fiber

Tuna and White Bean Salad ☻

4 ounces drained canned tuna
2 ounces rinsed drained canned
   white kidney (cannellini) beans
2 tablespoons finely diced celery
1 tablespoon *each* finely diced
   red onion and minced fresh
   parsley
2 tablespoons canned ready-
   to-serve chicken broth
2 teaspoons *each* olive oil and
   red wine vinegar
1 teaspoon water
⅛ teaspoon salt
Dash pepper

In salad bowl combine tuna, beans, celery, onion, and parsley and toss to combine. Using a wire whisk, in small mixing bowl combine remaining ingredients; pour over tuna mixture and toss to coat. Cover and refrigerate until ready to serve.

MAKES 2 SERVINGS

Each serving provides: 2 Protein Exchanges;
   ½ Bread Exchange; ⅛ Vegetable Exchange;
   1 Fat Exchange; 3 Optional Calories
Per serving: 190 calories; 19 g protein; 9 g fat;
   7 g carbohydrate; 29 mg calcium; 507 mg sodium
   (estimated); 10 mg cholesterol; 1 g dietary fiber

Did you know that rinsing canned tuna for about a minute washes away at least half the sodium without affecting the taste? Try it next time you use canned tuna.

Warm Fresh Tuna Salad Ⓜ

5 ounces cubed fresh tuna
½ cup *each* diced celery and red
    onion
2 tablespoons diced green bell
    pepper
2 teaspoons olive *or* vegetable oil
½ medium tomato, diced
2 teaspoons apple cider vinegar
1 teaspoon freshly squeezed
    lemon juice
¼ teaspoon salt
⅛ teaspoon grated lemon peel
Dash pepper
4 lettuce leaves

In 2-cup microwavable casserole combine tuna, celery, onion, bell pepper, and oil and stir to thoroughly coat. Microwave on Medium-High (70%) for 4 minutes. Add remaining ingredients except lettuce and stir to thoroughly combine. Let stand until fish is cooked through and flakes easily when tested with a fork and flavors blend, about 5 minutes.

To serve, line serving platter with lettuce; toss tuna mixture and arrange on lettuce.

MAKES 2 SERVINGS

Each serving provides: 2 Protein Exchanges;
    2⅛ Vegetable Exchanges; 1 Fat Exchange
Per serving: 172 calories; 18 g protein; 8 g fat;
    7 g carbohydrate; 37 mg calcium; 329 mg sodium;
    27 mg cholesterol; 2 g dietary fiber

Poultry

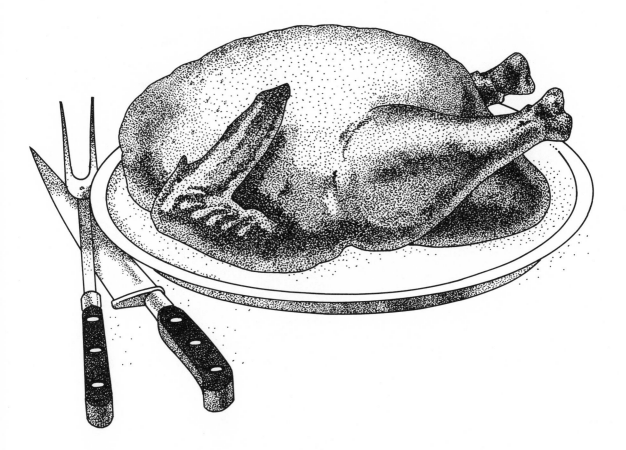

Busy cooks know that, besides being easy to prepare, poultry dishes fit today's health-conscious life-style. Our poultry chapter has something for everyone. And talk about fast! When you use the microwave oven, elegant dishes such as Chicken in Red Wine Sauce or Stuffed Chicken Rolls with Mushroom Gravy are just minutes away. Conventional cooking methods will also yield mouth-watering meals in a hurry. Try Madeira Duck with Plum or Turkey Cutlets with Apricots. They're sure to become family favorites.

Chicken and Pistachio Pâté

Add a touch of elegance to your next gathering with this rich pâté.

5 ounces chicken cutlets, sliced
½ cup diced onion
1 tablespoon cognac
1 small garlic clove, crushed
1 ounce shelled pistachio nuts
  (reserve 8 nuts for garnish)
2 tablespoons *each* whipped
  butter and white wine
  Worcestershire sauce
1 tablespoon whipping cream
⅛ teaspoon *each* ground red
  pepper and hot sauce

In small saucepan combine chicken, onion, cognac, and garlic; cover and cook over medium heat, stirring occasionally, until chicken is cooked, about 5 minutes. Transfer to work bowl of food processor and process until smooth, scraping down sides of container as necessary. Add remaining ingredients except reserved nuts and process until combined, about 30 seconds. Transfer to serving bowl and garnish with reserved nuts; cover and refrigerate at least 20 minutes or overnight.

MAKES 4 SERVINGS

Each serving provides: 1½ Protein Exchanges;
  ¼ Vegetable Exchange; ½ Fat Exchange;
  45 Optional Calories
Per serving: 138 calories; 10 g protein; 8 g fat;
  5 g carbohydrate; 23 mg calcium; 122 mg sodium;
  32 mg cholesterol; 0.2 g dietary fiber (this figure does
  not include pistachio nuts; nutrition analysis not
  available)

Curried Cream of Chicken Soup ⓒⓜ

1 tablespoon whipped butter
1 teaspoon margarine
1 garlic clove, minced
1 tablespoon plus 1½ teaspoons
    all-purpose flour
1 cup water
½ cup evaporated skimmed milk
1 packet instant chicken broth
    and seasoning mix
1 ounce diced cooked chicken
    (¼-inch pieces)
¼ teaspoon curry powder

In medium microwavable bowl combine butter, margarine, and garlic and microwave on High (100%) for 1 minute, until butter and margarine are melted. Sprinkle flour over butter mixture and, using a wire whisk, stir to combine. Gradually stir in water and milk; stir in broth mix. Microwave on High for 3 minutes, stirring every minute. Add chicken and curry powder and stir to combine; microwave on High for 30 seconds, until chicken is heated through.

MAKES 2 SERVINGS, ABOUT ¾ CUP EACH

Each serving provides: ½ Protein Exchange;
    ¼ Bread Exchange; ½ Fat Exchange; ½ Milk Exchange;
    30 Optional Calories
Per serving: 147 calories; 10 g protein; 6 g fat;
    13 g carbohydrate; 194 mg calcium; 633 mg sodium;
    23 mg cholesterol; 0.2 g dietary fiber

Curry powder is actually a blend of many herbs and spices: turmeric, coriander, black and red peppers, cumin, cardamom, cinnamon, ginger, mace, fenugreek, bay leaves, saffron, and mustard seed. In India, curry powders are blended by hand so every household has it own unique mixture.

Minted Chicken and Rice Soup Ⓒ Ⓜ

5 ounces skinned and boned
  chicken, cut into 1-inch cubes
2 cups water
1 ounce uncooked long-grain rice
¼ cup *each* diced onion, celery,
  and carrot
1 tablespoon freshly squeezed
  lemon juice
2 packets instant chicken broth
  and seasoning mix
1 tablespoon chopped fresh mint
⅛ teaspoon white pepper

In 1-quart microwavable shallow casserole combine all ingredients except mint and pepper; microwave on High (100%) for 13 minutes, stirring halfway through cooking, until chicken is cooked through. Stir in mint and pepper.

MAKES 2 SERVINGS, ABOUT 1½ CUPS EACH

Each serving provides: 2 Protein Exchanges;
    ½ Bread Exchange; ¾ Vegetable Exchange;
    10 Optional Calories
Per serving: 162 calories; 18 g protein; 2 g fat;
    17 g carbohydrate; 28 mg calcium; 1,064 mg sodium;
    50 mg cholesterol; 1 g dietary fiber

Chickado 'wiches

Turn leftover chicken into this winning sandwich.

2 slices Italian bread (1 ounce each), toasted
1 tablespoon Thousand Island salad dressing, divided
2 ounces thinly sliced cooked chicken
2 slices crisp bacon, crumbled
¼ cup *each* chopped scallions (green onions) and tomato
⅛ medium avocado (about 1 ounce), pared and thinly sliced
2 ounces sliced Swiss cheese

On baking sheet arrange bread slices in a single layer and spread each with ½ teaspoon dressing. Top each slice of bread with half of the chicken, bacon, scallions, and tomato, then top each with 1 teaspoon of the remaining dressing. Arrange half of the avocado slices and half of the cheese on each sandwich. Broil 6 inches from heat source until sandwich is hot and cheese is melted, about 2 minutes.

MAKES 2 SERVINGS

Each serving provides: 2 Protein Exchanges; 1 Bread Exchange; ½ Vegetable Exchange; 1½ Fat Exchanges; 45 Optional Calories
Per serving: 329 calories; 21 g protein; 18 g fat; 21 g carbohydrate; 293 mg calcium; 423 mg sodium; 57 mg cholesterol; 2 g dietary fiber

Arroz con Pollo Ⓜ

¼ cup *each* finely chopped onion,
   finely chopped green bell
   pepper, and seeded and finely
   chopped tomato
2 teaspoons olive *or* vegetable oil
2 garlic cloves, minced
1½ cups water
1 packet instant chicken broth
   and seasoning mix
1 teaspoon rinsed drained capers
3 large pimiento-stuffed green
   olives, cut into halves
3 ounces uncooked long-grain
   rice
2 chicken breasts (6 ounces each),
   skinned
1 teaspoon chopped fresh cilantro
   (Chinese parsley) *or* Italian
   (flat-leaf) parsley
⅛ teaspoon *each* pepper and
   ground cumin

In 4-quart microwavable casserole combine onion, bell pepper, tomato, oil, and garlic and stir to thoroughly coat. Microwave on High (100%) for 3 minutes, until vegetables are softened, stirring every minute. Add water, broth mix, capers, and olives and microwave on High for 3 minutes, until mixture comes to a boil. Stir in rice; cover with vented plastic wrap and microwave on High for 8 minutes, rotating casserole ½ turn halfway through cooking. Arrange chicken in casserole with thicker portions toward edge of casserole; re-cover with vented plastic wrap and microwave on High for 5 minutes, rotating casserole ½ turn halfway through cooking, until chicken is cooked through. Stir in remaining ingredients.

MAKES 2 SERVINGS

Each serving provides: 3 Protein Exchanges;
   1½ Bread Exchanges; ¾ Vegetable Exchange;
   1¼ Fat Exchanges; 5 Optional Calories
Per serving: 349 calories; 30 g protein; 7 g fat;
   39 g carbohydrate; 41 mg calcium; 751 mg sodium;
   66 mg cholesterol; 1 g dietary fiber

Chicken 'n' Dumplings Ⓜ

½ cup *each* sliced carrots and
  canned ready-to-serve chicken
  broth
¼ cup *each* diced onion and
  sliced celery
½ pound skinned and boned
  chicken, diced
¼ cup low-fat milk (1% milk fat)
1 tablespoon all-purpose flour
¼ cup *each* frozen whole-kernel
  corn and frozen tiny peas
1 teaspoon chopped fresh parsley
⅛ teaspoon thyme leaves
3 tablespoons buttermilk baking
  mix
1 tablespoon plus 1 teaspoon
  water

In 1-quart microwavable shallow casserole combine carrots, broth, onion, and celery and microwave on High (100%) for 2 minutes, until vegetables are tender-crisp. Add chicken, cover with vented plastic wrap, and microwave on High for 5 minutes, until chicken is no longer pink. In 1-cup liquid measure combine milk and flour and stir to dissolve flour; pour over chicken mixture and stir to combine. Add corn and peas and stir to combine; microwave on High, uncovered, for 2 minutes, until mixture thickens, stirring every minute. Add parsley and thyme; stir to combine and set aside.

Using a fork, in small mixing bowl combine baking mix and water and stir until mixture is thick and smooth. Drop batter by heaping tablespoonfuls onto chicken mixture, making two dumplings. Cover with vented plastic wrap and microwave on High for 3 minutes, until a toothpick, inserted in center of dumplings, comes out clean.

MAKES 2 SERVINGS

Each serving provides: 3 Protein Exchanges;
  1 Bread Exchange; 1 Vegetable Exchange;
  50 Optional Calories
Per serving: 268 calories; 29 g protein; 6 g fat;
  24 g carbohydrate; 92 mg calcium; 541 mg sodium;
  81 mg cholesterol; 3 g dietary fiber

Creamy Cheddar Chicken Ⓜ

½ cup *each* low-fat milk (1% milk fat) and canned ready-to-serve chicken broth
1 tablespoon all-purpose flour
2 ounces Cheddar cheese, shredded
5 ounces chicken cutlets, cut into 1-inch cubes
¼ cup sliced scallions (green onions)
2 tablespoons seeded and diced tomato
1 slice crisp bacon, crumbled
1 cup cooked noodles (hot)

Using a wire whisk, in 1-quart microwavable shallow casserole combine milk, broth, and flour and stir until flour is dissolved. Microwave on High (100%) for 5 minutes, until mixture thickens, stirring every minute. Add cheese and stir until cheese is melted. Add chicken and scallions and stir to coat; microwave on High for 3 minutes, until chicken is cooked through. Stir in tomato and bacon.

To serve, on serving platter arrange noodles and top with chicken mixture.

MAKES 2 SERVINGS

Each serving provides: 3 Protein Exchanges;
    1 Bread Exchange; ¼ Vegetable Exchange;
    ¼ Milk Exchange; 50 Optional Calories
Per serving: 364 calories; 31 g protein; 14 g fat;
    27 g carbohydrate; 304 mg calcium; 557 mg sodium;
    101 mg cholesterol; 2 g dietary fiber

Flaky Herb Chicken

2 ounces round buttery crackers,
  made into crumbs
1 teaspoon grated Parmesan
  cheese
¼ teaspoon *each* basil leaves and
  oregano leaves
2 thin chicken cutlets (¼ pound
  each)
¼ cup plain low-fat yogurt
2 teaspoons vegetable oil, divided

Preheat oven to 425°F. On sheet of wax paper or a paper plate combine cracker crumbs, cheese, basil, and oregano. Dip 1 chicken cutlet into yogurt, then into crumb mixture, coating both sides evenly; repeat procedure with remaining cutlet, being sure to use all of the yogurt and crumb mixture.

Arrange chicken on nonstick baking sheet and drizzle each cutlet with ½ teaspoon oil. Bake until chicken is lightly browned, 7 to 8 minutes. Turn cutlets over, drizzle each with ½ teaspoon oil, and bake until cooked through and lightly browned, 7 to 8 minutes longer.

MAKES 2 SERVINGS

Each serving provides: 3 Protein Exchanges;
    1 Bread Exchange; 1 Fat Exchange; ¼ Milk Exchange;
    65 Optional Calories
Per serving: 328 calories; 30 g protein; 15 g fat;
    20 g carbohydrate; 123 mg calcium; 350 mg sodium;
    68 mg cholesterol; dietary fiber data not available

Glazed Chicken Bits ⒸⓂ

If time permits, you may wish to substitute cooked long-grain rice for
the instant rice.

2 teaspoons *each* honey,
  ketchup, and reduced-sodium
  soy sauce
1 teaspoon freshly squeezed
  lemon juice
½ teaspoon grated pared
  gingerroot
1 garlic clove, minced
5 ounces skinned and boned
  chicken breast, cut into 1-inch
  cubes
1 cup cooked instant rice (hot)

Using a wire whisk, in small mixing bowl
combine honey, ketchup, soy sauce, lemon
juice, gingerroot, and garlic. In 8-inch microwavable glass pie plate arrange chicken
cubes. Pour honey mixture over chicken;
cover with plastic wrap and refrigerate for
30 minutes.

Vent plastic wrap and microwave chicken
mixture on High (100%) for 2 minutes, stirring halfway through cooking. Let stand for
1 minute, until chicken is cooked through.
Serve chicken mixture over rice.

MAKES 2 SERVINGS

Each serving provides: 2 Protein Exchanges;
    1 Bread Exchange; 25 Optional Calories
Per serving: 202 calories; 19 g protein; 1 g fat;
    28 g carbohydrate; 17 mg calcium; 307 mg sodium;
    41 mg cholesterol; 1 g dietary fiber

Hawaiian Chicken

2 teaspoons peanut *or vegetable* oil

7 ounces chicken cutlets, cut into 2 x ½-inch strips

¼ cup *each* cubed red and green bell peppers

1 teaspoon minced pared gingerroot

1 cup Chinese pea pods (snow peas), stem ends and strings removed

⅓ cup pineapple juice (no sugar added)

2 tablespoons teriyaki sauce

1 teaspoon cornstarch

½ cup drained canned pineapple chunks (no sugar added)

½ ounce macadamia nuts, toasted and chopped

In 10-inch nonstick skillet heat oil; add chicken and cook over high heat, stirring frequently, until chicken is lightly browned on all sides, 2 to 3 minutes. Transfer to plate and set aside.

In same skillet combine bell peppers and gingerroot and cook over medium heat, stirring frequently, until bell peppers are tender-crisp, 2 to 3 minutes. Add pea pods and cook, stirring occasionally, until tender-crisp, about 1 minute.

In 1-cup liquid measure combine pineapple juice, teriyaki sauce, and cornstarch and stir to dissolve cornstarch; add to vegetable mixture, along with chicken and pineapple chunks, and cook, stirring constantly, until sauce is thickened and chicken is cooked through, 2 to 3 minutes.

To serve, transfer chicken mixture to serving platter and sprinkle with nuts.

MAKES 2 SERVINGS

Each serving provides: 3 Protein Exchanges; 1½ Vegetable Exchanges; 1 Fat Exchange; 1 Fruit Exchange; 25 Optional Calories
Per serving: 315 calories; 27 g protein; 11 g fat; 27 g carbohydrate; 66 mg calcium; 760 mg sodium; 58 mg cholesterol; 2 g dietary fiber (this figure does not include macadamia nuts; nutrition analysis not available)

When is a nut not really a nut? When it's a macadamia nut, which is actually a seed. Macadamias are grown in Hawaii and California, and are considered a gourmet delight.

Kung Pao Chicken

2 tablespoons *each*
  reduced-sodium soy sauce and
  dry sherry
1 garlic clove, minced
1 teaspoon minced pared
  gingerroot
5 ounces chicken cutlets, cut into
  1-inch cubes
1 teaspoon peanut *or* vegetable oil
2 to 3 mild dried chili peppers
1 ounce unsalted shelled roasted
  peanuts
1 medium red bell pepper, cut
  into matchstick pieces
¼ cup *each* diagonally sliced
  scallions (green onions) and
  canned ready-to-serve chicken
  broth
1 teaspoon cornstarch

In small glass or stainless-steel mixing bowl combine soy sauce, sherry, garlic, and gingerroot; add chicken and turn to coat. Cover with plastic wrap and refrigerate at least 30 minutes.

In 12-inch nonstick skillet heat oil; add chili peppers and cook over medium-high heat, stirring frequently, until peppers are browned, about 1 minute. Remove and discard peppers.

To same skillet add peanuts and cook over medium-high heat, stirring frequently, until nuts are lightly browned, about 1 minute. Transfer nuts to plate; set aside. Using a slotted spoon, transfer chicken to same skillet, reserving marinade. Cook chicken over medium-high heat, stirring frequently, until browned on all sides and cooked through, 2 to 3 minutes. Transfer chicken to plate with peanuts; set aside. Add bell pepper and scallions to skillet and cook over medium-high heat, stirring frequently, until tender-crisp, 1 to 2 minutes.

Add broth and cornstarch to reserved marinade and stir to dissolve cornstarch; add to bell pepper-scallion mixture in skillet, along with chicken and peanuts, and cook, stirring constantly, until mixture comes to a boil and thickens, 2 to 3 minutes.

MAKES 2 SERVINGS

Each serving provides: 3 Protein Exchanges;
    1¼ Vegetable Exchanges; 1½ Fat Exchanges;
    25 Optional Calories
Per serving: 245 calories; 22 g protein; 11 g fat;
    12 g carbohydrate; 27 mg calcium; 775 mg sodium;
    41 mg cholesterol; 2 g dietary fiber

Stuffed Chicken Rolls with Mushroom Gravy Ⓜ

1 cup sliced mushrooms
2 teaspoons *each* margarine, divided, and all-purpose flour
1 packet instant chicken broth and seasoning mix, dissolved in ½ cup hot water
½ teaspoon lemon juice
¼ cup *each* diced onion, celery, and green bell pepper
1 small garlic clove, minced
1 ounce onion and garlic-flavored croutons
1 egg, beaten
2 thin chicken cutlets (3 ounces each), pounded to ⅛-inch thickness

In 1-quart microwavable shallow casserole combine mushrooms and 1 teaspoon margarine and microwave on High (100%) for 4 minutes, until softened, stirring once halfway through cooking. Sprinkle flour over mushrooms and stir to combine; microwave on High for 1 minute. Add dissolved broth mix and lemon juice and stir to combine. Microwave on High for 2 minutes, stirring once halfway through cooking. Transfer to bowl and set aside.

In same casserole combine vegetables, remaining teaspoon margarine, and the garlic; cover with vented plastic wrap and microwave on High for 3 minutes, until vegetables are softened, stirring once halfway through cooking. Add croutons and egg and stir to combine. Spread half of crouton mixture onto center of each chicken cutlet; carefully roll each cutlet crosswise to enclose filling and secure each with a toothpick. Arrange chicken rolls, seam-side down in same casserole; cover with vented plastic wrap and microwave on High for 3½ minutes, until chicken is tender, rotating casserole ½ turn halfway through cooking. Pour mushroom mixture over chicken and microwave on High for 30 seconds, until thoroughly heated.

MAKES 2 SERVINGS

Each serving provides: 2½ Protein Exchanges;
    1 Bread Exchange; 1¾ Vegetable Exchanges;
    1 Fat Exchange; 15 Optional Calories
Per serving: 216 calories; 25 g protein; 8 g fat;
    9 g carbohydrate; 40 mg calcium; 688 mg sodium;
    186 mg cholesterol; 1 g dietary fiber

Sweet 'n' Spicy Chicken ⒸⓂ

If you like the speed of the microwave oven but the crispness the broiler can produce, you might want to use both appliances for this recipe. Cook the chicken in the microwave oven as the recipe directs, then top with the spicy sauce, and broil on a rack in the broiling pan for 2 to 3 minutes.

1 cup sliced onions
2 chicken breasts (6 ounces each), skinned
3 tablespoons ketchup
1 tablespoon *each* apple cider vinegar and freshly squeezed lemon juice
1 teaspoon light *or* dark molasses
1 garlic clove, minced
¼ teaspoon *each* Worcestershire sauce and hot sauce

In 8 x 8 x 2-inch microwavable baking dish arrange onions; set chicken breasts, skinned-side up, over onions. Cover with vented plastic wrap and microwave on High (100%) for 5 minutes, until chicken is cooked through.

In small mixing bowl combine remaining ingredients; spread over chicken breasts. Microwave on High for 2 minutes until sauce is heated through.

MAKES 2 SERVINGS

Each serving provides: 3 Protein Exchanges;
    1 Vegetable Exchange; 35 Optional Calories
Per serving: 209 calories; 28 g protein; 3 g fat;
    16 g carbohydrate; 53 mg calcium; 358 mg sodium;
    72 mg cholesterol; 1 g dietary fiber

Szechuan Chicken

2 teaspoons peanut *or* vegetable
   oil
2 chicken cutlets (3 ounces each)
1 cup *each* thoroughly washed
   sliced leeks (white portion only)
   and shiitake *or* white
   mushrooms
½ cup *each* red bell pepper strips
   (3 x ½ inch) and Chinese pea
   pods (snow peas), stem ends
   and strings removed
1 medium mild chili pepper,
   seeded and minced
2 garlic cloves, sliced
1 teaspoon grated pared
   gingerroot
½ cup water
1 tablespoon reduced-sodium soy
   sauce
1 packet instant chicken broth
   and seasoning mix
1 teaspoon cornstarch
⅛ teaspoon powdered mustard
4 drops hot sauce

In 9-inch nonstick skillet heat oil; add chicken and cook over high heat, turning once, until browned on both sides and cooked through, about 2 minutes each side. Transfer chicken to a plate and set aside.

In same skillet combine leeks, mushrooms, bell pepper, pea pods, chili pepper, garlic, and gingerroot and cook over medium heat, stirring quickly and frequently until tender-crisp, about 5 minutes.

In 1-cup liquid measure combine water, soy sauce, broth mix, cornstarch, mustard, and hot sauce and stir to dissolve cornstarch; add to vegetables in skillet and cook, stirring constantly, until mixture comes to a boil. Reduce heat to low; return chicken to skillet and turn to coat with sauce. Cover and let simmer until chicken is heated through and flavors blend, about 3 minutes.

MAKES 2 SERVINGS

Each serving provides: 2 Protein Exchanges;
   3½ Vegetable Exchanges; 1 Fat Exchange;
   10 Optional Calories
Per serving: 223 calories; 24 g protein; 6 g fat;
   19 g carbohydrate; 70 mg calcium; 872 mg sodium;
   49 mg cholesterol; 2 g dietary fiber

Chicken and Sausage Casserole Ⓜ

1 tablespoon plus 1½ teaspoons
    all-purpose flour
¼ teaspoon paprika
10 ounces chicken thighs,
    skinned
2 teaspoons vegetable oil
½ cup chopped onion
¼ cup tomato puree
3 tablespoons water
2 tablespoons dry red table wine
1 packet instant beef broth and
    seasoning mix
1 bay leaf
1 ounce cooked veal sausage link,
    thinly sliced

On sheet of wax paper or a paper plate combine flour and paprika; dredge chicken in flour mixture coating all sides and reserving any remaining flour mixture.

In 3-quart microwavable casserole microwave oil on High (100%) for 1 minute; add onion. Arrange chicken in casserole with thickest portion toward edge of casserole. Cover with vented plastic wrap and microwave on High for 4 minutes, turning chicken over halfway through cooking. Add tomato puree, water, wine, broth mix, bay leaf, and reserved remaining flour mixture and stir to combine. Re-cover with vented plastic wrap and microwave on High for 5 minutes. Add sausage and stir to combine; re-cover with vented plastic wrap and microwave on High for 2 minutes. Let stand for 3 minutes, until chicken is cooked through. Remove and discard bay leaf.

MAKES 2 SERVINGS

Each serving provides: 3 Protein Exchanges;
    ¼ Bread Exchange; ¾ Vegetable Exchange;
    1 Fat Exchange; 20 Optional Calories
Per serving: 273 calories; 28 g protein; 11 g fat;
    12 g carbohydrate; 34 mg calcium; 873 mg sodium
    (estimated); 108 mg cholesterol; 2 g dietary fiber

Skillet Chicken and Potatoes ☺

2 teaspoons olive *or* vegetable oil
6 ounces thinly sliced pared
   all-purpose potatoes
5 ounces ground chicken
1 tablespoon whipped butter
½ cup *each* diced onion, diced
   green bell pepper, and sliced
   carrot
1 small garlic clove, minced
1 cup canned Italian tomatoes
   (with liquid); drain and chop
   tomatoes, reserving liquid
1 tablespoon chopped fresh
   Italian (flat-leaf) parsley
¼ teaspoon *each* thyme leaves,
   salt, and pepper

In 10-inch nonstick skillet heat oil; add potatoes and chicken and cook over high heat, stirring constantly, until chicken is lightly browned, about 2 minutes. Transfer to plate; set aside.

In same skillet melt butter; add onion, bell pepper, carrot, and garlic and sauté over high heat until tender-crisp, 2 to 3 minutes. Return potato-chicken mixture to skillet; add tomatoes, reserved tomato liquid, parsley, thyme, salt, and pepper and stir to thoroughly combine. Cook until mixture comes to a boil. Reduce heat to low, cover, and let simmer, stirring occasionally, until flavors blend and potatoes are tender, about 10 minutes.

MAKES 2 SERVINGS

Each serving provides: 2 Protein Exchanges;
   1 Bread Exchange; 2½ Vegetable Exchanges;
   1 Fat Exchange; 25 Optional Calories
Per serving: 275 calories; 19 g protein; 10 g fat;
   28 g carbohydrate; 74 mg calcium; 566 mg sodium;
   57 mg cholesterol; 4 g dietary fiber

Variation: Skillet Turkey and Potatoes — Substitute 5 ounces ground turkey for the chicken.

Per serving: 306 calories; 17 g protein; 15 g fat;
   28 g carbohydrate; 88 mg calcium; 578 mg sodium;
   55 mg cholesterol; 4 g dietary fiber

Keep peeled potatoes white by placing them in a bowl of water to which 1 teaspoon of lemon juice or vinegar has been added. Be sure to dry them thoroughly before placing them into a skillet of hot oil so oil doesn't spatter.

Chicken and Mushrooms in Parmesan Cream

For an elegant meal, pair this flavorful dish with cooked rice, noodles, or pasta.

2 chicken cutlets (¼ pound each),
   pounded to ¼-inch thickness
2 tablespoons all-purpose flour
1 teaspoon *each* margarine and
   olive *or* vegetable oil
1 cup sliced mushrooms
¼ cup evaporated skimmed milk
2 tablespoons half-and-half (blend
   of milk and cream)
½ ounce grated Parmesan cheese
1 tablespoon chopped fresh
   parsley
Dash white pepper

On sheet of wax paper or a paper plate dredge cutlets in flour, lightly coating both sides.

In 10-inch nonstick skillet combine margarine and oil and heat until margarine is melted; add cutlets and cook over medium-high heat, turning once, until lightly browned, 2 to 3 minutes on each side. Transfer chicken to plate and set aside.

In same skillet sauté mushrooms over high heat, stirring frequently, until tender-crisp, 1 to 2 minutes. Stir in milk and half-and-half. Reduce heat to medium-low and cook, stirring frequently, until mixture is heated through, 1 to 2 minutes. Stir in remaining ingredients and cook until cheese is melted. Return chicken to skillet and cook until heated through, 1 to 2 minutes.

MAKES 2 SERVINGS

Each serving provides: 3¼ Protein Exchanges;
   1 Vegetable Exchange; 1 Fat Exchange;
   ¼ Milk Exchange; 55 Optional Calories
Per serving: 276 calories; 34 g protein; 10 g fat;
   12 g carbohydrate; 225 mg calcium; 273 mg sodium;
   78 mg cholesterol; 1 g dietary fiber

Chicken in Red Wine Sauce Ⓜ

Perfect with cooked long-grain rice or noodles.

1 pound 2 ounces chicken parts, skinned
¼ cup dry red table wine
1 tablespoon brandy
2 garlic cloves, minced
½ cup *each* frozen pearl onions and water
1 tablespoon tomato paste
1 packet instant beef broth and seasoning mix
½ cup halved mushrooms
1 tablespoon all-purpose flour
1 bay leaf
1 tablespoon chopped fresh parsley
⅛ teaspoon *each* pepper and thyme leaves (optional)

In 4-quart microwavable casserole arrange chicken parts in a single layer in center of casserole. In 1-cup liquid measure combine wine, brandy, and garlic and pour evenly over chicken. Cover with vented plastic wrap and microwave on Medium-High (75%) for 5 minutes. Turn chicken pieces over; add onions, re-cover with vented plastic wrap, and cook on Medium-High for 5 minutes, until inside of chicken is still pink.

In 1-cup liquid measure combine water, tomato paste, and broth mix and stir to combine. Arrange mushrooms around chicken in casserole and sprinkle with flour; add tomato paste mixture and bay leaf. Re-cover with vented plastic wrap and microwave on Medium-High for 5 minutes, until chicken is tender and, when pierced with a fork, juices run clear. Stir in parsley, pepper, and, if desired, thyme and let stand 1 minute. Remove and discard bay leaf.

MAKES 2 SERVINGS

Each serving provides: 3 Protein Exchanges;
    1⅛ Vegetable Exchanges; 70 Optional Calories
Per serving: 227 calories; 27 g protein; 4 g fat;
    12 g carbohydrate; 49 mg calcium; 625 mg sodium;
    79 mg cholesterol; 1 g dietary fiber

Chicken with Carbonara Sauce

1 teaspoon *each* margarine and
    olive *or* vegetable oil
2 thin chicken cutlets (¼ pound
    each)
½ cup thinly sliced onion
¼ cup evaporated skimmed milk
2 tablespoons half-and-half (blend
    of milk and cream)
3 large pitted black olives, sliced
1 tablespoon grated Parmesan
    cheese
1 slice crisp bacon, crumbled
Dash white pepper

In 10-inch nonstick skillet combine margarine and oil and heat until margarine is melted; add chicken and cook over medium-high heat, turning once, until cooked through and lightly browned, 2 to 3 minutes on each side. Transfer to plate and set aside.

In same skillet sauté onion over medium-high heat, stirring frequently, until lightly browned, 2 to 3 minutes. Reduce heat to low, stir in milk and half-and-half and cook, stirring frequently, until tiny bubbles begin to form around edge of skillet. Stir in remaining ingredients; continuing to stir, cook, until cheese is melted and mixture thickens, 1 to 2 minutes. Return chicken to skillet and cook until heated through, 1 to 2 minutes longer.

MAKES 2 SERVINGS

Each serving provides: 3 Protein Exchanges;
    ½ Vegetable Exchange; 1¼ Fat Exchanges;
    ¼ Milk Exchange; 60 Optional Calories
Per serving: 261 calories; 32 g protein; 11 g fat;
    8 g carbohydrate; 173 mg calcium; 283 mg sodium;
    77 mg cholesterol; 1 g dietary fiber

Chicken with Creamy Chive Sauce Ⓒ Ⓜ

2 chicken breasts (6 ounces each)
⅛ teaspoon pepper
⅛ teaspoon salt, divided
¼ cup evaporated skimmed milk
1 teaspoon all-purpose flour
1 tablespoon *each* whipped
    cream cheese and half-and-half
    (blend of milk and cream)
2 teaspoons chopped chives
Dash ground nutmeg

In 9 x 9 x 2-inch microwavable baking dish arrange chicken breasts, skin-side up; sprinkle with pepper and half the salt. Cover with vented plastic wrap and microwave on High (100%) for 5 minutes until chicken is cooked through, rotating dish ½ turn halfway through cooking. Set aside and keep warm.

In 1-cup microwavable liquid measure combine milk and flour and stir to dissolve flour. Microwave, uncovered, on High for 2 minutes, stirring every 30 seconds. Add cream cheese and half-and-half and stir until smooth; microwave on High for 1 minute. Stir in chives, nutmeg, and remaining salt.

To serve, remove and discard skin from chicken; transfer to serving platter and top with sauce.

MAKES 2 SERVINGS

Each serving provides: 3 Protein Exchanges;
    ¼ Milk Exchange; 35 Optional Calories
Per serving: 197 calories; 29 g protein; 6 g fat;
    5 g carbohydrate; 119 mg calcium; 259 mg sodium;
    81 mg cholesterol; 0.1 g dietary fiber

Chicken with Port and Gorgonzola

A wonderful recipe to serve over cooked rice.

2 chicken cutlets (¼ pound each)
1 ounce Gorgonzola cheese
1 teaspoon *each* olive *or* vegetable oil and margarine
2 tablespoons chopped shallot *or* onion
2 teaspoons all-purpose flour
¼ cup *each* canned ready-to-serve chicken broth and port wine
⅛ teaspoon salt
Dash white pepper

Using a sharp knife, cut a 2 x 2-inch pocket into thickest portion of each cutlet; press half of the cheese into each pocket and gently press edges of each pocket to enclose filling.

In 10-inch nonstick skillet combine oil and margarine and heat until margarine is melted; add chicken and cook over medium-high heat, turning once, until lightly browned and cooked through, 2 to 3 minutes on each side. Transfer to plate and set aside.

In same skillet sauté shallot (or onion) over medium-high heat until softened, about 1 minute. Sprinkle flour over shallot (or onion) and stir quickly to combine; cook, stirring constantly, for 1 minute. Add remaining ingredients and bring mixture to a boil. Reduce heat to low and cook until mixture thickens and flavors blend, 2 to 3 minutes. Return chicken to skillet and cook until heated through, 1 to 2 minutes.

MAKES 2 SERVINGS

Each serving provides: 3½ Protein Exchanges; ⅛ Vegetable Exchange; 1 Fat Exchange; 65 Optional Calories
Per serving: 279 calories; 30 g protein; 10 g fat; 8 g carbohydrate; 96 mg calcium; 562 mg sodium; 76 mg cholesterol; 0.2 g dietary fiber

Chicken with Wine and Vinegar

1 tablespoon plus 1½ teaspoons
  all-purpose flour
⅛ teaspoon salt
Dash pepper
1 pound 2 ounces chicken parts,
  skinned
2 teaspoons olive *or* vegetable oil
1 garlic clove, minced
¾ cup water
⅓ cup dry red table wine
1 tablespoon balsamic *or* red wine
  vinegar
1 packet instant beef broth and
  seasoning mix
1 bay leaf
½ cup *each* frozen pearl onions,
  sliced carrot, and sliced
  mushrooms
2 tablespoons dark raisins

On sheet of wax paper or a paper plate combine flour, salt, and pepper; dredge chicken in flour mixture, coating all sides.

In 2-quart nonstick saucepan heat oil; add chicken and cook over high heat, turning occasionally, until browned, about 3 minutes on each side. Reduce heat to medium-high; add garlic and cook until golden, about 15 seconds. Add water, wine, vinegar, broth mix, and bay leaf and stir to combine. Increase heat to high and bring mixture to a boil; add vegetables and raisins. Reduce heat to medium-low, cover, and let simmer, stirring occasionally, until vegetables are tender and chicken is cooked through, about 15 minutes. Remove and discard bay leaf.

MAKES 2 SERVINGS

Each serving provides: 3 Protein Exchanges;
  ¼ Bread Exchange; 1½ Vegetable Exchanges;
  1 Fat Exchange; ½ Fruit Exchange;
  45 Optional Calories
Per serving: 320 calories; 27 g protein; 11 g fat;
  22 g carbohydrate; 54 mg calcium; 695 mg sodium;
  76 mg cholesterol; 2 g dietary fiber

Lemon Chicken with Mushrooms

2 chicken cutlets (¼ pound each), pounded to ¼-inch thickness
3 tablespoons all-purpose flour
1 teaspoon *each* margarine and olive *or* vegetable oil
1 cup sliced mushrooms
1 garlic clove, minced
½ cup canned ready-to-serve chicken broth
2 tablespoons *each* freshly squeezed lemon juice and dry white table wine
1 teaspoon chopped fresh parsley
⅛ teaspoon white pepper

On sheet of wax paper or a paper plate dredge cutlets in flour, lightly coating both sides and reserving remaining flour.

In 10-inch nonstick skillet combine margarine and oil and heat until margarine is melted; add cutlets and cook over medium-high heat, turning once, until lightly browned, 2 to 3 minutes on each side. Transfer chicken to plate and set aside.

In same skillet combine mushrooms and garlic and sauté over medium-high heat, until mushrooms are softened, 1 to 2 minutes. Sprinkle with reserved flour and stir quickly to combine; stir in remaining ingredients and bring to a boil. Reduce heat to low and let simmer, stirring frequently, until mixture thickens and flavors blend, 3 to 4 minutes. Return chicken to skillet and cook until heated through, 1 to 2 minutes.

MAKES 2 SERVINGS

Each serving provides: 3 Protein Exchanges;
    ½ Bread Exchange; 1 Vegetable Exchange;
    1 Fat Exchange; 25 Optional Calories
Per serving: 238 calories; 29 g protein; 6 g fat;
    13 g carbohydrate; 23 mg calcium; 350 mg sodium;
    66 mg cholesterol; 1 g dietary fiber

Chicken with Caper-Lemon Sauce

1 skinned and boned chicken
   breast (½ pound)
Dash *each* salt and pepper
2 teaspoons olive *or* vegetable oil
1 garlic clove, minced
2 tablespoons *each* dry white
   table wine and rinsed drained
   capers
2 teaspoons lemon juice
1½ teaspoons whipped butter

Sprinkle chicken with salt and pepper. In 9-inch nonstick skillet heat oil; add chicken to skillet and cook over high heat, turning once, until lightly browned, about 3 minutes on each side. Remove chicken to plate; set aside and keep warm.

To same skillet add garlic and cook over medium heat, stirring constantly, until golden, about 30 seconds. Add wine, capers, and lemon juice and bring mixture to a boil. Turn off heat; add butter and stir constantly, until melted.

To serve, diagonally slice chicken and arrange on serving platter; top with caper-lemon sauce.

MAKES 2 SERVINGS

Each serving provides: 3 Protein Exchanges;
   1 Fat Exchange; 30 Optional Calories
Per serving: 191 calories; 26 g protein; 7 g fat;
   1 g carbohydrate; 18 mg calcium; 376 mg sodium;
   70 mg cholesterol; dietary fiber data not available

Chicken-Corn Bread Pies ☻

2 teaspoons margarine
5 ounces diced cooked chicken
½ cup *each* diced carrot and
   celery
¼ cup diced onion
1 tablespoon chopped fresh
   parsley
1 garlic clove, minced
⅛ teaspoon *each* pepper and
   thyme leaves
¼ cup all-purpose flour, divided
1 cup canned ready-to-serve
   chicken broth
½ cup buttermilk
1 egg
2¼ ounces uncooked yellow
   cornmeal
¼ teaspoon baking soda

Preheat oven to 400°F. In 2-quart saucepan melt margarine; add chicken, carrot, celery, onion, parsley, garlic, pepper, and thyme and sauté over medium-high heat, stirring frequently, until vegetables are tender-crisp, 1 to 2 minutes. Sprinkle 1 tablespoon flour over vegetables and stir quickly to combine; stir in broth. Reduce heat to low and cook, stirring frequently, until vegetables are softened and mixture thickens, 5 to 6 minutes.

In medium mixing bowl combine buttermilk and egg; set aside. In small mixing bowl combine cornmeal, baking soda, and remaining 3 tablespoons flour; add to buttermilk mixture and stir until smooth.

Spray two 1½-cup casseroles with nonstick cooking spray and spoon half of the chicken mixture into each; top each with half of the cornmeal mixture and spread evenly over chicken mixture. Bake until cornmeal mixture is cooked through and lightly browned, 10 to 12 minutes.

MAKES 2 SERVINGS, 1 PIE EACH

Each serving provides: 3 Protein Exchanges;
   2 Bread Exchanges; 1¼ Vegetable Exchanges;
   1 Fat Exchange; 65 Optional Calories
Per serving: 449 calories; 32 g protein; 14 g fat;
   47 g carbohydrate; 132 mg calcium; 846 mg sodium;
   203 mg cholesterol; 4 g dietary fiber

Hen with Lemon-Dill Sauce Ⓜ

An elegant recipe for that special dinner.

1 Cornish hen (1¼ pounds*),
   cut in half
½ cup canned ready-to-serve
   chicken broth
1 tablespoon *each* all-purpose
   flour, freshly squeezed lemon
   juice, and sour cream
1 teaspoon chopped fresh dill
   or ½ teaspoon dillweed
⅛ teaspoon *each* salt and
   white pepper

On microwavable baking sheet arrange hen halves skin-side up; cover with vented plastic wrap and microwave on High (100%) for 10 minutes, until cooked through, rotating baking sheet ½ turn halfway through cooking. Set aside and keep warm.

In small microwavable mixing bowl combine broth and flour and stir to dissolve flour; microwave on High for 2 minutes, stirring halfway through cooking. Stir in remaining ingredients.

To serve, remove and discard skin from hen. Arrange hen halves on serving platter and top with sauce.

MAKES 2 SERVINGS

Each serving provides: 4 Protein Exchanges;
   40 Optional Calories
Per serving: 256 calories; 34 g protein; 10 g fat;
   5 g carbohydrate; 32 mg calcium; 491 mg sodium;
   104 mg cholesterol; 0.1 g dietary fiber

*A 1¼-pound Cornish hen will yield about ½ pound cooked poultry.

Oriental Citrus Hen

Celebrate a special occasion with this delicious recipe.

3 tablespoons teriyaki sauce
1 tablespoon *each* honey and
freshly squeezed lemon juice
¼ teaspoon *each* grated orange
peel and grated lemon peel
1 Cornish hen (1¼ pounds*), cut
in half
¼ cup canned ready-to-serve
chicken broth
1 teaspoon *each* cornstarch and
sesame seed, toasted

In shallow medium mixing bowl (not aluminum†) combine teriyaki sauce, honey, lemon juice, orange peel, and lemon peel; stir to combine. Add hen halves and turn to thoroughly coat with marinade. Cover with plastic wrap and refrigerate at least 30 minutes.

Preheat broiler. Arrange hen halves skin-side up on rack in broiling pan, reserving marinade, and broil 6 to 8 inches from heat source for 12 to 15 minutes; turn halves over and broil until lightly browned and cooked through, 12 to 15 minutes.

While hen is broiling prepare sauce. Transfer marinade mixture to small nonstick saucepan; add broth and cornstarch and stir to dissolve cornstarch. Cook over medium-high heat, stirring constantly, until mixture comes to a boil and thickens, 2 to 3 minutes.

To serve, remove and discard skin from hen; transfer hen halves to serving platter, top with sauce, and sprinkle with sesame seed.

MAKES 2 SERVINGS

Each serving provides: 4 Protein Exchanges;
    50 Optional Calories
Per serving: 282 calories; 35 g protein; 9 g fat;
    14 g carbohydrate; 38 mg calcium; 1,124 mg sodium;
    101 mg cholesterol; dietary fiber data not available

*A 1¼-pound Cornish hen yields about ½ pound cooked poultry.
†It's best to marinate in glass or stainless-steel containers; ingredients such as teriyaki sauce and lemon juice may react with aluminum, causing color and flavor changes in food.

Hoisin Duck with Eggplant

¼ cup canned ready-to-serve
   chicken broth
2 tablespoons *each* teriyaki sauce
   and dry sherry
1 tablespoon hoisin sauce
1 teaspoon cornstarch
1½ teaspoons peanut *or*
   vegetable oil
½ teaspoon Chinese sesame oil
½ pound skinned and boned duck
   breast, cut into 2 x ½-inch strips
1 tablespoon minced pared
   gingerroot
1 garlic clove, minced
1½ cups diced eggplant
½ cup diced red bell pepper
¼ cup sliced scallions (green
   onions)

In small mixing bowl combine broth, teriyaki sauce, sherry, hoisin sauce, and cornstarch and stir to dissolve cornstarch; set aside.

In 12-inch nonstick skillet heat oils; add duck, gingerroot, and garlic and cook over medium heat, stirring frequently, until duck is cooked through, 2 to 3 minutes. Transfer duck to plate and set aside.

In same skillet combine eggplant, bell pepper, and scallions and cook over medium heat, stirring frequently, until eggplant is tender, 1 to 2 minutes. Stir in reserved broth mixture; return duck to skillet and cook, stirring frequently, until mixture thickens and duck is heated through, about 1 minute.

MAKES 2 SERVINGS

Each serving provides: 3 Protein Exchanges;
   2¼ Vegetable Exchanges; 1 Fat Exchange;
   40 Optional Calories
Per serving: 278 calories; 24 g protein; 12 g fat;
   15 g carbohydrate; 54 mg calcium; 1,160 mg sodium;
   87 mg cholesterol; 2 g dietary fiber

Variation: Hoisin Chicken with Eggplant —
Substitute ½ pound skinned and boned chicken breast for the duck.

Per serving: 252 calories; 29 g protein; 6 g fat;
   15 g carbohydrate; 54 mg calcium; 1,150 mg sodium;
   66 mg cholesterol; 2 g dietary fiber

Hoisin sauce, also known as Peking sauce, is a soybean-based mixture that includes garlic and other spices.

Madeira Duck with Plum

For an elegant presentation and accompaniment, arrange sautéed bok choy and long-grain and wild rice on a serving platter with the duck.

1 teaspoon *each* margarine and olive *or* vegetable oil
½ pound skinned and boned duck breast
1 tablespoon chopped shallot *or* onion
1 teaspoon all-purpose flour
½ cup canned ready-to-serve chicken broth
¼ cup medium-dry Madeira wine
1 tablespoon raspberry vinegar
1 medium plum (about 2½ ounces), pitted and sliced

In 10-inch nonstick skillet heat margarine and oil until margarine is melted; add duck and cook over medium-high heat, turning once, until lightly browned, 2 to 3 minutes on each side. Transfer to plate and set aside.

In same skillet sauté shallot (or onion) over medium heat until translucent, about 1 minute. Sprinkle flour over shallot (or onion) and stir quickly to combine. Stir in broth, wine, and vinegar and cook, stirring frequently, until mixture thickens, 2 to 3 minutes. Reduce heat to low; add duck and plum slices and turn to coat with sauce. Cook until duck and plum slices are heated through, about 1 minute.

To serve, slice duck and arrange on serving platter; top with sauce and plum slices.

MAKES 2 SERVINGS

Each serving provides: 3 Protein Exchanges;
    1 Fat Exchange; ¼ Fruit Exchange;
    45 Optional Calories
Per serving: 268 calories; 22 g protein; 12 g fat;
    11 g carbohydrate; 20 mg calcium; 361 mg sodium;
    87 mg cholesterol; 1 g dietary fiber

Variation: Madeira Chicken with Plum — Substitute ½ pound skinned and boned chicken breast for the duck.

Per serving: 244 calories; 27 g protein; 6 g fat;
    11 g carbohydrate; 19 mg calcium; 351 mg sodium;
    66 mg cholesterol; 1 g dietary fiber

Sautéed Duck Breast with Peaches and Juniper Sauce

Juniper, a small evergreen shrub, provides berries that add a pleasant flavor to game, venison, rabbit, and duck. Juniper berries can be found in the dried spice section of your supermarket.

2 teaspoons olive *or* vegetable oil
½ pound skinned and boned duck breast
½ cup sliced shallots *or* onions
¼ cup dry red table wine
6 dried juniper berries,* crushed
½ cup water
1 packet instant chicken broth and seasoning mix
1 teaspoon *each* firmly packed brown sugar and cornstarch
1 cup drained canned peach slices (no sugar added)

In 9-inch nonstick skillet heat oil; add duck and cook over medium-high heat, turning once, until browned and cooked through, 3 to 4 minutes on each side. Transfer duck to plate and set aside.

In same skillet cook shallots (or onions) over medium heat, stirring frequently, until translucent, about 1 minute; stir in wine and juniper berries. Reduce heat to low and let simmer until flavors blend, about 2 minutes. In 1-cup liquid measure combine remaining ingredients except peaches and stir to dissolve cornstarch; add to juniper mixture in skillet and cook over high heat, stirring constantly, until mixture comes to a boil. Reduce heat to low; add peaches and duck to skillet and turn to coat with sauce. Cover and let simmer until flavors blend and mixture is thoroughly heated, about 3 minutes.

To serve, thinly slice duck and decoratively arrange slices on serving platter; top with peach mixture.

MAKES 2 SERVINGS

Each serving provides: 3 Protein Exchanges;
⅓ Vegetable Exchange; 1 Fat Exchange;
1 Fruit Exchange; 50 Optional Calories
Per serving: 312 calories; 23 g protein; 11 g fat;
25 g carbohydrate; 39 mg calcium; 591 mg sodium;
87 mg cholesterol; 1 g dietary fiber

*Nutritional data for juniper berries not available.

Cherry Fruit Soup

Nutty Oatmeal with Raisins
Blueberry Pancakes
Ginger-Pear Pancake
Prosciutto-Cheese Omelet

Pepper and Leek Soup
Gingered Onion-Apple Soup
Ham and Cheese Corn Bread Rolls

Shrimp Gruyère
Broccoli and Walnut Sauté

Kir Spritzer

Stir-Fry Duck with Vegetables

2 teaspoons peanut *or* vegetable
  oil
1 cup sliced shiitake *or* white
  mushrooms
1 tablespoon minced pared
  gingerroot
1 small garlic clove, minced
¼ pound cooked sliced duck
  (3 x ½-inch strips)
½ cup *each* red bell pepper strips
  (3 x ½-inch pieces) and Chinese
  pea pods (snow peas), stem
  ends and strings removed
¼ cup diagonally sliced scallions
  (green onions), white and green
  portions
¼ cup water
1 tablespoon reduced-sodium soy
  sauce
1 packet instant chicken broth
  and seasoning mix
1 teaspoon dark corn syrup

In 10-inch nonstick skillet or wok heat oil; add mushrooms, gingerroot, and garlic and cook over high heat, stirring quickly and frequently until mushrooms begin to soften, about 1 minute. Add duck, bell pepper, pea pods, and scallions and cook, stirring occasionally, until duck is heated through and vegetables are tender-crisp, 2 to 3 minutes.

In 1-cup liquid measure combine remaining ingredients and stir to combine; stir into skillet and cook, stirring constantly, until mixture is thoroughly heated, 1 to 2 minutes.

MAKES 2 SERVINGS

Each serving provides: 2 Protein Exchanges;
  2¼ Vegetable Exchanges; 1 Fat Exchange;
  15 Optional Calories
Per serving: 209 calories; 17 g protein; 11 g fat;
  11 g carbohydrate; 38 mg calcium; 839 mg sodium;
  51 mg cholesterol; 2 g dietary fiber

Variation: Stir-Fry Chicken with Vegetables — Substitute ¼ pound cooked sliced chicken for the duck.

Per serving: 203 calories; 20 g protein; 9 g fat;
  11 g carbohydrate; 40 mg calcium; 851 mg sodium;
  51 mg cholesterol; 2 g dietary fiber

To be labeled "reduced-sodium" a product must contain 75 percent less sodium than the original product.

Creamy Turkey Patties ☉

5 ounces ground turkey
3 tablespoons seasoned dried
  bread crumbs
1 egg white
2 tablespoons chopped onion
1 tablespoon chopped fresh
  parsley, divided
1 garlic clove, minced
2 teaspoons vegetable oil
1 tablespoon whipped butter
2 teaspoons all-purpose flour
½ cup low-fat milk (1% milk fat)
¼ cup water
1 packet instant chicken broth
  and seasoning mix

In medium mixing bowl combine turkey, bread crumbs, egg white, onion, 2 teaspoons parsley, and the garlic and mix well. Shape mixture into 4 equal patties; set aside.

In 9-inch nonstick skillet heat oil; add patties to skillet and cook over medium heat, turning once, until browned and cooked through, about 4 minutes on each side. Transfer patties to plate and set aside.

In same skillet melt butter; sprinkle with flour and stir quickly to combine. Cook over medium-high heat, stirring constantly, for 1 minute. Gradually stir in milk, water, broth mix, and remaining teaspoon parsley. Increase heat to high and cook, stirring constantly, until mixture comes to a boil. Reduce heat to low and let simmer until mixture thickens, 2 to 3 minutes. Return turkey patties to skillet and cook until heated through, about 2 minutes.

MAKES 2 SERVINGS, 2 PATTIES EACH

Each serving provides: 2 Protein Exchanges;
  ½ Bread Exchange; ⅛ Vegetable Exchange;
  1 Fat Exchange; ¼ Milk Exchange; 55 Optional Calories
Per serving: 274 calories; 19 g protein; 16 g fat;
  15 g carbohydrate; 118 mg calcium; 945 mg sodium;
  58 mg cholesterol; 1 g dietary fiber

Mexican Turkey Pitas Ⓜ

5 ounces ground turkey
¼ cup tomato sauce
2 tablespoons *each* chopped onion and green bell pepper
1 tablespoon *each* seeded and minced jalapeño *or* mild *or* hot chili pepper, and taco seasoning mix
1 garlic clove, minced
2 ounces rinsed drained canned red kidney beans
2 pitas (1 ounce each), heated
1 ounce Cheddar cheese, shredded
¼ medium avocado (about 2 ounces), pared, pitted, and diced

Using a fork, in 1-quart microwavable shallow casserole combine turkey, tomato sauce, onion, peppers, seasoning mix, and garlic and mix to thoroughly combine. Cover with vented plastic wrap and microwave on High (100%) for 2 minutes, until softened. Stir in beans. Re-cover with vented plastic wrap and microwave on High for 3 minutes, until turkey is cooked through, rotating casserole ½ turn after microwaving for 2 minutes. Let stand for 1 minute.

Using a sharp knife, cut top side of each pita into quarters, cutting to outer edge of each pita. Gently pull each quarter up and away from center to create starburst pattern. Spoon half of the turkey mixture into center of each pita and top each with half of the cheese and avocado.

MAKES 2 SERVINGS

Each serving provides: 3 Protein Exchanges;
    1 Bread Exchange; ¾ Vegetable Exchange;
    1 Fat Exchange
Per serving: 362 calories; 23 g protein; 16 g fat;
    33 g carbohydrate; 157 mg calcium; 852 mg sodium
    (estimated); 62 mg cholesterol; 3 g dietary fiber

Buy an avocado two to three days before you plan to use it since it will usually need some time to ripen. You can speed the ripening process by placing the avocado in a closed paper bag with air holes.

Microwave Turkey Loaf Ⓜ

¼ cup *each* finely chopped onion and red bell pepper
1 small jalapeño pepper, seeded and minced
1 garlic clove, minced
5 ounces ground turkey
¼ cup part-skim ricotta cheese
1 teaspoon *each* chili powder and chopped fresh cilantro (Chinese parsley) *or* Italian (flat-leaf) parsley
⅛ teaspoon *each* salt and pepper
4 tomato slices
1 ounce Cheddar cheese, shredded
2 large pitted black olives, sliced

In medium microwavable mixing bowl combine onion, peppers, and garlic; cover with vented plastic wrap and microwave on High (100%) for 1 minute, until vegetables are tender-crisp. Add turkey, ricotta cheese, chili powder, cilantro (or parsley), salt, and pepper; mix well until thoroughly combined. Transfer mixture to microwavable roasting rack and shape into a loaf; cover with vented plastic wrap and microwave on High for 3 minutes. Rotate rack ½ turn, uncover, and microwave on High, for 3 minutes. Top loaf with tomato slices and then sprinkle with Cheddar cheese; microwave on High for 1 minute, until cheese melts. Top with olive slices.

MAKES 2 SERVINGS

Each serving provides: 3 Protein Exchanges;
   1½ Vegetable Exchanges; 5 Optional Calories
Per serving: 245 calories; 21 g protein; 15 g fat;
   7 g carbohydrate; 229 mg calcium; 377 mg sodium;
   72 mg cholesterol; 1 g dietary fiber

Turkey Cutlets with Apricots

1 teaspoon *each* margarine and
olive *or* vegetable oil
½ pound turkey cutlets
1 tablespoon minced shallot
or onion
¼ teaspoon minced pared
gingerroot
1 tablespoon all-purpose flour
⅓ cup apricot nectar
¼ cup canned ready-to-serve
chicken broth
6 dried apricot halves, diced
1 tablespoon dried currants *or*
dark raisins
⅛ teaspoon *each* salt and white
pepper

In 10-inch nonstick skillet heat margarine
and oil until margarine is melted; add turkey
and cook over high heat, turning once, until
lightly browned and cooked through, 2 to 3
minutes on each side. Transfer turkey to
serving platter; set aside and keep warm.

In same skillet combine shallot (or onion)
and gingerroot and sauté over medium-high
heat, stirring frequently, until softened,
about 1 minute. Sprinkle flour over gingerroot mixture and stir quickly to combine; stir
in nectar and broth. Reduce heat to medium-
low and cook, stirring frequently, until mixture thickens, 2 to 3 minutes. Add remaining
ingredients and stir to combine; cook until
fruits are plumped and heated through, 1 to
2 minutes. Pour fruit mixture over turkey.

MAKES 2 SERVINGS

Each serving provides: 3 Protein Exchanges;
    1 Fat Exchange; 1½ Fruit Exchanges;
    20 Optional Calories
Per serving: 251 calories; 28 g protein; 6 g fat;
    20 g carbohydrate; 28 mg calcium; 366 mg sodium;
    70 mg cholesterol; 1 g dietary fiber

Turkey Shepherd's Pie ☉

2 teaspoons vegetable oil
½ cup chopped onion
1 garlic clove, minced
5 ounces ground turkey
1 tablespoon all-purpose flour
Water
1 tablespoon plus 1 teaspoon dry
    red table wine
1 packet instant beef broth and
    seasoning mix
1 tablespoon chopped fresh
    parsley
⅔ cup potato flakes (instant
    mashed potatoes)
1 teaspoon butter

In 10-inch nonstick skillet heat oil; add onion and garlic and cook over high heat, stirring frequently, until onion is translucent, about 1 minute. Add turkey, reduce heat to medium-high, and cook, stirring with a wooden spoon to break up large pieces, until turkey is no longer pink, about 6 minutes. Sprinkle flour over turkey mixture and stir quickly to combine; cook, stirring constantly, for 1 minute. Add ¼ cup water, the wine, and broth mix and cook over high heat until mixture comes to a boil. Stir in parsley; reduce heat to medium-low and let simmer for 3 minutes.

While turkey mixture simmers prepare potatoes. Using a fork, in small mixing bowl combine potato flakes, ⅔ cup boiling water, and the butter and mix until light and fluffy.

Preheat broiler. Transfer turkey mixture to 1-quart flameproof casserole; top with potato mixture and spread over casserole. Broil until potato mixture is golden brown, about 2 minutes.

MAKES 2 SERVINGS

Each serving provides: 2 Protein Exchanges;
    1 Bread Exchange; ½ Vegetable Exchange;
    1 Fat Exchange; 45 Optional Calories
Per serving: 286 calories; 16 g protein; 14 g fat;
    24 g carbohydrate; 47 mg calcium; 580 mg sodium;
    53 mg cholesterol; 1 g dietary fiber (this figure does not
    include potato flakes; nutrition analysis not available)

Nutty Turkey Salad Pitas

3 ounces diced cooked turkey
¼ cup diced celery
2 tablespoons *each* golden raisins
 and sour cream
1 tablespoon plus 1 teaspoon
 reduced-calorie mayonnaise
1 teaspoon *each* freshly squeezed
 lemon juice and pickle relish
Dash *each* salt and white pepper
2 pitas (1 ounce each), cut in half
 horizontally
¼ ounce unsalted roasted shelled
 almonds, chopped
¼ cup alfalfa sprouts

In small mixing bowl combine all ingredients except pitas, almonds, and alfalfa sprouts; mix well until thoroughly combined. Onto bottom half of each pita spread half of the turkey mixture, then top each with half of the almonds and alfalfa sprouts. Set top half of each pita over sprouts; cut each pita in half crosswise.

MAKES 2 SERVINGS

Each serving provides: 1¾ Protein Exchanges;
 1 Bread Exchange; ½ Vegetable Exchange;
 1¼ Fat Exchanges; ½ Fruit Exchange;
 40 Optional Calories
Per serving: 272 calories; 17 g protein; 10 g fat;
 29 g carbohydrate; 55 mg calcium; 394 mg sodium;
 42 mg cholesterol; 1 g dietary fiber

Harvest Turkey-Chestnut Salad

Turkey salad is a well-known way to serve leftover roast turkey; but our version, with fresh leeks, chestnuts, and bacon, is far from humdrum. If you have the time, purchase fresh chestnuts and roast and peel them yourself.

3 cups assorted mixed lettuce leaves (red leaf lettuce, radicchio, frisée, and mache)*
¼ pound cubed cooked turkey (2-inch cubes)
½ cup julienne-cut thoroughly washed leeks (white portion only), matchstick pieces
3 small canned chestnuts (no sugar added), cut into halves
2 slices crisp bacon, broken into pieces
⅓ cup apple juice (no sugar added)
2 tablespoons apple cider vinegar
2 teaspoons olive oil
Dash *each* salt and pepper

On serving platter decoratively arrange assorted lettuce leaves; top with turkey, leeks, chestnuts, and bacon.

In cup or small bowl combine remaining ingredients and stir well to combine; pour evenly over salad.

MAKES 2 SERVINGS

Each serving provides: 2 Protein Exchanges; ¼ Bread Exchange; 3½ Vegetable Exchanges; 1 Fat Exchange; ½ Fruit Exchange; 45 Optional Calories
Per serving: 238 calories; 20 g protein; 11 g fat; 15 g carbohydrate; 97 mg calcium; 226 mg sodium; 49 mg cholesterol; 1 g dietary fiber (this figure does not include chestnuts; nutrition analysis not available)

Variation: Harvest Turkey Salad — Omit chestnuts from recipe. Omit Bread Exchange from Exchange Information.

Per serving: 224 calories; 20 g protein; 11 g fat; 12 g carbohydrate; 92 mg calcium; 223 mg sodium; 49 mg cholesterol; 1 g dietary fiber

*Three cups assorted mixed greens of your choice may be substituted for the red leaf lettuce, radicchio, frisée, and mache.

Warm Chicken Salad with Rosemary

2 teaspoons olive *or* vegetable oil
½ pound chicken cutlets, cut into
    2 x ½-inch pieces
1 medium red bell pepper, seeded
    and cut into matchstick pieces
1 garlic clove, minced
1 cup thawed frozen artichoke
    hearts
¼ cup canned ready-to-serve
    chicken broth
1 tablespoon balsamic *or* red wine
    vinegar
1 teaspoon rinsed drained capers
¼ teaspoon crushed rosemary
    leaves
⅛ teaspoon *each* salt and pepper
4 escarole *or* romaine lettuce
    leaves

In 10-inch nonstick skillet heat oil; add chicken and cook over high heat until chicken is lightly browned on all sides, 3 to 4 minutes. Transfer to plate and set aside.

In same skillet combine bell pepper and garlic and cook over medium heat until pepper is softened, 2 to 3 minutes. Return chicken to skillet; add remaining ingredients except escarole (or romaine lettuce) leaves and cook, stirring occasionally, until artichokes and chicken are cooked through and flavors blend, 2 to 3 minutes.

To serve, line serving platter with escarole (or romaine lettuce) leaves; using a slotted spoon, spoon chicken mixture onto center of platter and pour liquid in skillet evenly over escarole (or romaine lettuce) leaves.

MAKES 2 SERVINGS

Each serving provides: 3 Protein Exchanges;
    2½ Vegetable Exchanges; 1 Fat Exchange;
    5 Optional Calories
Per serving: 218 calories; 29 g protein; 7 g fat;
    10 g carbohydrate; 44 mg calcium; 417 mg sodium;
    66 mg cholesterol; 4 g dietary fiber

Tostada Salad

Don't let the long list of ingredients intimidate you. This recipe cooks up in about 10 minutes.

2 teaspoons olive *or* vegetable oil
1 cup *each* diced onions and
    green bell peppers
1 tablespoon thinly sliced mild *or*
    hot chili pepper
2 garlic cloves, minced
7 ounces julienne-cut chicken
    cutlets (matchstick pieces)
6 ounces (¾ cup) canned baked
    beans (without meat)
1 tablespoon *each* chopped
    cilantro (Chinese parsley) *or*
    chopped Italian (flat-leaf)
    parsley and lime juice (no sugar
    added)
1 medium tomato, chopped
1 cup torn romaine lettuce
1 ounce Monterey Jack *or*
    Cheddar cheese, shredded
1 tablespoon sour cream
3 pitted black olives, sliced
1½ tostada shells, broken into
    pieces

In 9-inch skillet heat oil; add onions, bell peppers, chili pepper, and garlic and cook over medium heat, stirring frequently, until onion is translucent, 2 to 3 minutes. Add chicken and cook, stirring frequently, until chicken is no longer pink, 2 to 3 minutes. Add beans, cilantro (or parsley), and lime juice and stir to combine. Reduce heat to low and let simmer until chicken is cooked and mixture is thoroughly heated, about 1 minute. Remove from heat and stir in tomato.

To serve, on serving platter arrange lettuce; top with chicken mixture and sprinkle with cheese. Top with sour cream and olives. Serve with tostada pieces.

MAKES 2 SERVINGS

Each serving provides: 3 Protein Exchanges;
    1½ Bread Exchanges; 4 Vegetable Exchanges;
    1¼ Fat Exchanges; 50 Optional Calories
Per serving with Monterey Jack cheese: 413 calories;
    34 g protein; 16 g fat; 36 g carbohydrate;
    218 mg calcium; 584 mg sodium; 73 mg cholesterol;
    5 g dietary fiber (this figure does not include tostada
    shells; nutrition analysis not available)
With Cheddar cheese: 417 calories; 34 g protein; 16 g fat;
    37 g carbohydrate; 215 mg calcium; 596 mg sodium;
    76 mg cholesterol; 5 g dietary fiber (this figure does not
    include tostada shells; nutrition analysis not available)

Sweet and Sour Chicken Salad

5 ounces diced cooked chicken
   (¼-inch pieces)
½ cup minced celery
1 medium apricot (about
   1¼ ounces), pitted and diced,
   or 2 dried apricot halves, diced
2 tablespoons *each* minced
   scallion (green onion) and sour
   cream
1 tablespoon plus 1 teaspoon
   reduced-calorie mayonnaise
1 tablespoon apple cider vinegar
2 teaspoons apricot preserves
⅛ teaspoon salt

In serving bowl combine chicken, celery, apricot, and scallion. In small bowl combine remaining ingredients; pour over chicken mixture and stir well to combine.

MAKES 2 SERVINGS

Each serving provides: 2½ Protein Exchanges;
   ½ Vegetable Exchange; 1 Fat Exchange;
   ¼ Fruit Exchange; 50 Optional Calories
Per serving with fresh apricot: 226 calories; 22 g protein;
   11 g fat; 10 g carbohydrate; 47 mg calcium;
   309 mg sodium; 73 mg cholesterol; 1 g dietary fiber
With dried apricot: 226 calories; 21 g protein; 11 g fat;
   10 g carbohydrate; 46 mg calcium; 310 mg sodium;
   73 mg cholesterol; 1 g dietary fiber

Meat and Veal

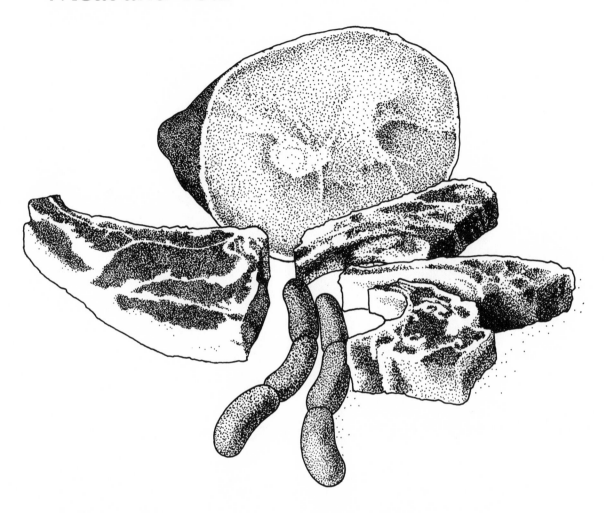

Do you think that "quick" and "delicious" are mutually exclusive? You'll toss out that old notion when you sample some of the hearty, classic dishes here that used to take hours to prepare. Because we've revamped some old favorites to fit in with today's busy life-styles, you can now prepare Beef Bourguignonne and Old-Fashioned Beef Soup in the microwave oven. Stove-top and conventional oven methods also yield dishes that are fast and tasty. From Dijon Pork Chops to Lamb Chops with Minted Horseradish Sauce, from Gyros to Warm Spinach and Ham Salad, there's a dish to please every palate.

Old-Fashioned Beef Soup Ⓒ Ⓜ

Use leftover cooked beef in this hearty vegetable soup.

2 cups water
1 cup canned Italian tomatoes (with liquid); drain, seed, and dice tomatoes, reserving liquid
4½ ounces pared all-purpose potato, cut into ½-inch cubes
3 ounces diced cooked beef
½ cup *each* sliced carrot, celery, and mushrooms
¼ cup *each* chopped onion and frozen whole-kernel corn
2 packets instant beef broth and seasoning mix
1 tablespoon chopped fresh parsley
⅛ teaspoon pepper

In 3-quart microwavable casserole combine all ingredients except parsley and pepper; microwave on High (100%) for 15 minutes, until potato is fork-tender, stirring halfway through cooking. Stir in parsley and pepper.

MAKES 2 SERVINGS, ABOUT 1½ CUPS EACH

Each serving provides: 1½ Protein Exchanges;
    1 Bread Exchange; 2¾ Vegetable Exchanges;
    10 Optional Calories
Per serving: 211 calories; 17 g protein; 4 g fat;
    28 g carbohydrate; 66 mg calcium; 1,196 mg sodium;
    34 mg cholesterol; 4 g dietary fiber

Beef Bourguignonne Ⓜ

1 cup quartered mushrooms
½ cup *each* frozen pearl onions,
    sliced carrot, and canned
    ready-to-serve beef broth
¼ cup *each* dry red table wine
    and canned crushed tomatoes
1 tablespoon tomato paste
2 teaspoons all-purpose flour
1 garlic clove, minced
½ pound boneless beef sirloin,
    cut into 1-inch cubes; broiled
    until medium
¼ teaspoon rosemary leaves
⅛ teaspoon *each* salt and pepper

In 1-quart microwavable casserole combine all ingredients except beef, rosemary, salt, and pepper and stir to dissolve tomato paste and flour. Microwave on High (100%) for 5 minutes, until mixture thickens and vegetables are tender, stirring every 2 minutes. Add remaining ingredients and stir to combine; microwave on High for 1 minute until beef is heated through.

MAKES 2 SERVINGS

Each serving provides: 3 Protein Exchanges;
    2¼ Vegetable Exchanges; 55 Optional Calories
Per serving: 269 calories; 29 g protein; 8 g fat;
    15 g carbohydrate; 55 mg calcium; 532 mg sodium;
    76 mg cholesterol; 2 g dietary fiber

The leanest cuts of beef are top round, eye of the round, tip round, sirloin, top loin, and tenderloin. Look for them when you shop.

Philadelphia Cheese-Steak Hoagie

While the steak is broiling for this hearty sandwich, sauté the onion and pepper and prepare the cheese sauce.

1 teaspoon olive *or* vegetable oil
½ cup *each* sliced onion and green bell pepper
2 ounces sharp Cheddar cheese, shredded
1 tablespoon *each* whipped cream cheese and half-and-half (blend of milk and cream)
5 ounces top round steak, broiled until done to taste
2 hero *or* hoagie rolls (2 ounces each), each cut lengthwise into halves

In 9-inch nonstick skillet heat oil; add onion and bell pepper and sauté over medium-high heat, stirring frequently, until vegetables are tender, 3 to 4 minutes. Set aside and keep warm.

In small nonstick saucepan combine cheeses and half-and-half and cook over low heat, stirring constantly, until cheeses melt and mixture is smooth and thickened, 2 to 3 minutes. Set aside and keep warm.

To serve, thinly slice steak across the grain. Onto bottom half of each roll arrange half of the steak slices, half of the onion mixture, and then half of the cheese mixture; cover with top half of roll.

MAKES 2 SERVINGS

Each serving provides: 3 Protein Exchanges;
    2 Bread Exchanges; 1 Vegetable Exchange;
    ½ Fat Exchange; 30 Optional Calories
Per serving: 454 calories; 31 g protein; 20 g fat;
    36 g carbohydrate; 255 mg calcium; 561 mg sodium;
    87 mg cholesterol; 2 g dietary fiber

Quick Veal Paprikash

½ cup water
1 tablespoon *each* sour cream,
  tomato paste, and dry white
  table wine
1 packet instant chicken broth
  and seasoning mix
1 teaspoon sweet Hungarian
  paprika
1 teaspoon *each* olive *or*
  vegetable oil and margarine
1 cup sliced onions
5 ounces ground veal

In 1-cup liquid measure combine water, sour cream, tomato paste, wine, broth mix, and paprika and stir well to combine; set aside. In 9-inch nonstick skillet combine oil and margarine and heat until margarine is melted; add onions and sauté over high heat until tender-crisp, about 1 minute. Add veal and cook, stirring constantly, until veal is no longer pink, about 1 minute. Add sour cream mixture; stir to combine and bring to a boil. Reduce heat to low and let simmer, stirring occasionally, until flavors blend, 2 to 3 minutes.

MAKES 2 SERVINGS

Each serving provides: 2 Protein Exchanges;
    1⅛ Vegetable Exchanges; 1 Fat Exchange;
    30 Optional Calories
Per serving: 232 calories; 18 g protein; 13 g fat;
    9 g carbohydrate; 42 mg calcium; 616 mg sodium;
    60 mg cholesterol; 1 g dietary fiber

Quick Veal Stew Ⓜ

1 cup *each* sliced mushrooms and
   celery
2 teaspoons margarine
1 small garlic clove, minced
5 ounces cubed veal (½-inch
   pieces)
2 tablespoons dry red table wine
1 packet instant chicken broth
   and seasoning mix
2 cups frozen pearl onions
1 cup canned crushed tomatoes

In 2-quart microwavable casserole combine mushrooms, celery, margarine, and garlic; cover with vented plastic wrap and microwave on High (100%) for 2 minutes, until vegetables are soft. Add veal, wine, and broth mix and stir to combine; re-cover with vented plastic wrap and microwave on High for 2 minutes. Add onions and tomatoes and stir to combine; re-cover with vented plastic wrap and microwave on High for 2 minutes, stirring once halfway through cooking.

MAKES 2 SERVINGS

Each serving provides: 2 Protein Exchanges;
   5 Vegetable Exchanges; 1 Fat Exchange;
   25 Optional Calories
Per serving: 293 calories; 20 g protein; 12 g fat;
   26 g carbohydrate; 134 mg calcium; 836 mg sodium;
   57 mg cholesterol; 2 g dietary fiber

Veal Chops Italiana

1 tablespoon *each* all-purpose
   flour, grated Parmesan cheese,
   and chopped fresh parsley
2 veal loin *or* rib chops (5 ounces
   each)
2 teaspoons olive *or* vegetable oil
1 cup *each* julienne-cut red bell
   peppers (matchstick pieces)
   and quartered mushrooms
2 garlic cloves, minced
½ cup drained canned Italian
   tomatoes, seeded and diced
¼ cup dry white table wine
½ teaspoon crushed rosemary
   leaves
⅛ teaspoon *each* salt and pepper

On sheet of wax paper or a paper plate combine flour, Parmesan cheese, and parsley; dredge veal in flour mixture, coating both sides.

In 10-inch nonstick skillet heat oil; add chops and cook over medium-high heat, turning once, until lightly browned on both sides, 2 to 3 minutes on each side. Transfer chops to plate and set aside.

In same skillet combine bell peppers, mushrooms, and garlic and sauté over medium-high heat, stirring frequently, until vegetables are softened, 1 to 2 minutes. Stir in remaining ingredients; return chops to skillet. Reduce heat to low, cover, and cook, stirring occasionally, for 10 minutes. Uncover and cook until chops are cooked through and liquid is reduced and slightly thickened, about 5 minutes longer.

MAKES 2 SERVINGS

Each serving provides: 3 Protein Exchanges;
    2½ Vegetable Exchanges; 1 Fat Exchange;
    60 Optional Calories
Per serving with loin chops: 324 calories; 26 g protein;
    17 g fat; 11 g carbohydrate; 80 mg calcium;
    344 mg sodium; 88 mg cholesterol; 2 g dietary fiber
With rib chops: 354 calories; 27 g protein; 20 g fat;
    11 g carbohydrate; 81 mg calcium; 345 mg sodium;
    88 mg cholesterol; 2 g dietary fiber

Don't store fresh garlic in the refrigerator. Not only will it sprout, it will also both give off and absorb odors. Garlic keeps best in a dry, cool, dark spot that is also well ventilated.

Veal Sausage with Peppers

Because the roasted peppers in this recipe will need about 15 minutes to cool, make sure you roast the peppers before doing anything else.

2 medium red bell peppers
2 teaspoons olive *or* vegetable oil
4 veal sausage links (about
   2 ounces each)
1 cup sliced onions
2 garlic cloves, minced
¼ cup dry white table wine
¼ teaspoon crushed rosemary
   leaves
⅛ teaspoon pepper

On baking sheet lined with heavy-duty foil broil peppers 3 inches from heat source, turning frequently, until charred on all sides; let stand until cool enough to handle, about 15 minutes.

Fit strainer into small mixing bowl; peel peppers over strainer, removing and discarding stem ends and seeds and allowing juice from peppers to drip into bowl. Cut peppers into thin strips and add to bowl with juice; set aside.

In 10-inch nonstick skillet heat oil; add sausage and cook over medium-high heat, turning occasionally, until sausage is well browned on all sides, 5 to 6 minutes. Add onions and garlic and sauté, stirring frequently, until softened, 2 to 3 minutes. Stir in roasted peppers and juice, the wine, rosemary, and pepper. Reduce heat to low and let simmer, stirring frequently, until flavors blend, 4 to 5 minutes.

MAKES 2 SERVINGS

Each serving provides: 3 Protein Exchanges;
   3 Vegetable Exchanges; 1 Fat Exchange;
   30 Optional Calories
Per serving: 311 calories; 26 g protein; 16 g fat;
   11 g carbohydrate; 45 mg calcium; 1,106 mg sodium
   (estimated); 86 mg cholesterol; 1 g dietary fiber

Nearly every country boasts its own special kind of sausage. For instance, there's chorizo *from Spain and Mexico,* kielbasa *from Poland, and* wursts *from Germany.*

Veal Scaloppine with Tomato-Cream Sauce

½ pound veal scallops *or* thin veal
   cutlets
1 tablespoon all-purpose flour
1 teaspoon *each* margarine and
   olive *or* vegetable oil
1 cup sliced mushrooms
¼ cup *each* dry white table wine
   and canned ready-to-serve
   chicken broth
1 tablespoon tomato paste
2 tablespoons half-and-half (blend
   of milk and cream)
2 teaspoons *each* chopped fresh
   parsley and fresh basil *or*
   ½ teaspoon basil leaves
⅛ teaspoon *each* salt and pepper

On sheet of wax paper or a paper plate dredge veal in flour, coating both sides.

In 10-inch nonstick skillet combine margarine and oil and heat until margarine is melted; add veal and sauté over medium-high heat, turning once, until cooked through and lightly browned on both sides, 1 to 2 minutes on each side. Transfer to plate and set aside.

In same skillet sauté mushrooms over medium-high heat, until mushrooms are lightly browned, 2 to 3 minutes. In 1-cup liquid measure combine wine, broth, and tomato paste and stir until smooth. Stir into skillet; continuing to stir, cook, until mixture thickens and is slightly reduced, 3 to 4 minutes. Stir in remaining ingredients; return veal to skillet and cook until heated through, 1 to 2 minutes.

MAKES 2 SERVINGS

Each serving provides: 3 Protein Exchanges;
   1⅛ Vegetable Exchanges; 1 Fat Exchange;
   75 Optional Calories
Per serving: 289 calories; 25 g protein; 15 g fat;
   8 g carbohydrate; 48 mg calcium; 439 mg sodium;
   86 mg cholesterol; 1 g dietary fiber

Sweet and Sour Meat Balls

1 tablespoon plus 1 teaspoon
  vegetable oil, divided
¼ cup *each* finely chopped onion
  and celery
1 small garlic clove, minced
9 ounces ground veal
⅓ cup plus 2 teaspoons seasoned
  dried bread crumbs
1 egg, lightly beaten
1 tablespoon plus 1 teaspoon
  grated Parmesan cheese
2 tablespoons ketchup
1 tablespoon *each* reduced-
  calorie apricot and grape
  spreads (16 calories per
  2 teaspoons)
1 teaspoon apple cider vinegar
1 cup sliced mushrooms
2 tablespoons *each* red and green
  bell peppers

In 9-inch nonstick skillet heat 1 teaspoon oil; add onion, celery, and garlic and cook over high heat, stirring frequently, until tender-crisp, about 30 seconds. Transfer to medium mixing bowl; add veal, bread crumbs, egg, and cheese and mix well. Shape into 16 equal balls.

In same skillet heat remaining tablespoon oil; add meat balls and cook over medium heat, turning occasionally, until browned on all sides, 5 to 8 minutes. Transfer meat balls to plate; set aside.

In cup or small bowl combine ketchup, apricot and grape spreads, and vinegar and stir to combine; set aside. In same skillet combine mushrooms and bell peppers and cook, stirring frequently, until tender-crisp, about 1 minute. Reduce heat to low and stir in ketchup mixture. Return meat balls to skillet and turn to coat with sauce. Cook until flavors blend and meat balls are heated through, about 5 minutes.

MAKES 4 SERVINGS, 4 MEAT BALLS EACH

Each serving provides: 2 Protein Exchanges;
  ½ Bread Exchange; ¾ Vegetable Exchange;
  1 Fat Exchange; 30 Optional Calories
Per serving: 250 calories; 17 g protein; 13 g fat;
  15 g carbohydrate; 58 mg calcium; 487 mg sodium;
  116 mg cholesterol; 1 g dietary fiber

Veal and Rice Balls Ⓜ

2 tablespoons *each* finely
  chopped onion, green bell
  pepper, and celery
2 teaspoons margarine
1 small garlic clove, minced
5 ounces ground veal
1 ounce uncooked instant rice
⅛ teaspoon oregano leaves
½ cup *each* tomato sauce and
  water
1 packet instant chicken broth
  and seasoning mix
¼ teaspoon marjoram leaves

In 1-quart microwavable casserole combine onion, bell pepper, celery, margarine, and garlic; microwave on High (100%) for 1 minute. Add veal, rice, and oregano and mix well. Shape into 8 equal balls.

In same casserole arrange veal balls and microwave on High for 3 minutes. In 1-cup liquid measure combine remaining ingredients; pour over veal balls. Cover with vented plastic wrap and microwave on Medium (50%) for 12 minutes, turning veal balls over every 3 minutes. Let stand for 2 minutes.

MAKES 2 SERVINGS, 4 VEAL BALLS EACH

Each serving provides: 2 Protein Exchanges;
  ½ Bread Exchange; ¾ Vegetable Exchange;
  1 Fat Exchange; 5 Optional Calories
Per serving: 240 calories; 16 g protein; 11 g fat;
  18 g carbohydrate; 29 mg calcium; 964 mg sodium;
  50 mg cholesterol; 2 g dietary fiber

Dijon Pork Chops

For an attractive presentation, arrange each pork chop on a dinner plate with sautéed sliced zucchini, sliced mushrooms, diced red bell pepper, cooked carrot chunks, and rosemary sprigs.

3 tablespoons plain dried bread crumbs
1 tablespoon *each* grated Parmesan cheese and chopped fresh parsley
1 teaspoon vegetable oil
⅛ teaspoon pepper
2 pork loin chops (5 ounces each)
2 teaspoons Dijon-style mustard

In shallow mixing bowl combine bread crumbs, Parmesan cheese, parsley, oil, and pepper; mix well and set aside.

Spread both sides of each pork chop with mustard; then press each pork chop into bread crumb mixture, coating both sides and using all of mixture.

Spray rack in broiling pan with nonstick cooking spray; arrange chops on rack and broil 5 to 6 inches from heat source, turning once, until thoroughly cooked and lightly browned, 5 to 6 minutes on each side.

MAKES 2 SERVINGS

Each serving provides: 3 Protein Exchanges;
    ½ Bread Exchange; ½ Fat Exchange;
    15 Optional Calories
Per serving: 272 calories; 29 g protein; 13 g fat;
    8 g carbohydrate; 53 mg calcium; 333 mg sodium;
    86 mg cholesterol; 0.1 g dietary fiber

Pork Chops with Brandied Fruits

2 pork loin chops (5 ounces each)
2 teaspoons *each* country Dijon-style mustard, divided, and margarine
1 small Bartlett pear (about 5 ounces), cored and diced
1 small Granny Smith apple (about ¼ pound), cored and diced
¼ cup diced onion
2 teaspoons freshly squeezed lemon juice
2 tablespoons *each* apple brandy (calvados) and water
¼ teaspoon fennel seed
⅛ teaspoon pepper

On rack in broiling pan arrange chops and spread top side of each with ½ teaspoon mustard. Broil 5 to 6 inches from heat source until lightly browned, 5 to 6 minutes; turn chops over, spread with remaining mustard and broil until thoroughly cooked and lightly browned, about 5 to 6 minutes.

While chops are broiling prepare fruit mixture. In 9-inch nonstick skillet melt margarine; add pear, apple, onion, and lemon juice and sauté over medium-high heat, stirring frequently, until fruits are lightly browned and tender-crisp, 2 to 3 minutes. Stir in remaining ingredients and cook until flavors blend, 2 to 3 minutes. Serve with pork chops.

MAKES 2 SERVINGS

Each serving provides: 3 Protein Exchanges;
¼ Vegetable Exchange; 1 Fat Exchange;
1 Fruit Exchange; 40 Optional Calories
Per serving: 355 calories; 28 g protein; 14 g fat;
25 g carbohydrate; 25 mg calcium; 262 mg sodium;
83 mg cholesterol; 3 g dietary fiber

Pork Chops with Salsa

2 teaspoons vegetable oil
1 garlic clove, minced
1 teaspoon seeded and minced
  jalapeño pepper
1 cup canned Italian tomatoes
  (with liquid); drain, seed, and
  chop tomatoes, reserving liquid
¼ cup dry red table wine
1 teaspoon chopped cilantro
  (Chinese parsley) or Italian
  (flat-leaf) parsley
¼ teaspoon chili powder
Dash hot sauce
2 pork loin chops (5 ounces each),
  broiled until rare

In 9-inch skillet heat oil; add garlic and jalapeño pepper and cook over high heat, stirring frequently, until softened, about 1 minute. Add remaining ingredients except pork chops and cook, stirring frequently, until mixture comes to a boil. Reduce heat to medium-low; add chops and let simmer for 15 minutes or until tender.

MAKES 2 SERVINGS

Each serving provides: 3 Protein Exchanges;
   1 Vegetable Exchange; 1 Fat Exchange;
   30 Optional Calories
Per serving: 286 calories; 29 g protein; 14 g fat;
   6 g carbohydrate; 42 mg calcium; 271 mg sodium;
   83 mg cholesterol; 1 g dietary fiber

A common ingredient in Tex-Mex cookery is the jalapeño pepper, a small, hot chili pepper named for Jalapa, the capital of Veracruz, Mexico. When handling the jalapeño or any chili pepper, wear rubber gloves and be careful not to touch your face or eyes.

Pork Medallions with Cran-Orange Sauce

1 teaspoon margarine
2 tablespoons chopped shallot
   or onion
2 teaspoons all-purpose flour
¼ cup *each* port wine, orange
   juice (no sugar added), orange
   sections, halved, and
   cranberries
⅛ teaspoon *each* salt and pepper
2 boneless pork loin chops
   (¼ pound each), each cut in half
   horizontally

In 1-quart saucepan melt margarine; add shallot (or onion) and sauté over medium-high heat, stirring frequently, until softened, about 1 minute. Sprinkle with flour and stir quickly to combine; stir in wine and orange juice and cook, stirring occasionally, until mixture begins to thicken, about 3 minutes. Reduce heat to low; add orange sections, cranberries, salt, and pepper and cook until cranberries are softened but still retain their shape, 2 to 3 minutes. Set aside and keep warm.

On rack in broiling pan broil pork, turning once, until thoroughly cooked and lightly browned, 2 to 3 minutes on each side. Serve topped with cranberry-orange mixture.

MAKES 2 SERVINGS

Each serving provides: 3 Protein Exchanges;
   ⅛ Vegetable Exchange; ½ Fat Exchange;
   ½ Fruit Exchange; 70 Optional Calories
Per serving: 298 calories; 28 g protein; 11 g fat;
   13 g carbohydrate; 25 mg calcium; 231 mg sodium;
   83 mg cholesterol; 1 g dietary fiber (this figure does not
   include cranberries; nutrition analysis not available)

Stock up on fresh cranberries in season and freeze them for future use. When a recipe calls for cranberries, just measure out the amount you need and put the rest back in the freezer.

Fruited Ham Salad

¼ pound diced boiled *or* cooked
    smoked ham
2 tablespoons *each* golden raisins,
    diced green bell pepper, diced
    celery, and diced red onion *or*
    scallion (green onion)
2 teaspoons country Dijon-style
    mustard
1 teaspoon honey
8 lettuce leaves
½ medium tomato, sliced

In small mixing bowl combine all ingredients except lettuce and tomato and stir until thoroughly blended.

    To serve, line center of serving platter with lettuce leaves and arrange tomato slices along side of platter; top lettuce with ham mixture.

MAKES 2 SERVINGS

Each serving provides: 2 Protein Exchanges;
    1¾ Vegetable Exchanges; ½ Fruit Exchange;
    10 Optional Calories
Per serving: 163 calories; 14 g protein; 6 g fat;
    15 g carbohydrate; 39 mg calcium; 1,015 mg sodium;
    33 mg cholesterol; 2 g dietary fiber

Ham with Port and Red Grapes

2 teaspoons margarine, divided
2 slices "fully cooked" boneless smoked ham (2 ounces each)
1 cup diced red onions
2 tablespoons port wine
20 small *or* 12 large red seedless grapes

In 9-inch nonstick skillet melt 1 teaspoon margarine; add ham and cook over high heat, turning once, about 1 minute on each side. Transfer ham to serving platter; set aside and keep warm.

In same skillet melt remaining teaspoon margarine; add onions and sauté over high heat until tender, about 1 minute. Stir in wine and bring mixture to a boil. Reduce heat to low; add grapes and stir to combine. Let simmer until flavors blend, about 1 minute. Spoon grape mixture over ham.

MAKES 2 SERVINGS

Each serving provides: 2 Protein Exchanges;
    1 Vegetable Exchange; 1 Fat Exchange;
    ½ Fruit Exchange; 25 Optional Calories
Per serving: 206 calories; 14 g protein; 9 g fat;
    13 g carbohydrate; 32 mg calcium; 900 mg sodium;
    33 mg cholesterol; 1 g dietary fiber (this figure does not
    include grapes; nutrition analysis not available)

Smoked Ham and Squash Gratin Ⓜ

¼ **pound** *each* **julienne-cut pared butternut squash and cooked smoked ham (matchstick pieces)**
2 ounces Gruyère *or* Swiss cheese, shredded, divided
¼ **cup thoroughly washed sliced leek (white portion only)**
1 tablespoon all-purpose flour
½ **cup evaporated skimmed milk, divided**
⅛ **teaspoon white pepper**
Dash ground nutmeg
3 tablespoons plain dried bread crumbs

In medium mixing bowl combine squash, ham, 1 ounce cheese, and the leek; sprinkle flour over squash-ham mixture and mix well. Add milk and stir well to thoroughly combine. Spray 8 x 8 x 2-inch flameproof microwavable baking dish with nonstick cooking spray; spread squash-ham mixture in baking dish and microwave on High (100%) for 4 minutes until leek is tender-crisp, stirring mixture and rotating baking dish ½ turn halfway through cooking. Add pepper and nutmeg and stir to combine. In small bowl combine remaining 1 ounce cheese and the bread crumbs; sprinkle over squash-ham mixture.

Preheat broiler. Transfer baking dish to broiler and broil 5 to 6 inches from heat source until crumb mixture is lightly browned, 1 to 2 minutes.

MAKES 2 SERVINGS

Each serving provides: 3 Protein Exchanges; 1 Bread Exchange; ¼ Vegetable Exchange; ½ Milk Exchange; 15 Optional Calories
Per serving with Gruyère cheese: 353 calories; 28 g protein; 15 g fat; 26 g carbohydrate; 524 mg calcium; 1,094 mg sodium; 68 mg cholesterol; 1 g dietary fiber (this figure does not include butternut squash; nutrition analysis not available)
With Swiss cheese: 343 calories; 28 g protein; 14 g fat; 27 g carbohydrate; 509 mg calcium; 1,073 mg sodium; 63 mg cholesterol; 1 g dietary fiber (this figure does not include butternut squash; nutrition analysis not available)

Warm Spinach and Ham Salad ⒸⓂ

Try this winning salad when you have leftover cooked sweet potato or yam.

3 ounces cooked smoked ham
2 tablespoons plus 2 teaspoons
   apple juice (no sugar added)
1 tablespoon apple cider vinegar
2 teaspoons olive oil
1 teaspoon Dijon-style mustard
3 cups spinach leaves, trimmed,
   thoroughly washed, drained,
   and torn into bite-size pieces
3 ounces diced cooked sweet
   potato _or_ yam
1 ounce Swiss cheese, shredded

On microwavable plate arrange ham and microwave on High (100%) for 1 minute, until heated through; dice and set aside.

In microwavable cup or small bowl combine apple juice, vinegar, oil, and mustard and microwave on High for 1 minute, until heated through.

To serve, in serving bowl combine spinach, potato, and ham and toss to combine. Pour vinegar mixture over salad and toss to coat. Sprinkle with cheese.

MAKES 2 SERVINGS

Each serving provides: 2 Protein Exchanges;
  ½ Bread Exchange; 3 Vegetable Exchanges;
  1 Fat Exchange; ¼ Fruit Exchange
Per serving: 226 calories; 15 g protein;
  11 g fat; 17 g carbohydrate; 233 mg calcium;
  792 mg sodium; 33 mg cholesterol; 4 g dietary fiber

Cooking a potato in its skin retains the nutrients; if need be, the skin can easily be removed after cooking.

Ground Lamb Lyonnaise

2 teaspoons olive *or* vegetable oil
6 ounces shredded pared
   all-purpose potato
1 cup minced onions
¼ pound cooked ground lamb,
   crumbled
½ cup *each* sliced celery and
   diced red bell pepper
1 tablespoon red wine vinegar
1 teaspoon honey
⅛ teaspoon rosemary leaves,
   crushed
Dash *each* salt and pepper

In 9-inch skillet heat oil; add potato and cook over medium heat, stirring constantly, until lightly browned, 4 to 5 minutes. Add onions and stir to combine. Reduce heat to low, cover, and cook until potato is soft, 2 to 3 minutes. Add remaining ingredients and stir to combine. Cover and cook until celery and bell pepper are soft and flavors blend, about 2 minutes.

MAKES 2 SERVINGS

Each serving provides: 2 Protein Exchanges;
   1 Bread Exchange; 2 Vegetable Exchanges;
   1 Fat Exchange; 10 Optional Calories
Per serving: 274 calories; 18 g protein; 11 g fat;
   27 g carbohydrate; 47 mg calcium; 138 mg sodium;
   57 mg cholesterol; 3 g dietary fiber

Gyros

1/4 cup minced onion
1 small garlic clove, minced
1/2 pound ground lamb
2 tablespoons lemon juice
1/2 teaspoon *each* oregano leaves
  and ground cumin
1/2 cup seeded pared cucumber,
  diced
1/4 cup plain low-fat yogurt
1 tablespoon chopped fresh mint
2 pitas (2 ounces each)
1/2 cup *each* shredded lettuce
  and diced tomato

Spray small skillet with nonstick cooking spray; add onion and garlic and cook over medium heat, stirring constantly, until softened, about 30 seconds. Transfer to medium mixing bowl; add lamb, lemon juice, oregano, and cumin and mix to thoroughly combine. Shape into 2 equal patties.

Spray rack in broiling pan with nonstick cooking spray and broil patties, turning once, for 3 to 5 minutes on each side or until done to taste. In small serving bowl combine cucumber, yogurt, and mint and stir to combine; set aside.

To serve, using a sharp knife, cut 1/4 of the way around edge of each pita; open to form pocket. Fill each pita with half of the lettuce and tomato, 1 lamb patty, and half of the yogurt mixture.

MAKES 2 SERVINGS

Each serving provides: 3 Protein Exchanges;
  2 Bread Exchanges; 1 3/4 Vegetable Exchanges;
  1/4 Milk Exchange
Per serving: 397 calories; 31 g protein; 10 g fat;
  45 g carbohydrate; 111 mg calcium; 451 mg sodium;
  87 mg cholesterol; 2 g dietary fiber

Lamb Chops with Minted Horseradish Sauce

1 teaspoon margarine
1 tablespoon chopped shallot
   or onion
¼ cup *each* dry vermouth and
   canned ready-to-serve chicken
   broth
2 tablespoons sour cream
1 tablespoon chopped fresh mint
   or 1 teaspoon mint flakes
2 teaspoons all-purpose flour
1 teaspoon prepared horseradish
2 lamb loin chops (5 ounces each)

In small nonstick saucepan melt margarine; add shallot (or onion) and sauté over medium-high heat, stirring frequently, until softened, about 1 minute. Reduce heat to low; add vermouth and broth and cook, stirring occasionally, until liquid is reduced by half, 3 to 4 minutes.

In cup or small bowl combine sour cream, mint, flour, and horseradish and stir until thoroughly combined; stir into vermouth mixture. Cook, stirring frequently, until mixture thickens, 3 to 4 minutes. Keep warm.

On rack in broiling pan broil chops, turning once, until medium-rare, 3 to 4 minutes on each side, or until done to taste. Serve lamb chops topped with sauce.

MAKES 2 SERVINGS

Each serving provides: 3 Protein Exchanges;
   ½ Fat Exchange; 80 Optional Calories
Per serving: 295 calories; 27 g protein; 13 g fat;
   8 g carbohydrate; 25 mg calcium; 233 mg sodium;
   86 mg cholesterol; 0.1 g dietary fiber

Scrubbing a broiling pan is a time-consuming task. To speed cleanup, spray the rack of your broiling pan with nonstick cooking spray before broiling foods.

Marinated Lamb Chops with Ginger

½ cup orange juice (no sugar added)
1 tablespoon *each* Dijon-style mustard, teriyaki sauce, and freshly squeezed lemon juice
1 teaspoon minced pared gingerroot
2 lamb loin chops (5 ounces each)
1 teaspoon cornstarch

In a shallow bowl (not aluminum*) large enough to hold lamb in a single layer combine orange juice, mustard, teriyaki sauce, lemon juice, and gingerroot and mix well; add lamb and turn to coat. Cover with plastic wrap and refrigerate for at least 30 minutes.

Arrange lamb chops on rack in broiling pan, reserving marinade, and broil, turning once, 3 to 4 minutes on each side or until done to taste.

While lamb chops are broiling prepare sauce. In small saucepan combine reserved marinade and cornstarch and stir to dissolve cornstarch; cook over medium-high heat, stirring constantly, until mixture comes to a boil. Reduce heat to low and cook, stirring frequently, until sauce is thickened, 3 to 4 minutes. Serve lamb chops topped with sauce.

MAKES 2 SERVINGS

Each serving provides: 3 Protein Exchanges;
  ½ Fruit Exchange; 5 Optional Calories
Per serving: 235 calories; 26 g protein; 9 g fat;
  11 g carbohydrate; 9 mg calcium; 642 mg sodium;
  80 mg cholesterol; 0.3 g dietary fiber

*It's best to marinate in glass or stainless-steel containers; ingredients such as orange juice and lemon juice may react with aluminum, causing color and flavor changes in food.

If you've never tried fresh ginger, you're in for a wonderful surprise. It's much better tasting than the dried, powdered ginger you keep on your spice shelf. Store unpeeled fresh ginger in a sealed plastic bag in your refrigerator vegetable crisper.

Microwave Moussaka Ⓜ

1 medium eggplant (about
   1 pound), pared and cut
   lengthwise into eight ¼-inch-
   thick slices, divided
1½ cups tomato sauce
¼ cup diced onion
⅛ teaspoon *each* ground
   cinnamon, garlic powder, and
   oregano leaves
Dash ground nutmeg
½ cup part-skim ricotta cheese
1 egg
6 ounces cooked ground lamb
1 ounce grated Parmesan cheese,
   divided

Line 10-inch round microwavable plate with 3 paper towels; arrange 4 of the eggplant slices in a circle on towels with narrow ends in center of plate and wide ends facing edge of plate. Cover with sheet of paper towel and microwave on High (100%) for 4 minutes, turning slices over halfway through cooking. Repeat procedure with remaining eggplant slices.

In medium mixing bowl combine tomato sauce, onion, cinnamon, garlic powder, oregano, and nutmeg and stir to combine; set aside. In separate medium mixing bowl combine ricotta cheese and egg and stir to combine; set aside.

In 2-quart microwavable casserole combine lamb and half of the tomato sauce mixture; stir to combine and spread over bottom of casserole. Arrange half of the eggplant slices in a single layer over meat mixture; sprinkle with ½ ounce of the Parmesan cheese. Top with remaining tomato sauce mixture and then with remaining eggplant slices. Spread ricotta cheese mixture over eggplant slices; sprinkle with remaining ½ ounce Parmesan cheese. Microwave, uncovered, on High for 13 minutes, rotating casserole ½ turn halfway through cooking. Let stand for 2 minutes.

MAKES 4 SERVINGS

Each serving provides: 2½ Protein Exchanges;
   2¼ Vegetable Exchanges
Per serving: 297 calories; 20 g protein; 18 g fat;
   16 g carbohydrate; 247 mg calcium; 768 mg sodium;
   125 mg cholesterol; 3 g dietary fiber

Portuguese Lamb Ⓜ

¾ cup canned ready-to-serve beef
   broth
½ cup julienne-cut red bell pepper
   (matchstick pieces)
¼ cup *each* sliced onion and dry
   red table wine
1 ounce diced prosciutto (Italian-
   style ham)
2 garlic cloves, minced
2 teaspoons all-purpose flour
½ teaspoon paprika
7 ounces lamb cubes (½-inch
   cubes), broiled until medium
Dash pepper

In 1-quart microwavable shallow casserole
combine all ingredients except lamb and
dash pepper and stir until flour is dissolved;
microwave on High (100%) for 5 minutes,
until mixture thickens, stirring every 2 minutes. Add lamb and stir to combine; microwave on High for 1 minute, until lamb is
heated through. Stir in pepper.

MAKES 2 SERVINGS

Each serving provides: 3 Protein Exchanges;
   ¾ Vegetable Exchange; 55 Optional Calories
Per serving: 217 calories; 24 g protein; 7 g fat;
   7 g carbohydrate; 25 mg calcium; 646 mg sodium
   (estimated); 79 mg cholesterol; 1 g dietary fiber

Rabbit Cacciatore Ⓜ

½ cup sliced onions
2 teaspoons olive oil
2 garlic cloves, minced
½ cup canned Italian tomatoes
(with liquid); drain, seed, and
dice tomatoes, reserving liquid
¼ cup *each* dry white table wine
and canned ready-to-serve
chicken broth
1 tablespoon all-purpose flour
1 cup quartered mushrooms
1 pound 1¼ ounces rabbit parts,*
skinned
2 teaspoons chopped fresh
parsley
⅛ teaspoon *each* salt and pepper

In 1-quart microwavable shallow casserole combine onions, oil, and garlic and stir to thoroughly coat; microwave on High (100%) for 3 minutes, stirring halfway through cooking. Add tomatoes with liquid, wine, broth, and flour and stir to dissolve flour; microwave on High for 5 minutes, stirring halfway through cooking. Add mushrooms and stir to combine. Arrange rabbit in casserole over vegetable mixture with thickest portions toward edge of casserole; cover with vented plastic wrap and microwave on Medium-High (75%) for 15 minutes, until rabbit is cooked through, rotating casserole halfway through cooking. Add parsley, salt, and pepper and stir to combine.

MAKES 2 SERVINGS

Each serving provides: 3 Protein Exchanges;
2 Vegetable Exchanges; 1 Fat Exchange;
50 Optional Calories
Per serving: 302 calories; 28 g protein; 14 g fat;
12 g carbohydrate; 57 mg calcium; 401 mg sodium;
77 mg cholesterol; 2 g dietary fiber

*One pound 1¼ ounces rabbit parts will yield about
6 ounces boned cooked rabbit.

Variation: Chicken Cacciatore — Substitute 1 pound 2 ounces chicken parts, skinned, for the rabbit.

Per serving: 279 calories; 27 g protein; 11 g fat;
12 g carbohydrate; 52 mg calcium; 440 mg sodium;
76 mg cholesterol; 2 g dietary fiber

Rabbit with Pignolias and Raisins ⓜ

½ cup canned ready-to-serve
  chicken broth
¼ cup dry white table wine
2 teaspoons all-purpose flour
2 tablespoons golden raisins
¼ ounce pignolias (pine nuts),
  toasted
1 teaspoon freshly squeezed
  lemon juice
¼ teaspoon *each* rosemary
  leaves, crushed, grated lemon
  peel, and browning sauce
1 pound 1¼ ounces rabbit parts,*
  skinned
⅛ teaspoon *each* salt and white
  pepper

In 1-quart microwavable shallow casserole combine broth, wine, and flour and stir to dissolve flour; microwave on High (100%) for 4 minutes, until mixture thickens, stirring every minute. Add raisins, pignolias, lemon juice, rosemary, lemon peel, and browning sauce and stir to combine; microwave on High for 2 minutes, stirring every minute.

Arrange rabbit in casserole over raisin mixture with thickest portions toward edge of casserole; cover with vented plastic wrap and microwave on Medium-High (75%) for 15 minutes, until rabbit is cooked through, rotating casserole halfway through cooking. Stir in salt and pepper.

MAKES 2 SERVINGS

Each serving provides: 3¼ Protein Exchanges;
  ¼ Fat Exchange; ½ Fruit Exchange;
  50 Optional Calories
Per serving: 270 calories; 27 g protein; 11 g fat;
  11 g carbohydrate; 30 mg calcium; 432 mg sodium;
  77 mg cholesterol; 1 g dietary fiber (this figure does
  not include pignolias; nutrition analysis not available)

*One pound 1¼ ounces rabbit parts will yield about
6 ounces boned cooked rabbit.

Variation: Chicken with Pignolias and Raisins — Substitute 1 pound 2 ounces chicken parts, skinned, for the rabbit.

Per serving: 248 calories; 27 g protein; 9 g fat;
  11 g carbohydrate; 25 mg calcium; 470 mg sodium;
  76 mg cholesterol; 1 g dietary fiber (this figure does
  not include pignolias; nutrition analysis not available)

Legume Entrées

Versatile, tasty, and economical, legumes are a low-fat, high-fiber source of protein. They're also simple to prepare, making them ideal for today's busy life-styles. The secret to shortcut legume cookery is canned beans, which you'll find in such delicious dishes as Chick-Pea and Sausage Sauté, Three-Bean Salad, and Microwave Black Bean Soup. You'll find these and many more wonderfully quick legume dishes right in this chapter.

Autumn Soup

2 teaspoons margarine
½ cup *each* diced onion and
   sliced celery
2 cups water
1½ cups frozen cubed butternut
   squash
1 packet instant chicken broth
   and seasoning mix
8 ounces rinsed drained canned
   small white beans
2 slices crisp bacon, crumbled

In 1-quart saucepan melt margarine; add vegetables and sauté over high heat, stirring frequently, until tender-crisp, about 1 minute. Add water, squash, and broth mix and stir to combine; cook until mixture comes to a full boil. Reduce heat to low, cover, and let simmer until squash is soft, about 15 minutes. Using a wooden spoon, press some of the squash against inside of saucepan to mash; stir in beans and bacon and let simmer until flavors blend, about 5 minutes longer.

MAKES 2 SERVINGS, ABOUT 1⅔ CUPS EACH

Each serving provides: 2 Protein Exchanges;
    1½ Bread Exchanges; 1 Vegetable Exchange;
    1 Fat Exchange; 55 Optional Calories
Per serving: 279 calories; 14 g protein; 7 g fat;
    43 g carbohydrate; 144 mg calcium; 1,056 mg sodium
    (estimated); 5 mg cholesterol; 1 g dietary fiber (this
    figure does not include butternut squash and white
    beans; nutrition analyses not available)

Bean Chowder

6 ounces rinsed drained canned white kidney (cannellini) beans, divided
2 teaspoons margarine
½ cup *each* diced onion, green bell pepper, carrot, and celery
1 ounce Canadian-style bacon, diced
1 cup *each* frozen *or* drained canned whole-kernel corn and whole milk

Using a fork, in small mixing bowl mash 3 ounces kidney beans and set aside. In 1½-quart saucepan melt margarine; add vegetables and bacon and sauté over medium-high heat, stirring frequently, until vegetables are tender-crisp, 2 to 3 minutes. Add mashed and remaining whole beans, the corn, and milk and stir to combine. Reduce heat to medium-low and cook, stirring frequently, until flavors blend and mixture is thoroughly heated, about 8 minutes.

MAKES 2 SERVINGS, ABOUT 2 CUPS EACH

Each serving provides: 2 Protein Exchanges;
    1 Bread Exchange; 2 Vegetable Exchanges;
    1 Fat Exchange; ½ Milk Exchange; 30 Optional Calories
Per serving with frozen corn: 334 calories; 17 g protein;
    10 g fat; 48 g carbohydrate; 221 mg calcium;
    636 mg sodium (estimated); 24 mg cholesterol;
    7 g dietary fiber
With canned corn: 328 calories; 17 g protein; 10 g fat;
    46 g carbohydrate; 218 mg calcium; 634 mg sodium
    (estimated); 24 mg cholesterol; 6 g dietary fiber

If you're adding more fiber to your diet, remember to do it gradually, and drink plenty of water.

Bean and Bacon Soup Ⓜ

A wonderful cold-weather warmer. Just serve with a slice of crusty bread and a tossed salad for a weekend lunch or light dinner.

½ cup diced red onion
¼ cup *each* diced celery and red bell pepper
1 small garlic clove, minced
1 teaspoon olive *or* vegetable oil
1 cup canned Italian tomatoes (with liquid), pureed
4 ounces rinsed drained canned white kidney (cannellini) beans
2 slices crisp bacon, crumbled

In 1-quart microwavable casserole combine onion, celery, bell pepper, garlic, and oil; cover with vented plastic wrap and microwave on High (100%) for 3 minutes, until softened, stirring once halfway through cooking. Add remaining ingredients and stir to combine; re-cover with vented plastic wrap and microwave on High for 1 minute, until thoroughly heated.

MAKES 2 SERVINGS, ABOUT 1 CUP EACH

Each serving provides: 1 Protein Exchange;
    2 Vegetable Exchanges; ½ Fat Exchange;
    45 Optional Calories
Per serving: 164 calories; 8 g protein; 6 g fat;
    21 g carbohydrate; 77 mg calcium; 496 mg sodium
    (estimated); 5 mg cholesterol; 4 g dietary fiber

Bean and Vegetable Soup with Pesto Topping Ⓜ

1 cup chopped thoroughly
   washed leeks (white portion
   and some green)
½ cup *each* sliced carrot, celery,
   green beans, and zucchini
3 ounces diced pared all-purpose
   potato
¾ ounce uncooked thin spaghetti
   or vermicelli, broken into pieces
1 tablespoon plus 1 teaspoon olive
   or vegetable oil, divided
2 small garlic cloves, minced,
   divided
2 cups *each* canned crushed
   tomatoes and water
2 tablespoons tomato paste,
   divided
1 ounce grated Parmesan cheese,
   divided
¼ cup fresh basil *or* 1 tablespoon
   basil leaves
Dash *each* salt and pepper
14 ounces rinsed drained canned
   red kidney beans

In 4-quart microwavable casserole combine leeks, carrot, celery, green beans, zucchini, potato, pasta, 2 teaspoons oil, and half of the minced garlic. Cover with vented plastic wrap and microwave on High (100%) for 4 minutes, stirring once halfway through cooking. Stir in tomatoes, water, and 1 tablespoon tomato paste and microwave on High for 16 minutes, stirring every 5 minutes through cooking.

While soup is cooking prepare pesto topping. In work bowl of food processor combine ½ ounce Parmesan cheese, the basil, salt and pepper, the remaining 2 teaspoons oil, the remaining garlic, and the remaining tablespoon tomato paste and process until smooth; set aside.

Add beans to soup and stir to combine; re-cover with vented plastic wrap and microwave on High for 1 minute, until heated through.

To serve, divide soup into 4 soup bowls and top each portion with ¼ of the pesto topping and remaining Parmesan cheese.

MAKES 4 SERVINGS, ABOUT 1¾ CUPS EACH

Each serving provides: 2 Protein Exchanges;
   ½ Bread Exchange; 2½ Vegetable Exchanges;
   1 Fat Exchange
Per serving: 283 calories; 14 g protein; 7 g fat;
   42 g carbohydrate; 239 mg calcium; 792 mg sodium
   (estimated); 6 mg cholesterol; 6 g dietary fiber

Frijole-Cheese Soup

2 teaspoons olive *or* vegetable oil
½ cup diced onion
1 tablespoon seeded and minced
    jalapeño pepper
1 small garlic clove, mashed
1½ cups canned Italian tomatoes
    (with liquid); drain and chop
    tomatoes, reserving liquid
2 slices crisp bacon, crumbled
Dash *each* chili powder, ground
    cumin, and oregano leaves
6 ounces rinsed drained canned
    pinto beans, mashed
1 ounce Cheddar cheese,
    shredded

In 1-quart saucepan heat oil; add onion, pepper, and garlic and cook over medium heat, stirring occasionally, until tender, about 1 minute. Add tomatoes with liquid, bacon, chili powder, cumin, and oregano and stir to combine; cook for 5 minutes. Add beans, increase heat to medium-high, and cook, stirring constantly, until mixture is thoroughly heated.

To serve, ladle soup into 2 soup bowls and top each portion with ½ ounce cheese.

MAKES 2 SERVINGS, ABOUT 1½ CUPS EACH

Each serving provides: 2 Protein Exchanges;
    2 Vegetable Exchanges; 1 Fat Exchange;
    45 Optional Calories
Per serving: 283 calories; 14 g protein; 13 g fat;
    30 g carbohydrate; 198 mg calcium; 772 mg sodium
    (estimated); 20 mg cholesterol; 6 g dietary fiber

Green Pigeon Pea Soup ⓒ

You'll need boiling water to blanch the tomato in order to peel it, so start the water cooking before doing anything else.

1 teaspoon olive *or* vegetable oil
¼ cup *each* chopped onion and green bell pepper
1 small jalapeño pepper, seeded and minced
1 garlic clove, minced
1 medium tomato, blanched, peeled, seeded, and chopped
½ cup thawed frozen cooked pureed squash
1½ cups water
2 packets instant chicken broth and seasoning mix
6 ounces rinsed drained canned green pigeon peas
1 tablespoon chopped fresh parsley
⅛ teaspoon pepper

In 2-quart saucepan heat oil; add onion, peppers, and garlic and sauté over medium-high heat, stirring frequently, until vegetables are softened, 1 to 2 minutes. Stir in tomato and squash and cook 1 minute longer. Add water and broth mix; cover and bring mixture to a boil. Let cool slightly.

Pour half of mixture into blender container and process at low speed until smooth; transfer mixture to 1-quart bowl and process remaining soup. Pour soup back into saucepan; stir in remaining ingredients and cook over medium heat until peas are heated through and flavors blend, 8 to 10 minutes.

MAKES 2 SERVINGS, ABOUT 2 CUPS EACH

Each serving provides: 1½ Protein Exchanges;
 ½ Bread Exchange; 1¾ Vegetable Exchanges;
 ½ Fat Exchange; 10 Optional Calories
Per serving: 175 calories; 9 g protein; 3 g fat;
 30 g carbohydrate; 66 mg calcium; 1,287 mg sodium
 (estimated); 0 mg cholesterol; 5 g dietary fiber

Microwave Black Bean Soup Ⓒ Ⓜ

¼ cup *each* minced onion, green
    bell pepper, and seeded and
    diced tomato
2 teaspoons olive *or* vegetable oil
1 garlic clove, minced
1 cup canned ready-to-serve
    chicken broth
1 teaspoon all-purpose flour
8 ounces rinsed drained canned
    black beans
1 tablespoon chopped fresh
    parsley
⅛ teaspoon *each* ground
    coriander, ground cumin, and
    salt
Dash pepper
2 tablespoons sour cream

In 2-quart microwavable casserole combine onion, bell pepper, tomato, oil, and garlic and stir to thoroughly coat. Microwave on High (100%) for 2 minutes, until vegetables are tender; transfer to plate and set aside.

In 1-cup liquid measure combine broth and flour and stir to dissolve flour; pour into casserole. Add beans and parsley and microwave on High for 5 minutes, stirring once every minute.

Transfer half of the bean mixture to blender container and process until smooth; return to casserole. Add vegetable mixture and stir to combine. Microwave on High for 8 minutes, until flavors blend. Stir in coriander, cumin, salt, and pepper.

To serve, divide soup into 2 soup bowls and top each portion with 1 tablespoon sour cream.

MAKES 2 SERVINGS, ABOUT 1¼ CUPS EACH

Each serving provides: 2 Protein Exchanges;
    ¾ Vegetable Exchange; 1 Fat Exchange;
    60 Optional Calories
Per serving: 239 calories; 11 g protein; 9 g fat;
    30 g carbohydrate; 78 mg calcium; 1,034 mg sodium
    (estimated); 6 mg cholesterol; 6 g dietary fiber

Catalan Chick-Peas ©

1 teaspoon olive *or* vegetable oil
¼ cup *each* finely chopped onion and green bell pepper
2 garlic cloves, minced
1 medium tomato, blanched, peeled, seeded, and finely chopped
6 ounces rinsed drained canned chick-peas
2 ounces diced cooked smoked ham
½ cup water
1 teaspoon *each* chopped fresh cilantro (Chinese parsley) *or* Italian (flat-leaf) parsley, and rinsed drained capers
1½ cups cooked instant rice (hot)

In 2-quart saucepan heat oil; add onion, bell pepper, and garlic and cook over medium-high heat, stirring frequently, until vegetables are softened, 1 to 2 minutes. Add tomato and cook, stirring frequently, until flavors blend, 1 to 2 minutes. Add remaining ingredients except rice and stir to combine; reduce heat to low and cook, stirring occasionally, until flavors blend and mixture thickens, 15 to 20 minutes. Serve over rice.

MAKES 2 SERVINGS

Each serving provides: 2½ Protein Exchanges; 1½ Bread Exchanges; 1½ Vegetable Exchanges; ½ Fat Exchange
Per serving: 335 calories; 16 g protein; 7 g fat; 53 g carbohydrate; 51 mg calcium; 760 mg sodium (estimated); 17 mg cholesterol; 4 g dietary fiber

Chick-Pea and Sausage Sauté ☉

2 teaspoons olive *or* vegetable oil
½ cup *each* diced onion and
   green bell pepper strips
1 small garlic clove, minced
3 ounces veal sausage links, sliced
½ cup canned Italian tomatoes
   (with liquid); drain and cut
   tomatoes into quarters,
   reserving liquid
1 tablespoon *each* chopped fresh
   basil and fresh Italian (flat-leaf)
   parsley
¼ teaspoon *each* oregano leaves
   and fennel seed
Dash *each* salt and pepper
8 ounces rinsed drained canned
   chick-peas

In 9-inch nonstick skillet heat oil; add onion, bell pepper, and garlic and cook over high heat, stirring occasionally, until tender-crisp, 1 to 2 minutes. Add remaining ingredients except chick-peas and cook, stirring frequently, until sausage is no longer pink, 5 to 6 minutes. Add chick-peas and stir to combine; cook until thoroughly heated, 1 to 2 minutes.

MAKES 2 SERVINGS

Each serving provides: 3 Protein Exchanges;
   1½ Vegetable Exchanges; 1 Fat Exchange
Per serving: 279 calories; 17 g protein; 11 g fat;
   30 g carbohydrate; 90 mg calcium; 922 mg sodium
   (estimated); 29 mg cholesterol; 3 g dietary fiber

Variation: Chick-Pea Sauté — Omit sausage. Decrease Protein Exchange to 2 Exchanges.

Per serving: 212 calories; 9 g protein; 7 g fat;
   30 g carbohydrate; 87 mg calcium; 555 mg sodium
   (estimated); 0 mg cholesterol; 3 g dietary fiber

Greek Chick-Peas with Vegetables

2 teaspoons olive *or* vegetable oil

1 Japanese *or* tiny eggplant (6 ounces), sliced

¼ cup *each* diced onion and red *or* yellow bell pepper

2 garlic cloves, minced

½ cup canned Italian tomatoes (with liquid); drain, seed, and dice tomatoes, reserving liquid

8 ounces rinsed drained canned chick-peas

¼ cup tomato sauce

4 Calamata *or* black olives, pitted and sliced

1 tablespoon chopped fresh dill *or* ½ teaspoon dillweed

⅛ teaspoon pepper

2 ounces feta cheese, crumbled

In 12-inch nonstick skillet heat oil; add eggplant, onion, bell pepper, and garlic and cook over medium-high heat, stirring occasionally, until vegetables are tender-crisp, 2 to 3 minutes. Add tomatoes with liquid, chick-peas, tomato sauce, olives, dill, and pepper and stir to combine. Reduce heat to medium-low, cover, and cook, stirring occasionally, until vegetables are softened and flavors blend, 4 to 5 minutes.

Into each of two 1¼-cup flameproof au gratin dishes spoon half of the vegetable mixture; top each portion with half of the feta cheese. Broil 5 to 6 inches from heat source until cheese is lightly browned, 1 to 2 minutes.

MAKES 2 SERVINGS

Each serving provides: 3 Protein Exchanges; 2¼ Vegetable Exchanges; 1 Fat Exchange; 15 Optional Calories

Per serving: 324 calories; 14 g protein; 15 g fat; 38 g carbohydrate; 254 mg calcium; 1,047 mg sodium (estimated); 25 mg cholesterol; 5 g dietary fiber

Sweet Potato and Chick-Pea Sauté

2 teaspoons margarine
1 cup chopped onions
6 ounces pared sweet potato, cut
    into ½-inch cubes
½ cup canned ready-to-serve
    chicken broth
1 teaspoon freshly squeezed
    lemon juice
4 ounces rinsed drained canned
    chick-peas
⅛ teaspoon thyme leaves
¼ teaspoon grated lemon peel
Dash pepper

In 10-inch nonstick skillet melt margarine; add onions and sauté over high heat, until translucent, about 1 minute. Add sweet potato and cook over medium-high heat, stirring occasionally, for 2 minutes. Add chicken broth and lemon juice and stir to combine. Reduce heat to medium; cover and let simmer for 5 minutes. Add chick-peas, thyme, lemon peel, and pepper and stir to combine; cover and let simmer until mixture is heated through and liquid is absorbed, about 5 minutes.

MAKES 2 SERVINGS

Each serving provides: 1 Protein Exchange;
    1 Bread Exchange; 1 Vegetable Exchange;
    1 Fat Exchange; 10 Optional Calories
Per serving: 229 calories; 7 g protein; 6 g fat;
    39 g carbohydrate; 62 mg calcium; 493 mg sodium
    (estimated); 0 mg cholesterol; 5 g dietary fiber

Variation: Yam and Chick-Pea Sauté —
Substitute 6 ounces pared yam for the sweet potato.

Per serving: 240 calories; 6 g protein; 6 g fat;
    42 g carbohydrate; 58 mg calcium; 490 mg sodium
    (estimated); 0 mg cholesterol; 6 g dietary fiber

Sweet and Sour Beans ©Ⓜ

½ cup *each* diced red onion, red
   bell pepper strips, and green
   bell pepper strips (3 x ½-inch
   pieces)
2 teaspoons vegetable oil
1 small garlic clove, minced
1 cup canned pineapple chunks
   (no sugar added); drain and
   reserve ¼ cup liquid
1 tablespoon reduced-sodium
   soy sauce
1 teaspoon *each* cornstarch and
   honey
¼ teaspoon apple cider vinegar
6 ounces rinsed drained canned
   chick-peas

In 2-cup microwavable casserole combine onion, bell peppers, oil, and garlic and stir to thoroughly coat; microwave on High (100%) for 1 minute, until tender-crisp.

In 1-cup liquid measure combine reserved pineapple liquid, the soy sauce, cornstarch, honey, and vinegar and stir to dissolve cornstarch; stir into vegetable mixture. Microwave on High for 2 minutes, until mixture thickens, stirring halfway through cooking. Add pineapple chunks and chick-peas and stir to combine; microwave on High for 1 minute, until flavors blend and mixture is thoroughly heated.

MAKES 2 SERVINGS

Each serving provides: 1½ Protein Exchanges;
    1½ Vegetable Exchanges; 1 Fat Exchange;
    1 Fruit Exchange; 15 Optional Calories
Per serving: 266 calories; 7 g protein; 7 g fat;
    48 g carbohydrate; 64 mg calcium; 596 mg sodium
    (estimated); 0 mg cholesterol; 4 g dietary fiber

When storing leftover canned fruit or juice, always transfer it to a plastic or glass container. Never leave fruit or juice in the open can because the metal will leach into the contents, affecting the food and its flavor.

Vegetarian Chick-Pea Pitas

1 tablespoon *each* chopped fresh
    dill *or* ½ teaspoon dillweed,
    tahini (sesame paste), sour
    cream, and half-and-half (blend
    of milk and cream)
3 ounces rinsed drained canned
    chick-peas
1½ ounces feta cheese, crumbled
2 pitas (2 ounces each), heated
1 cup shredded lettuce
4 tomato slices

In small mixing bowl combine dill, tahini, sour cream, and half-and-half and stir until smooth and creamy; add chick-peas and feta cheese and stir to combine.

Cut each pita in half crosswise, making 4 halves; open each half to form a pocket. Fill each pita half with ¼ cup lettuce, 1 tomato slice, and ¼ of the chick-pea mixture (about ¼ cup).

MAKES 2 SERVINGS

Each serving provides: 2 Protein Exchanges;
    2 Bread Exchanges; 1¾ Vegetable Exchanges;
    ½ Fat Exchange; 30 Optional Calories
Per serving: 361 calories; 13 g protein; 12 g fat;
    50 g carbohydrate; 201 mg calcium; 767 mg sodium
    (estimated); 25 mg cholesterol; 2 g dietary fiber

Bean 'wiches ☉

4 ounces canned pink beans
2 slices crisp bacon, crumbled
1 tablespoon chili sauce
2 flour tortillas (6-inch diameter each), toasted
1 tablespoon plus 1 teaspoon whipped cream cheese
2 tablespoons chopped scallion (green onion)

In small saucepan combine beans, bacon, and chili sauce and cook over high heat, stirring constantly, until mixture comes to a boil.

On nonstick baking sheet arrange tortillas in a single layer; spread half of the cream cheese over each tortilla, then top each with half of the bean mixture and half of the scallion. Broil until cheese is melted, about 2 minutes. Cut each tortilla into 4 equal wedges.

MAKES 2 SERVINGS

Each serving provides: 1 Protein Exchange;
1 Bread Exchange; ⅛ Vegetable Exchange;
75 Optional Calories
Per serving: 203 calories; 9 g protein; 7 g fat;
27 g carbohydrate; 75 mg calcium; 560 mg sodium
(estimated); 12 mg cholesterol; 3 g dietary fiber

Black Bean Terrine

2 envelopes unflavored gelatin
1 cup spicy mixed vegetable juice
16 ounces rinsed drained canned
  black beans, divided
¼ pound chèvre (French goat
  cheese)
2 tablespoons *each* finely
  chopped red bell pepper, green
  bell pepper, red onion, and
  celery
1 tablespoon *each* seeded and
  minced mild *or* hot chili pepper
  and minced fresh cilantro
  (Chinese parsley) *or* Italian
  (flat-leaf) parsley
1 garlic clove, minced
⅓ cup plus 2 teaspoons
  sour cream

In small saucepan sprinkle gelatin over vegetable juice and let stand 1 minute to soften. Cook over medium-low heat, stirring constantly, until gelatin is dissolved, about 2 minutes. Fill medium mixing bowl with ice water; pour dissolved gelatin into small mixing bowl and set small bowl in bowl of ice water; set aside.

In work bowl of food processor puree half of the beans; transfer to large mixing bowl. Add remaining beans and gelatin mixture; stir to combine and set aside. In small mixing bowl combine cheese, bell peppers, onion, celery, chili pepper, cilantro (or parsley), and garlic; set aside.

Line bottom and sides of 7⅜ x 3⅝ x 2¼-inch loaf pan with plastic wrap. Spread half of the bean mixture over bottom of prepared pan. Carefully spread cheese mixture over bean mixture in pan, then top with remaining bean mixture. Tap loaf pan on counter top to settle mixture. Cover loaf pan with plastic wrap and set another 7⅜ x 3⅝ x 2¼-inch loaf pan over plastic wrap. Set two cans in second pan to weight it down. Refrigerate overnight or at least 1 hour.

To serve, unmold bean loaf onto serving platter; cut into 6 equal slices and top each portion with 1 tablespoon sour cream.

MAKES 6 SERVINGS

Each serving provides: 2 Protein Exchanges;
  ¼ Vegetable Exchange; 35 Optional Calories
Per serving: 204 calories; 12 g protein; 9 g fat;
  20 g carbohydrate; 84 mg calcium; 531 mg sodium
  (estimated); 24 mg cholesterol; 3 g dietary fiber (this
  figure does not include mixed vegetable juice; nutrition
  analysis not available)

Black beans, also called turtle beans, are a black-skinned, white-fleshed bean with a distinctive flavor that deepens during cooking. This bean is especially good in soups.

Black-Eyed Muffins

1 tablespoon plus 1 teaspoon
   margarine
½ cup *each* diced onion, celery,
   and carrot
1 small garlic clove, minced
10 ounces rinsed drained canned
   black-eyed peas
¾ cup seasoned dried bread
   crumbs
2 eggs, lightly beaten
1 ounce Monterey Jack cheese,
   shredded
4 drops hot sauce
Dash *each* salt and pepper

Preheat oven to 350°F. In small nonstick skillet melt margarine; add vegetables and garlic and sauté over high heat, stirring frequently, until vegetables are tender, about 2 minutes. Transfer to medium mixing bowl; add remaining ingredients and stir to combine.

Spray eight 2½-inch-diameter muffin pan cups with nonstick cooking spray; spoon ⅛ of batter into each sprayed cup and partially fill remaining cups with water (this will prevent pan from burning and/or warping). Bake in middle of center oven rack until golden brown, 15 to 20 minutes. Remove pan from oven and carefully drain off water (remember, it will be boiling hot). Let muffins cool in pan for 5 minutes. Remove muffins from pan and set on wire rack to cool.

MAKES 4 SERVINGS, 2 MUFFINS EACH

Each serving provides: 2 Protein Exchanges;
   1 Bread Exchange; ¾ Vegetable Exchange;
   1 Fat Exchange
Per serving: 275 calories; 14 g protein; 10 g fat;
   33 g carbohydrate; 129 mg calcium; 1,008 mg sodium
   (estimated); 144 mg cholesterol; 8 g dietary fiber

Caribbean Pigeon Peas and Rice

If time permits, you may want to substitute cooked long-grain rice for the instant rice.

2 teaspoons olive *or* vegetable oil, divided
3 ounces peeled plantain, sliced lengthwise
¼ cup *each* diced green bell pepper and onion
1 small jalapeño pepper, seeded and minced
1 garlic clove, minced
1 medium tomato, blanched, peeled, seeded, and diced
1 cup cooked instant rice
4 ounces rinsed drained canned green pigeon peas
¼ cup canned ready-to-serve chicken broth
1 ounce Canadian-style bacon, diced
⅛ teaspoon *each* salt and white pepper

In 10-inch nonstick skillet heat 1 teaspoon oil; add plantain and cook over medium-high heat, turning occasionally, until lightly browned, 2 to 3 minutes. Remove from skillet; dice and set aside.

In same skillet heat remaining teaspoon oil; add bell pepper, onion, jalapeño pepper, and garlic and sauté over medium-high heat, stirring frequently, until vegetables are tender-crisp, 1 to 2 minutes. Add tomato and stir to combine; continuing to stir, cook until vegetables are softened, 3 to 4 minutes longer. Add remaining ingredients and stir to combine. Reduce heat to medium-low and cook until liquid has evaporated and flavors blend, 3 to 5 minutes.

MAKES 2 SERVINGS

Each serving provides: 1½ Protein Exchanges; 1½ Bread Exchanges; 1¾ Vegetable Exchanges; 1 Fat Exchange; 5 Optional Calories
Per serving: 281 calories; 11 g protein; 6 g fat; 47 g carbohydrate; 44 mg calcium; 664 mg sodium (estimated); 7 mg cholesterol; 4 g dietary fiber (this figure does not include plantain; nutrition analysis not available)

No one knows how the pigeon pea got its name. This legume grows in the tropics and is also called the Congo pea, Goongoo pea, and no-eyed pea.

Microwave Golden Baked Beans Ⓒ Ⓜ

¼ cup finely chopped onion
2 tablespoons *each* ketchup and
  water
1 tablespoon firmly packed light
  brown sugar, divided
2 teaspoons *each* country Dijon-
  style mustard and light *or* dark
  molasses
8 ounces drained canned pink *or*
  navy beans
2 slices crisp bacon, broken into
  pieces
1 small orange (about 6 ounces),
  peeled and sectioned
Garnish: Italian (flat-leaf)
         parsley sprig

In 1-quart microwavable casserole combine onion, ketchup, water, 2 teaspoons sugar, the mustard, and molasses and stir well to combine. Cover with vented plastic wrap and microwave on High (100%) for 1 minute. Stir in beans; top with bacon pieces and microwave on High for 2 minutes until beans are heated through. Decoratively arrange orange sections over bean mixture in center of casserole. Sprinkle remaining teaspoon sugar over orange sections. Re-cover with vented plastic wrap and microwave on High for 1 minute, until sugar is melted. Garnish with parsley.

MAKES 4 SERVINGS

Each serving provides: 1 Protein Exchange;
  ⅛ Vegetable Exchange; ¼ Fruit Exchange;
  55 Optional Calories
Per serving: 133 calories; 6 g protein; 2 g fat;
  24 g carbohydrate; 58 mg calcium; 400 mg sodium
  (estimated); 3 mg cholesterol; 3 g dietary fiber

Once upon a time, there were no tomatoes in ketchup. Originally a seasoning made from the brine of pickled fish, ketsiap was first brought to England from the Orient by sailors in the seventeenth and eighteenth centuries.

Quick Cassoulet ©Ⓜ

6 ounces rinsed drained canned red kidney beans, divided
½ cup *each* diced celery, carrot, and onion
2 teaspoons margarine
2 small garlic cloves, mashed
⅓ cup water
1 ounce smoked beef sausage link, sliced
2 slices crisp bacon, crumbled
Dash thyme leaves

Using a fork, in small mixing bowl mash 3 ounces kidney beans and set aside. In 1-quart microwavable casserole combine vegetables, margarine, and garlic; cover with vented plastic wrap and microwave on High (100%) for 3 minutes, stirring halfway through cooking. Add mashed and remaining whole beans, the water, sausage, bacon, and thyme and stir to combine; re-cover with vented plastic wrap and microwave on High for 3 minutes. Let stand for 5 minutes.

MAKES 2 SERVINGS

Each serving provides: 2 Protein Exchanges;
1½ Vegetable Exchanges; 1 Fat Exchange;
45 Optional Calories
Per serving: 245 calories; 12 g protein; 12 g fat;
25 g carbohydrate; 76 mg calcium; 614 mg sodium
(estimated); 9 mg cholesterol; 5 g dietary fiber

White Beans and Escarole Sauté ◉

2 teaspoons olive *or* vegetable oil
2 garlic cloves, minced
2 cups chopped escarole
½ cup canned Italian tomatoes
   (with liquid); drain, seed, and
   dice tomatoes, reserving liquid
4 ounces rinsed drained canned
   white kidney (cannellini) beans
1 tablespoon chopped fresh
   parsley
⅛ teaspoon salt
Dash pepper
1 teaspoon grated Parmesan
   cheese

In 10-inch nonstick skillet heat oil; add garlic and sauté over medium-high heat, stirring frequently, for 1 minute (do not brown). Add escarole and sauté, stirring frequently, until escarole is wilted, 1 to 2 minutes. Add remaining ingredients except Parmesan cheese and stir to combine. Reduce heat to low, cover, and cook, stirring occasionally, until mixture is heated through and flavors blend, 3 to 4 minutes.

To serve, sprinkle with Parmesan cheese.

MAKES 2 SERVINGS

Each serving provides: 1 Protein Exchange;
   2½ Vegetable Exchanges; 1 Fat Exchange;
   5 Optional Calories
Per serving: 132 calories; 6 g protein; 5 g fat;
   17 g carbohydrate; 89 mg calcium; 448 mg sodium
   (estimated); 1 mg cholesterol; 4 g dietary fiber

Ranch-Style Frijoles ⓒⓜ

¼ cup *each* diced onion and seeded and chopped drained canned mild green chili pepper
1 teaspoon olive *or* vegetable oil
¾ cup drained canned Italian tomatoes (with liquid); drain, seed, and dice tomatoes, reserving liquid
6 ounces rinsed drained canned pinto beans
2 tablespoons barbecue sauce
1 teaspoon chili powder
1 corn tortilla (6-inch diameter), toasted and cut into 6 equal wedges

In 1-quart microwavable shallow casserole combine onion, chili pepper, and oil and stir to thoroughly coat; microwave on High (100%) for 1 minute, until onion is softened. Add tomatoes with liquid, beans, barbecue sauce, and chili powder and stir to combine; microwave on High for 3 minutes, until mixture is heated through and flavors blend. Serve each portion with 3 tortilla wedges.

MAKES 2 SERVINGS

Each serving provides: 1½ Protein Exchanges; ½ Bread Exchange; 1¼ Vegetable Exchanges; ½ Fat Exchange; 15 Optional Calories
Per serving: 194 calories; 9 g protein; 4 g fat; 33 g carbohydrate; 91 mg calcium; 705 mg sodium (estimated); 0 mg cholesterol; 6 g dietary fiber

Stewed Potatoes with Beans ☻

2 teaspoons olive *or* vegetable oil
½ cup diced onion
1 small garlic clove, minced
6 ounces cubed pared baking
   potatoes
2 cups canned Italian tomatoes
   (with liquid); drain, seed, and
   chop tomatoes, reserving liquid
1 tablespoon red wine vinegar
⅛ teaspoon *each* parsley flakes
   and oregano leaves
8 ounces rinsed drained canned
   white kidney (cannellini) beans
2 slices crisp bacon, crumbled

In 10-inch nonstick skillet heat oil; add onion and garlic and cook over high heat, stirring occasionally, until lightly browned, 1 to 2 minutes. Add potatoes and cook, stirring frequently, for 1 minute. Add tomatoes, reserved tomato liquid, vinegar, parsley, and oregano; stir to combine and bring mixture to a boil. Reduce heat to low, cover, and let simmer, stirring occasionally, until potatoes are tender and liquid is absorbed, 8 to 10 minutes. Stir in beans and bacon and let simmer until thoroughly heated, 1 to 2 minutes.

MAKES 2 SERVINGS

Each serving provides: 2 Protein Exchanges;
   1 Bread Exchange; 2½ Vegetable Exchanges;
   1 Fat Exchange; 45 Optional Calories
Per serving: 334 calories; 15 g protein; 9 g fat;
   52 g carbohydrate; 137 mg calcium; 887 mg sodium
   (estimated); 5 mg cholesterol; 8 g dietary fiber

Kung Pao Chicken

Tomato Risotto with Shrimp
Couscous Pilaf
Pasta Puttanesca

Madeira Duck with Plum
Fish Amandine

Banana-Yogurt Orleans
Minted Three-Berry Ice
Mint-Chocolate Pudding

Fisherman's Sausage

Lentils 'n' Sausage

If you have the time, you might want to prepare cooked long-grain rice rather than instant rice.

1 teaspoon olive *or* vegetable oil
½ cup *each* diced onion and red bell pepper
2 garlic cloves, minced
1 teaspoon all-purpose flour
¼ cup *each* dry red table wine and water
1 cup canned Italian tomatoes (with liquid); drain, seed, and dice tomatoes, reserving liquid
5 ounces veal sausage links, sliced
4 ounces rinsed drained canned lentils
1 tablespoon chopped fresh basil *or* 1 teaspoon basil leaves
⅛ teaspoon pepper
1 cup cooked instant rice (hot)

In 10-inch nonstick skillet heat oil; add onion, bell pepper, and garlic and sauté over medium-high heat, stirring frequently, until onion is translucent, 1 to 2 minutes. Sprinkle flour over vegetables and stir quickly to combine; stir in wine and water. Add remaining ingredients except rice and stir to combine. Reduce heat to low, cover, and cook, stirring occasionally, until sausage is cooked and flavors blend, 8 to 10 minutes. Serve over rice.

MAKES 2 SERVINGS

Each serving provides: 3 Protein Exchanges;
1 Bread Exchange; 2 Vegetable Exchanges;
½ Fat Exchange; 35 Optional Calories
Per serving: 383 calories; 25 g protein; 10 g fat;
43 g carbohydrate; 86 mg calcium; 1,125 mg sodium
(estimated); 57 mg cholesterol; 4 g dietary fiber

Lentil Stew with Franks Ⓜ

2 teaspoons olive *or* vegetable oil
6 ounces diced pared all-purpose
    potato
¼ cup *each* thinly sliced carrot,
    celery, onion, and green bell
    pepper
1 small garlic clove, minced
2 cups canned Italian tomatoes
    (with liquid); drain and chop
    tomatoes, reserving liquid
8 ounces rinsed drained canned
    lentils
2 ounces chicken frankfurters,
    sliced
2 tablespoons chopped fresh
    Italian (flat-leaf) parsley

In 2-quart saucepan heat oil; add potato,
carrot, celery, onion, bell pepper, and garlic
and cook over high heat, stirring frequently,
until vegetables are tender-crisp, about 3
minutes. Add tomatoes and reserved tomato
liquid and stir to combine. Reduce heat to
low, cover, and let simmer until potato is
soft, about 10 minutes. Add lentils and frankfurters and stir to combine; cook until thoroughly heated, 1 to 2 minutes. Sprinkle with
parsley and stir to combine.

MAKES 2 SERVINGS

Each serving provides: 3 Protein Exchanges;
    1 Bread Exchange; 3 Vegetable Exchanges;
    1 Fat Exchange
Per serving: 377 calories; 19 g protein; 11 g fat;
    54 g carbohydrate; 136 mg calcium; 1,189 mg sodium
    (estimated); 29 mg cholesterol; 9 g dietary fiber (this
    figure does not include chicken frankfurters; nutrition
    analysis not available)

Variation: Lentil Stew — Omit frankfurters.
Decrease Protein Exchange to 2 Exchanges.

Per serving: 304 calories; 15 g protein; 6 g fat;
    52 g carbohydrate; 109 mg calcium; 800 mg sodium
    (estimated); 0 mg cholesterol; 9 g dietary fiber

*The average person eats about 10
grams of fiber a day; most nutrition
experts recommend at least twice
that amount daily.*

Lentils and Vegetables ◓

½ cup sliced mushrooms
¼ cup *each* sliced carrot, celery,
  red bell pepper, and scallions
  (green onions)
2 teaspoons margarine
6 ounces rinsed drained canned
  lentils

In small microwavable casserole combine vegetables and margarine; cover with vented plastic wrap and microwave on High (100%) for 3 minutes, until softened. Add lentils and microwave on High, uncovered, for 30 seconds, until thoroughly heated.

MAKES 2 SERVINGS

Each serving provides: 1½ Protein Exchanges;
  1½ Vegetable Exchanges; 1 Fat Exchange
Per serving: 150 calories; 9 g protein; 4 g fat;
  21 g carbohydrate; 39 mg calcium; 353 mg sodium
  (estimated); 0 mg cholesterol; 5 g dietary fiber

Nutritious lentils are a food staple in India and the Middle East. Lentils are always used dried, never fresh, and range in color from brown to yellow-green.

Saucy Lentils 'n' Potatoes ©Ⓜ

½ cup water
½ packet (½ teaspoon) instant
  chicken broth and seasoning
  mix
6 ounces small new red potatoes,
  quartered
½ cup drained canned Italian
  tomatoes, seeded and diced
¼ cup diced onion
1 large garlic clove, minced
4 ounces rinsed drained canned
  lentils
1 tablespoon *each* grated
  Parmesan cheese and chopped
  fresh basil *or* ½ teaspoon basil
  leaves

In 1-quart microwavable shallow casserole combine water and broth mix and stir to dissolve broth mix. Add potatoes, cover with vented plastic wrap, and microwave on High (100%) for 5 minutes. Add tomatoes, onion, and garlic and stir to combine. Microwave on High, uncovered, for 3 minutes, until onion is tender and flavors blend. Add lentils and stir to combine; microwave on High, uncovered, for 2 minutes until lentils are heated through. Stir in Parmesan cheese and basil.

MAKES 2 SERVINGS

Each serving provides: 1 Protein Exchange;
    1 Bread Exchange; ¾ Vegetable Exchange;
    20 Optional Calories
Per serving: 169 calories; 9 g protein; 1 g fat;
    31 g carbohydrate; 76 mg calcium; 591 mg sodium
    (estimated); 2 mg cholesterol; 4 g dietary fiber

Bean Slaw

1 small apple (about ¼ pound),
  cored and diced
2 teaspoons lemon juice
2 cups shredded green cabbage
6 ounces rinsed drained canned
  small white beans
½ cup shredded carrot
1 ounce Swiss cheese, shredded
¼ cup *each* sliced scallions (green
  onions), diced red bell pepper,
  diced green bell pepper, and
  plain low-fat yogurt
1 tablespoon plus 1 teaspoon
  reduced-calorie mayonnaise
Dash *each* salt and pepper

In medium mixing bowl combine apple and lemon juice and turn to coat; add remaining ingredients and toss to combine. Cover with plastic wrap and refrigerate until flavors blend, about 1 hour. Toss again before serving.

MAKES 2 SERVINGS

Each serving provides: 2 Protein Exchanges;
   3¼ Vegetable Exchanges; 1 Fat Exchange;
   ½ Fruit Exchange; ¼ Milk Exchange
Per serving: 263 calories; 14 g protein; 8 g fat;
   37 g carbohydrate; 310 mg calcium; 511 mg sodium
   (estimated); 18 mg cholesterol; 4 g dietary fiber (this
   figure does not include white beans; nutrition analysis
   not available)

Cannellini Salad Giardeniera Ⓜ

4 sun-dried tomato halves (not packed in oil)
¼ cup water
6 ounces rinsed drained canned white kidney (cannellini) beans
1 cup drained prepared giardeniera (vegetable medley packed in vinegar), chopped
¼ cup diced pimiento
1 tablespoon chopped fresh basil or ½ teaspoon basil leaves
1 tablespoon balsamic or red wine vinegar
2 teaspoons olive oil
Dash pepper
8 lettuce leaves

In 1-quart microwavable shallow casserole combine tomatoes and water; cover with vented plastic wrap and microwave on High (100%) for 1 minute, until tomatoes are plumped. Dice tomatoes, reserving cooking liquid; return diced tomatoes to cooking liquid. Add kidney beans, giardeniera, and pimiento; cover with vented plastic wrap and microwave on High for 2 minutes, rotating casserole ½ turn halfway through cooking, until mixture is heated through. Add remaining ingredients except lettuce and stir to combine. Cover and refrigerate at least 30 minutes before serving.

To serve, line serving bowl with lettuce leaves and top with bean mixture.

MAKES 2 SERVINGS

Each serving provides: 1½ Protein Exchanges; 3¼ Vegetable Exchanges; 1 Fat Exchange
Per serving: 110 calories; 4 g protein; 5 g fat; 15 g carbohydrate; 63 mg calcium; 485 mg sodium (estimated); 0 mg cholesterol; 5 g dietary fiber (this figure does not include pimiento; nutrition analysis not available)

Chick-Pea and Artichoke Salad

8 ounces rinsed drained canned chick-peas
1 cup drained canned artichoke hearts, cut into quarters
1 medium tomato, cut into wedges
¼ cup sliced scallions (green onions)
1 tablespoon *each* minced fresh basil, minced fresh Italian (flat-leaf) parsley, red wine vinegar, and lemon juice
1 garlic clove, minced
2 teaspoons olive *or* vegetable oil
Dash *each* salt and pepper
2 teaspoons grated Parmesan cheese

In salad bowl combine chick-peas, artichoke hearts, tomato, and scallions; set aside. Using a wire whisk, in cup or small bowl combine remaining ingredients except Parmesan cheese and beat until blended. Pour over chick-pea mixture and toss to coat. Cover with plastic wrap and refrigerate until ready to serve.

To serve, toss salad and divide onto 2 serving plates; sprinkle each portion with half of the cheese.

MAKES 2 SERVINGS

Each serving provides: 2 Protein Exchanges;
2¼ Vegetable Exchanges; 1 Fat Exchange;
10 Optional Calories
Per serving: 238 calories; 11 g protein; 8 g fat;
34 g carbohydrate; 109 mg calcium; 534 mg sodium
(estimated); 1 mg cholesterol; 7 g dietary fiber

Fiber, a useful component of the diet, is found in plant foods. There are two types of fiber—soluble fiber, found in beans, barley, oats, and fruit, and insoluble fiber, found in bran cereals, whole-grain breads, and vegetables. Current research suggests that soluble fiber may lower blood cholesterol.

Citrus-Bean Salad

4 ounces rinsed drained canned
   chick-peas
1 small navel orange (about
   6 ounces), peeled and sectioned
¼ cup *each* sliced red onion,
   sliced celery, diced red bell
   pepper, and diced yellow bell
   pepper
1 tablespoon *each* rice vinegar
   and freshly squeezed lime juice
1 teaspoon honey
½ teaspoon *each* vegetable oil
   and Chinese sesame oil
Dash *each* salt and pepper
8 lettuce leaves

In medium mixing bowl combine chick-peas, orange sections, onion, celery, and bell peppers and toss to combine. In small mixing bowl combine remaining ingredients except lettuce; pour over chick-pea mixture and toss to coat.

To serve, line serving platter with lettuce and top with chick-pea mixture.

MAKES 2 SERVINGS

Each serving provides: 1 Protein Exchange;
   2 Vegetable Exchanges; ½ Fat Exchange;
   ½ Fruit Exchange; 10 Optional Calories
Per serving: 145 calories; 5 g protein; 4 g fat;
   25 g carbohydrate; 75 mg calcium; 268 mg sodium
   (estimated); 0 mg cholesterol; 4 g dietary fiber

Cannellini-Tuna Salad

6 ounces rinsed drained canned
    white kidney (cannellini) beans
3 ounces cooked tuna, flaked
2 tablespoons diced red onion
1 tablespoon *each* chopped fresh
    basil, freshly squeezed lemon
    juice, and water
2 teaspoons olive oil
1 cup chopped lettuce

In medium mixing bowl combine all ingredients except lettuce and toss to combine. Line serving platter with lettuce and top with bean mixture.

MAKES 2 SERVINGS

Each serving provides: 3 Protein Exchanges;
    1⅛ Vegetable Exchanges; 1 Fat Exchange
Per serving: 228 calories; 20 g protein; 8 g fat;
    20 g carbohydrate; 74 mg calcium; 317 mg sodium
    (estimated); 22 mg cholesterol; 3 g dietary fiber

Hoppin' John Salad Ⓜ

You might want to substitute cooked long-grain rice for the instant rice.

2 cups chopped escarole
6 ounces rinsed drained canned
    black-eyed peas
2 ounces cooked smoked ham,
    diced
¼ cup water
2 tablespoons chopped onion
1 cup cooked instant rice
½ cup seeded diced tomato
1 tablespoon *each* apple cider
    vinegar and olive oil
1 teaspoon country Dijon-style
    mustard
¼ teaspoon *each* hot sauce and
    salt

In 1-quart microwavable shallow casserole combine escarole, peas, ham, water, and onion; stir to combine. Cover with vented plastic wrap and microwave on High (100%) for 4 minutes, rotating casserole ½ turn halfway through cooking. Add rice and tomato; stir to combine and set aside.

In cup or small bowl combine remaining ingredients; add to escarole-pea mixture and stir to thoroughly combine. Cover with plastic wrap and refrigerate until flavors blend and salad is chilled, at least 30 minutes.

MAKES 2 SERVINGS

Each serving provides: 2½ Protein Exchanges;
    1 Bread Exchange; 2½ Vegetable Exchanges;
    1½ Fat Exchanges
Per serving: 307 calories; 15 g protein; 9 g fat;
    42 g carbohydrate; 70 mg calcium; 1,071 mg sodium
    (estimated); 13 mg cholesterol; 4 g dietary fiber

Southwestern Black Bean and Corn Salad ☉

5 ounces rinsed drained canned
  black (turtle) beans
1 hard-cooked egg, chopped
½ cup *each* thawed frozen
  whole-kernel corn and seeded
  and diced tomato
¼ cup finely chopped red onion
½ ounce Monterey Jack cheese,
  shredded
1 tablespoon sour cream
1 teaspoon *each* chopped fresh
  cilantro (Chinese parsley),*
  chopped fresh parsley,
  safflower *or* vegetable oil,
  and red wine vinegar
4 lettuce leaves

In small mixing bowl combine all ingredients
except lettuce and mix well. Cover with
plastic wrap and refrigerate until flavors
blend and salad is chilled, at least 30 minutes.

To serve, line serving platter with lettuce
leaves and top with salad.

MAKES 2 SERVINGS

Each serving provides: 2 Protein Exchanges;
    ½ Bread Exchange; 1¼ Vegetable Exchanges;
    ½ Fat Exchange; 15 Optional Calories
Per serving: 234 calories; 12 g protein; 9 g fat;
    27 g carbohydrate; 115 mg calcium; 320 mg sodium
    (estimated); 146 mg cholesterol; 5 g dietary fiber

*An additional 1 teaspoon chopped fresh parsley may
  be substituted for the cilantro (Chinese parsley).

Three-Bean Salad Ⓜ

Water
1 cup green beans, cut into 1-inch pieces
2 ounces *each* rinsed drained canned red kidney beans and chick-peas
2 tablespoons finely chopped shallot *or* onion
2 teaspoons *each* minced fresh parsley, red wine vinegar, and olive oil
⅛ teaspoon salt
Dash pepper

Fill bottom of microwavable steamer with ½ cup water; set top portion of steamer over water and arrange green beans in insert. Cover with steamer lid and microwave on High (100%) for 4 minutes.* Let stand for 1 minute, until beans are tender-crisp. Fill medium mixing bowl with ice water; immediately add beans to stop the cooking process. Drain beans well and transfer to serving bowl. Add kidney beans, chick-peas, shallot (or onion), and parsley.

In cup or small bowl combine vinegar, oil, 1 teaspoon water, the salt, and pepper; pour over bean mixture and toss well to coat. Cover and refrigerate until ready to serve.

MAKES 2 SERVINGS

Each serving provides: 1 Protein Exchange;
  1⅛ Vegetable Exchanges; 1 Fat Exchange
Per serving: 132 calories; 5 g protein; 5 g fat;
  17 g carbohydrate; 50 mg calcium; 328 mg sodium
  (estimated); 0 mg cholesterol; 3 g dietary fiber

*If you do not own a microwavable steamer, in 1-quart microwavable casserole combine green beans and ¼ cup water; cover with vented plastic wrap and microwave on High (100%) for 4 minutes. Proceed as recipe directs.

Tofu Waldorf Salad

7½ ounces firm-style tofu, diced
½ cup *each* diced red onion and
    sliced celery
1 small Golden Delicious *or*
    McIntosh apple (about
    ¼ pound), cored and diced
2 tablespoons golden raisins
¼ ounce chopped walnuts
¼ cup plain low-fat yogurt
1 tablespoon *each* reduced-
    calorie mayonnaise and lemon
    juice
½ teaspoon salt
Dash *each* white pepper, ground
    cinnamon, and ground nutmeg

In serving bowl combine tofu, onion, celery, apple, raisins, and walnuts; set aside. In small mixing bowl combine remaining ingredients and stir until blended; add to tofu mixture and toss to coat. Cover with plastic wrap and refrigerate until flavors blend, about 30 minutes. Toss again before serving.

MAKES 2 SERVINGS

Each serving provides: 1½ Protein Exchanges;
    1 Vegetable Exchange; 1 Fat Exchange;
    1 Fruit Exchange; ¼ Milk Exchange
Per serving: 294 calories; 20 g protein; 14 g fat;
    27 g carbohydrate; 308 mg calcium; 668 mg sodium;
    4 mg cholesterol; 4 g dietary fiber

Hoisin Tofu and Broccoli Ⓒ

½ cup water
1 tablespoon hoisin sauce
1 teaspoon cornstarch
½ packet (½ teaspoon) instant chicken broth and seasoning mix
1½ teaspoons peanut *or* vegetable oil
1 garlic clove, chopped
1 cup broccoli florets
9 ounces firm-style tofu, cut into 1-inch cubes
½ teaspoon Chinese sesame oil

In small mixing bowl combine water, hoisin sauce, cornstarch, and broth mix and stir well to dissolve cornstarch; set aside. In 12-inch nonstick skillet heat peanut (or vegetable) oil; add garlic and cook over high heat, stirring frequently, for 30 seconds. Add broccoli and cook, stirring frequently, until bright green, about 1 minute. Add tofu and cook, stirring frequently, until lightly golden, about 1 minute. Stir hoisin mixture and add to skillet; bring mixture to a boil. Reduce heat to medium and let simmer until mixture thickens and broccoli is tender-crisp, about 3 minutes; stir in sesame oil.

MAKES 2 SERVINGS

Each serving provides: 1½ Protein Exchanges; 1 Vegetable Exchange; 1 Fat Exchange; 25 Optional Calories
Per serving: 265 calories; 23 g protein; 16 g fat; 13 g carbohydrate; 293 mg calcium; 536 mg sodium; 0 mg cholesterol; 2 g dietary fiber

Tofu, which is the Japanese name for bean curd, is the main source of protein in many Oriental cuisines. Bean curd is excellent in stir-fry dishes because it picks up the flavors of the foods it is cooked with.

Vegetables

Today's vegetables aren't the mushy, boring foods our mothers forced us to eat. They're crunchy and colorful, quick-cooking, and full of pizzazz. This chapter features dozens of side dishes, salads, and soups that will complement any meal. Enjoy Zucchini Chowder or Mixed Vegetable Soup, steaming hot and so delicious. Skillet Jicama and Kohlrabi Slaw will introduce you to new taste sensations. And since nothing beats the microwave oven when it comes to vegetables, you'll find quite a few microwave recipes. Microwave Stuffed Onion, Butternut Squash Whip, and Microwave Scalloped Potatoes are just a few — you'll want to try them all!

Cream of Cucumber and Leek Soup Ⓜ

In a little more than 10 minutes you can cook up this homemade soup.

2 cups diced seeded pared
   cucumbers
1 cup chopped thoroughly
   washed leeks (white portion
   only)
1 tablespoon *each* whipped
   butter and all-purpose flour
1 cup water
1 packet instant vegetable broth
   and seasoning mix

In 1-quart microwavable casserole combine cucumbers, leeks, and butter; cover with vented plastic wrap and microwave on High (100%) for 6 minutes, until vegetables are softened, stirring every 2 minutes through cooking. Sprinkle flour over vegetables and stir to combine; microwave on High, uncovered, for 1 minute. Stir in water and broth mix and microwave on High, uncovered, for 2 minutes, until mixture thickens, stirring once halfway through cooking.

MAKES 2 SERVINGS, ABOUT 1½ CUPS EACH

Each serving provides: 3 Vegetable Exchanges;
   45 Optional Calories
Per serving: 97 calories; 2 g protein; 3 g fat;
   16 g carbohydrate; 56 mg calcium; 488 mg sodium;
   8 mg cholesterol; 1 g dietary fiber

Creamy Gazpacho

½ cup *each* spicy mixed
vegetable juice and plain
low-fat yogurt
½ cup chopped seeded pared
cucumber, divided
¼ cup *each* diced green and red
bell pepper, celery, scallions
(green onions), and tomato,
divided
1½ teaspoons *each* seeded and
minced mild *or* hot chili pepper
and fresh Italian (flat-leaf)
parsley
½ small garlic clove, minced
Dash *each* salt and pepper
1 ounce croutons, divided
1 tablespoon plus 1½ teaspoons
sour cream

In blender container combine juice and
yogurt and process until combined; add ⅓
cup of the cucumber, 2 tablespoons each of
the bell peppers, celery, scallions, and
tomato, the chili pepper, parsley, garlic,
salt, and pepper and process until smooth.
Refrigerate until chilled, at least 1 hour.

To serve, into each of 2 soup bowls pour
half of the gazpacho; top each portion with
half of the remaining cucumber, bell peppers,
celery, scallions, and tomato. Then top each
with half of the croutons and sour cream.

MAKES 2 SERVINGS, ABOUT 1 CUP EACH

Each serving provides: 1 Bread Exchange;
  2 Vegetable Exchanges; ½ Milk Exchange;
  25 Optional Calories
Per serving: 106 calories; 5 g protein; 4 g fat;
  14 g carbohydrate; 147 mg calcium; 394 mg sodium;
  8 mg cholesterol; 1 g dietary fiber (this figure does not
  include mixed vegetable juice; nutrition analysis not
  available)

Escarole and Vegetable Soup

For a satisfying lunch, tote this to the office in an insulated vacuum container, along with a sandwich and fresh fruit.

2 teaspoons *each* olive *or* vegetable oil and margarine
1 cup *each* chopped onions, celery, carrots, zucchini, and red bell peppers
2 small garlic cloves, sliced
1 quart water
1 medium tomato, blanched, peeled, seeded, and chopped
¼ cup tomato paste
2 packets instant vegetable broth and seasoning mix
4 cups thoroughly washed and drained escarole, torn into bite-size pieces*

In 4-quart saucepan combine oil and margarine and heat until margarine is melted; add onions, celery, carrots, zucchini, bell peppers, and garlic and cook over high heat, stirring occasionally, until tender-crisp, about 2 minutes. Add water, tomato, tomato paste, and broth mix and stir to thoroughly combine; bring mixture to a boil. Reduce heat to low; stir in escarole and let simmer until escarole is wilted and flavors blend, about 10 minutes.

MAKES 4 SERVINGS, ABOUT 2 CUPS EACH

Each serving provides: 3¾ Vegetable Exchanges; 1 Fat Exchange; 5 Optional Calories
Per serving: 114 calories; 3 g protein; 5 g fat; 17 g carbohydrate; 71 mg calcium; 644 mg sodium; 0 mg cholesterol; 3 g dietary fiber

*Four cups fresh escarole will yield about 1 cup cooked.

Gingered Onion-Apple Soup

½ pound McIntosh *or* Granny
  Smith apples, cored
2 teaspoons margarine
1 cup diced onions
½ teaspoon grated pared
  gingerroot
1 packet instant chicken broth
  and seasoning mix
1 teaspoon all-purpose flour
1¼ cups water
1 tablespoon *each* apple brandy
  (calvados) and chopped chives
4 trimmed chives

Cut 6 thin apple slices and reserve for garnish; pare and dice remaining apples. In small saucepan melt margarine; add diced apples, onions, and gingerroot and sauté, stirring constantly, over medium-high heat until onions are translucent, about 2 minutes. Sprinkle broth mix and flour over apple mixture and stir quickly to combine; cook, stirring constantly, for 1 minute. Add water and cook over high heat, stirring constantly, until mixture comes to a boil. Reduce heat to low and stir in brandy; partially cover and let simmer until flavors blend, 6 to 7 minutes. Pour soup into 2 soup bowls; top each portion with 3 reserved apple slices and 2 chives.

MAKES 2 SERVINGS, ABOUT 1 CUP EACH

Each serving provides: 1 Vegetable Exchange;
  1 Fat Exchange; 1 Fruit Exchange; 30 Optional Calories
Per serving: 156 calories; 2 g protein; 4 g fat;
  27 g carbohydrate; 29 mg calcium; 542 mg sodium;
  0 mg cholesterol; 4 g dietary fiber

Mixed Vegetable Soup Ⓒ Ⓜ

3 cups water
½ cup *each* diced onion, celery,
   carrot, and seeded drained
   canned Italian tomatoes
¼ cup *each* frozen baby lima
   beans and frozen whole kernel
   corn
2 packets instant chicken broth
   and seasoning mix
1 bay leaf
1 tablespoon chopped fresh
   parsley
⅛ teaspoon pepper

In 2-quart microwavable casserole combine all ingredients except parsley and pepper and stir to dissolve broth mix. Cover with vented plastic wrap and microwave on High (100%) for 17 minutes, until vegetables are tender, stirring halfway through cooking. Remove and discard bay leaf; stir in parsley and pepper.

MAKES 2 SERVINGS, ABOUT 1½ CUPS EACH

Each serving provides: ½ Bread Exchange;
   2 Vegetable Exchanges; 10 Optional Calories
Per serving: 98 calories; 5 g protein; 1 g fat;
   20 g carbohydrate; 59 mg calcium; 1,137 mg sodium;
   0 mg cholesterol; 2 g dietary fiber

Pepper and Leek Soup Ⓜ

2 cups chopped red bell peppers
   (reserve 1 teaspoon for garnish)
2 cups chopped thoroughly
   washed leeks (white portion
   and some green)
1 tablespoon seeded and chopped
   jalapeño pepper (reserve
   1 teaspoon for garnish)
1 tablespoon whipped butter
1 garlic clove, minced
½ cup water
2 packets instant chicken broth
   and seasoning mix
1 tablespoon sour cream

In 1-quart microwavable casserole combine bell peppers, leeks, jalapeño pepper, butter, and garlic. Cover with vented plastic wrap and microwave on High (100%) for 6 minutes, stirring once halfway through cooking. Add water and broth mix and stir to combine. Microwave, uncovered, on High for 2 minutes; let cool slightly.

Transfer mixture to blender container and process on low speed until pureed, scraping down sides of container as necessary. Pour soup into 2 soup bowls; top each with half of the sour cream and half of the reserved bell and jalapeño peppers.

MAKES 2 SERVINGS, ABOUT 1½ CUPS EACH

Each serving provides: 4 Vegetable Exchanges;
   50 Optional Calories
Per serving: 141 calories; 4 g protein; 5 g fat;
   22 g carbohydrate; 80 mg calcium; 1,047 mg sodium;
   11 mg cholesterol; 3 g dietary fiber

Zucchini-Buttermilk Soup ⓒⓜ

1 cup sliced zucchini
½ cup *each* sliced onion and water
3 ounces minced pared all-
    purpose potato
1 tablespoon chopped fresh
    Italian (flat-leaf) parsley
1 packet instant chicken broth
    and seasoning mix
½ small garlic clove, sliced
⅛ teaspoon powdered mustard
⅓ cup plus 2 teaspoons
    buttermilk

In 1-quart microwavable casserole combine all ingredients except buttermilk. Cover with vented plastic wrap and microwave on High (100%) for 5 minutes, until vegetables are softened, stirring once halfway through cooking.

Pour zucchini mixture into blender container and process at low speed until smooth. Pour soup back into casserole; stir in buttermilk. Cover with vented plastic wrap and microwave on High for 30 seconds, until thoroughly heated.

MAKES 2 SERVINGS, ABOUT 1 CUP EACH

Each serving provides: ½ Bread Exchange;
    1½ Vegetable Exchanges; ¼ Milk Exchange;
    5 Optional Calories
Per serving: 80 calories; 4 g protein; 1 g fat;
    15 g carbohydrate; 78 mg calcium; 549 mg sodium;
    2 mg cholesterol; 1 g dietary fiber

Zucchini Chowder ⒸⓂ

If you prefer, canned whole kernel corn can be substituted for the fresh or frozen.

2 cups sliced zucchini
½ cup sliced onion
1½ teaspoons whipped butter
½ small garlic clove, sliced
1 cup water
3 ounces diced pared sweet
    potato *or* yam
1 packet instant chicken broth
    and seasoning mix
½ cup fresh *or* frozen whole
    kernel corn
1 tablespoon half-and-half (blend
    of milk and cream)

In 2-quart microwavable casserole combine zucchini, onion, butter, and garlic; cover with vented plastic wrap and microwave on High (100%) for 2 minutes, until vegetables are softened. Add water, sweet potato (or yam), and broth mix and stir to combine; cover with vented plastic wrap and microwave on High for 2 minutes, until sweet potato (or yam) is soft, stirring once halfway through cooking.

Pour sweet potato mixture into blender container and process at low speed until smooth. Pour soup back into casserole; add corn and half-and-half and stir to combine. Cover with vented plastic wrap and microwave on High for 1 minute, until heated through.

MAKES 2 SERVINGS, ABOUT 1 CUP EACH

Each serving provides: 1 Bread Exchange;
   2½ Vegetable Exchanges; 30 Optional Calories
Per serving: 138 calories; 5 g protein; 3 g fat;
   25 g carbohydrate; 50 mg calcium; 529 mg sodium;
   7 mg cholesterol; 2 g dietary fiber

Shredded Beets with Raisins Ⓜ

A sweet and sour side dish that can't be beat!

2 cups shredded pared trimmed
    beets
¼ cup thinly sliced red onion
2 tablespoons golden raisins
2 teaspoons margarine
1½ teaspoons firmly packed
    brown sugar
½ teaspoon raspberry *or* apple
    cider vinegar
Dash *each* salt and pepper

In 1-quart microwavable casserole combine beets, onion, and raisins. Cover with vented plastic wrap and microwave on High (100%) for 3 minutes, until raisins are plumped and beets are softened, stirring halfway through cooking. Add remaining ingredients and stir to combine; cover and let stand for 1 minute.

MAKES 2 SERVINGS

Each serving provides: 2¼ Vegetable Exchanges;
    1 Fat Exchange; ½ Fruit Exchange; 15 Optional Calories
Per serving: 141 calories; 3 g protein; 4 g fat;
    26 g carbohydrate; 37 mg calcium; 211 mg sodium;
    0 mg cholesterol; 2 g dietary fiber

Broccoli and Walnut Sauté

Build an Oriental-style meal around this recipe with stir-fried sliced chicken and cooked rice.

1 teaspoon peanut *or* vegetable oil
1 cup sliced onions
1 ounce walnut halves
1 small garlic clove, thinly sliced
½ cup water
1 tablespoon reduced-sodium soy sauce
2 teaspoons cornstarch
1 packet instant chicken broth and seasoning mix
4 cups broccoli florets, blanched

In 9-inch nonstick skillet heat oil; add onions, walnuts, and garlic and sauté over high heat until onions are tender-crisp, about 1 minute. In 1-cup liquid measure combine water, soy sauce, cornstarch, and broth mix and stir to dissolve cornstarch; add to walnut mixture in skillet and cook, stirring constantly, until mixture comes to a boil. Reduce heat to low; add broccoli, stir to combine, and cook until thoroughly heated, 1 to 2 minutes.

MAKES 2 SERVINGS

Each serving provides: 1 Protein Exchange;
    5 Vegetable Exchanges; 1½ Fat Exchanges;
    15 Optional Calories
Per serving: 237 calories; 13 g protein; 12 g fat;
    27 g carbohydrate; 148 mg calcium; 860 mg sodium;
    0 mg cholesterol; 1 g dietary fiber (this figure does not
    include broccoli florets; nutrition analysis not available)

Beta-carotene, the plant source of vitamin A, is found in good supply in broccoli, carrots, winter squash, cantaloupe, sweet potatoes, collard greens, pink grapefruit, and vegetable and tomato juices.

Orange-Glazed Carrots and Onions Ⓜ

2 cups diagonally sliced carrots
¼ cup water
1 tablespoon *each* firmly packed
   light *or* dark brown sugar and
   whipped butter, softened
¼ teaspoon cornstarch
1 cup frozen pearl onions
¼ teaspoon *each* ground
   cinnamon and grated orange
   peel
⅛ teaspoon salt

In 1-quart microwavable shallow casserole combine carrots and water; cover with vented plastic wrap and microwave on High (100%) for 4 minutes, until carrots are tender-crisp. In cup or small bowl combine sugar, butter, and cornstarch and mix well to combine; stir into carrot mixture. Add remaining ingredients and stir to combine. Re-cover with vented plastic wrap and microwave on High for 3 minutes, until onions are heated through and mixture thickens.

MAKES 2 SERVINGS

Each serving provides: 3 Vegetable Exchanges;
   55 Optional Calories
Per serving: 134 calories; 2 g protein; 3 g fat;
   26 g carbohydrate; 75 mg calcium; 217 mg sodium;
   8 mg cholesterol; 4 g dietary fiber

When it comes to vegetable cookery, a short cooking time using as little water as possible means that valuable nutrients will be retained. So try to cook vegetables in the microwave whenever possible, or use a vegetable steamer.

Cauliflower Niçoise

2 cups cooked cauliflower florets
   (hot)
2 tablespoons water
2 teaspoons olive oil
1 tablespoon balsamic *or* red wine
   vinegar
3 large oil-cured black olives,
   pitted and minced
1 tablespoon *each* finely chopped
   rinsed drained capers and
   Italian (flat-leaf) parsley
1 garlic clove, minced
6 cherry tomatoes, cut into halves
4 drained canned anchovy fillets
1 egg, hard-cooked and chopped

On serving platter arrange cauliflower; set aside. Using a wire whisk, in small mixing bowl combine water, oil, and vinegar; add olives, capers, parsley, and garlic and stir to combine. Pour evenly over cauliflower. Arrange tomato halves and anchovy fillets decoratively over cauliflower; sprinkle with egg.

MAKES 2 SERVINGS

Each serving provides: ½ Protein Exchange;
   2½ Vegetable Exchanges; 1¼ Fat Exchanges;
   10 Optional Calories
Per serving: 151 calories; 8 g protein; 10 g fat;
   9 g carbohydrate; 77 mg calcium; 597 mg sodium;
   141 mg cholesterol; 3 g dietary fiber

Cauliflower in Parmesan-Wine Sauce

This saucy side dish will complement almost any meat, fish, or poultry entrée.

1 teaspoon olive *or* vegetable oil
¼ cup *each* chopped red bell pepper and scallions (green onions)
½ teaspoon all-purpose flour
¼ cup canned ready-to-serve chicken broth
1 teaspoon dry white table wine
2 cups cauliflower florets, blanched
½ ounce grated Parmesan cheese
1 slice crisp bacon, crumbled
1 teaspoon chopped fresh basil *or* ¼ teaspoon basil leaves

In 9-inch skillet heat oil; add bell pepper and scallions and cook over medium-high heat, stirring frequently, until bell pepper is tender-crisp, 1 to 2 minutes. Sprinkle flour over vegetables and stir quickly to combine; cook, stirring constantly, for 1 minute. Add broth and wine and, stirring constantly, bring mixture to a boil. Reduce heat to low and stir in remaining ingredients; cook until thoroughly heated, 2 to 3 minutes.

MAKES 2 SERVINGS

Each serving provides: ¼ Protein Exchange; 2½ Vegetable Exchanges; ½ Fat Exchange; 30 Optional Calories
Per serving: 105 calories; 6 g protein; 6 g fat; 7 g carbohydrate; 130 mg calcium; 306 mg sodium; 8 mg cholesterol; 4 g dietary fiber

Cauliflower with Pignolias and Currants Ⓜ

½ ounce pignolias (pine nuts)
2 tablespoons whipped butter
1 tablespoon dried currants
2 teaspoons freshly squeezed
   lemon juice
1 teaspoon olive or vegetable oil
1 garlic clove, minced
2 cups cooked cauliflower florets
   (hot)
Dash pepper

On paper plate arrange pignolias and microwave on High (100%) for 4 minutes, stirring every minute, until lightly golden; set aside. In microwavable small bowl combine butter, currants, lemon juice, oil, and garlic; microwave on High for 30 seconds, until butter is completely melted and mixture bubbles slightly.

To serve, in serving bowl combine cauliflower florets, pignolias, and currant mixture and toss to coat; sprinkle with pepper.

MAKES 2 SERVINGS

Each serving provides: ½ Protein Exchange;
   2 Vegetable Exchanges; 1 Fat Exchange;
   ¼ Fruit Exchange; 50 Optional Calories
Per serving: 153 calories; 4 g protein; 12 g fat;
   11 g carbohydrate; 44 mg calcium; 67 mg sodium;
   16 mg cholesterol; 3 g dietary fiber (this figure does not
   include pignolias; nutrition analysis not available)

Variation: Cauliflower with Pignolias and Raisins — Substitute 1 tablespoon dark raisins for the currants.

Per serving: 154 calories; 4 g protein; 12 g fat;
   12 g carbohydrate; 43 mg calcium; 68 mg sodium;
   16 mg cholesterol; 3 g dietary fiber (this figure does not
   include pignolias; nutrition analysis not available)

"Fried" Celeriac Chips ⓒ

2 teaspoons olive *or* vegetable oil
2 cups thinly sliced pared celeriac
   (celery root *or* knob)
2 tablespoons chopped scallion
   (green onion)
Dash *each* salt and white pepper

In 9-inch nonstick skillet heat oil; add celeriac and cook over high heat, stirring constantly, until golden brown, about 5 minutes. Add remaining ingredients; stir to combine and cook until heated through, about 30 seconds longer.

MAKES 2 SERVINGS

Each serving provides: 2⅛ Vegetable Exchanges;
   1 Fat Exchange
Per serving: 102 calories; 2 g protein; 5 g fat;
   15 g carbohydrate; 71 mg calcium; 222 mg sodium;
   0 mg cholesterol; 0.2 g dietary fiber (this figure does not
   include celeriac; nutrition analysis not available)

Celeriac, also known as celery root or celery knob, is a relative of celery and has a celery-like flavor. Celeriac is available from October through April and can be eaten raw in salads just like its more common cousin celery.

Creamy Cucumbers and Onions ⒸⓂ

2 cups thinly sliced cucumbers
1 cup thinly sliced onions
2 teaspoons olive *or* vegetable oil
1 small garlic clove, minced
2 tablespoons sour cream
1 tablespoon chopped fresh dill *or*
   ½ teaspoon dillweed
½ teaspoon salt
Dash white pepper

In 1-quart microwavable casserole combine cucumbers, onions, oil, and garlic and stir to thoroughly coat. Cover with vented plastic wrap and microwave on High (100%) for 2 minutes, stirring halfway through cooking. Let stand for 5 minutes, until onions are translucent. Stir in remaining ingredients.

MAKES 2 SERVINGS

Each serving provides: 3 Vegetable Exchanges;
   1 Fat Exchange; 35 Optional Calories
Per serving: 114 calories; 2 g protein; 8 g fat;
   10 g carbohydrate; 61 mg calcium; 559 mg sodium;
   6 mg cholesterol; 2 g dietary fiber

Greek Eggplant Rounds

6 thin eggplant slices (¼-inch-
thick slices)
1 teaspoon olive oil, divided
1 tablespoon tahini (sesame paste)
1 medium tomato, cut into six
¼-inch-thick slices
2 ounces feta cheese, crumbled
½ teaspoon oregano leaves
⅛ teaspoon pepper

On nonstick baking sheet arrange eggplant slices in a single layer and, using a pastry brush, lightly brush ½ teaspoon oil over top of eggplant slices. Broil 5 to 6 inches from heat source until eggplant is lightly browned, 2 to 3 minutes. Using a spatula, turn eggplant slices over and brush with remaining oil. Broil until lightly browned, 2 to 3 minutes. Spread ½ teaspoon tahini over each eggplant slice, then top each with 1 tomato slice. Broil until tomato is heated through, about 1 minute. Top each tomato slice with ⅙ of the feta cheese, then sprinkle with oregano and pepper. Broil until cheese is melted and lightly browned, 1 to 2 minutes.

MAKES 2 SERVINGS

Each serving provides: 1½ Protein Exchanges;
   1¾ Vegetable Exchanges; 1 Fat Exchange
Per serving: 167 calories; 7 g protein; 13 g fat;
   9 g carbohydrate; 203 mg calcium; 332 mg sodium;
   25 mg cholesterol; 1 g dietary fiber

Endives Gratinées Ⓜ

3 medium Belgian endives (about
   3 ounces each), each cut in half
   lengthwise and rinsed
½ cup water
¼ teaspoon salt
1 ounce Jarlsberg *or* Swiss
   cheese, shredded

In 8 x 8 x 2-inch microwavable baking dish arrange endive halves, cut-side down; add water and salt. Cover with vented plastic wrap and microwave on High (100%) for 4 minutes. Let stand for 1 minute; drain endives. Sprinkle endives with cheese and microwave on High, uncovered, for 1 minute, until cheese melts.

MAKES 2 SERVINGS

Each serving provides: ½ Protein Exchange;
   1½ Vegetable Exchanges
Per serving with Jarlsberg cheese: 69 calories; 5 g protein;
   3 g fat; 5 g carbohydrate; 102 mg calcium;
   342 mg sodium; 5 mg cholesterol; 3 g dietary fiber
With Swiss cheese: 72 calories; 5 g protein; 4 g fat;
   5 g carbohydrate; 138 mg calcium; 316 mg sodium;
   13 mg cholesterol; 3 g dietary fiber

The creamy white Belgian endive is related to curly endive and escarole. Peak season is September through May. To store Belgian endive, wrap in a paper towel and place in a plastic bag, or wrap in wax paper or aluminum foil.

Skillet Jicama

1 tablespoon whipped butter
2 teaspoons olive *or* vegetable oil
4 cups cubed pared jicama
1 cup *each* sliced red onions and
    red bell pepper strips
¼ cup water
1 packet instant chicken broth
    and seasoning mix
Dash crushed red pepper

In 10-inch skillet combine butter and oil and heat until butter is melted; add jicama and cook over medium-high heat, stirring frequently, until lightly browned, about 5 minutes. Add onions and bell pepper and cook, stirring occasionally, until onions are translucent, about 3 minutes. Stir in remaining ingredients; cover and cook over high heat until jicama is tender, 6 to 7 minutes.

MAKES 2 SERVINGS

Each serving provides: 6 Vegetable Exchanges;
    1 Fat Exchange; 30 Optional Calories
Per serving: 208 calories; 5 g protein; 8 g fat;
    30 g carbohydrate; 60 mg calcium; 542 mg sodium;
    8 mg cholesterol; 6 g dietary fiber

Here's news about a vegetable you may not be familiar with. Jicama (pronounced HEE-kah-mah) resembles a turnip but tastes more like water chestnuts. Try it raw in salads or with other crudités to accompany a dip.

Mushroom and Onion Sauté

2 teaspoons olive *or* vegetable oil
1 cup thinly sliced Spanish *or*
   Bermuda onions
1½ cups thinly sliced shiitake *or*
   white mushrooms
¼ cup canned ready-to-serve
   chicken broth
2 teaspoons balsamic *or* red wine
   vinegar
⅛ teaspoon salt
Dash pepper

In 9-inch nonstick skillet heat oil; add onions and cook over high heat, stirring frequently, for 1 minute. Reduce heat to medium-high; add mushrooms and sauté for 4 minutes. Stir in chicken broth and cook, stirring occasionally, until liquid has evaporated, about 2 minutes. Add remaining ingredients and cook until vinegar has evaporated, about 1 minute.

MAKES 2 SERVINGS

Each serving provides: 2½ Vegetable Exchanges;
   1 Fat Exchange; 5 Optional Calories
Per serving: 85 calories; 2 g protein; 5 g fat;
   9 g carbohydrate; 24 mg calcium; 268 mg sodium;
   0 mg cholesterol; 2 g dietary fiber

According to the National Mushroom Growers Association, most people today prefer fresh mushrooms, whereas 20 years ago, processed mushrooms were more popular. Try many of the more unusual mushrooms found in the produce section of your supermarket such as enoki, crimini, and shiitake.

Microwave Stuffed Onion Ⓜ

1 large Spanish onion (about
   ¾ pound)
¼ cup water
1½ ounces cooked veal sausage,
   crumbled
3 tablespoons seasoned dried
   bread crumbs
¼ ounce pignolias (pine nuts),
   toasted
1 tablespoon dried currants *or*
   dark raisins
1 egg white
2 teaspoons grated Parmesan
   cheese, divided
1 teaspoon chopped fresh parsley
¼ teaspoon salt

Cut onion in half from top to root end. In 1-quart microwavable casserole set each half, cut-side down; add water. Cover with vented plastic wrap and microwave on High (100%) for 4 minutes, until onion is tender-crisp, rotating casserole halfway through cooking. Set aside and let cool.

In medium mixing bowl combine sausage, bread crumbs, pignolias, currants (or raisins), egg white, 1 teaspoon cheese, the parsley, and salt; mix well and set aside.

Drain onion halves, discarding cooking liquid. Using a spoon, scoop out center of each onion half, reserving centers and leaving ¾-inch-thick shells. Finely dice onion centers; add to sausage mixture and stir to combine. Spoon half of the onion-sausage mixture into each reserved shell; sprinkle half of the remaining cheese evenly over stuffing portion of each onion. Set stuffed onions in same casserole and microwave on Medium-High (70%), uncovered, for 5 minutes, until stuffing mixture is heated through, rotating casserole halfway through cooking. Let stand for 2 minutes.

MAKES 2 SERVINGS, ½ ONION EACH

Each serving provides: 1 Protein Exchange;
   ½ Bread Exchange; 1¾ Vegetable Exchanges;
   ¼ Fat Exchange; ¼ Fruit Exchange;
   20 Optional Calories
Per serving with currants: 195 calories; 13 g protein;
   6 g fat; 24 g carbohydrate; 87 mg calcium;
   904 mg sodium (estimated); 23 mg cholesterol;
   3 g dietary fiber (this figure does not include pignolias;
   nutrition analysis not available)
With raisins: 196 calories; 13 g protein; 6 g fat;
   25 g carbohydrate; 86 mg calcium; 903 mg sodium
   (estimated); 23 mg cholesterol; 3 g dietary fiber (this
   figure does not include pignolias; nutrition analysis not
   available)

Peas and Lettuce Sauté

1 tablespoon whipped butter
½ cup sliced celery
1 cup *each* frozen tiny peas,
    frozen pearl onions, and torn
    green leaf lettuce
½ teaspoon granulated sugar
⅛ teaspoon *each* salt and white
    pepper
1 tablespoon chopped fresh mint

In 9-inch skillet melt butter; add celery and sauté over medium-high heat until tender, about 1 minute. Add peas and onions and stir to combine. Reduce heat to low, cover, and let simmer until heated through, about 2 minutes. Add lettuce, sugar, salt, and pepper and stir to combine; cook, uncovered, for 1 minute.

To serve, transfer vegetable mixture to serving bowl and sprinkle with mint.

MAKES 2 SERVINGS

Each serving provides: 1 Bread Exchange;
    2½ Vegetable Exchanges; 30 Optional Calories
Per serving: 135 calories; 6 g protein; 3 g fat;
    22 g carbohydrate; 83 mg calcium; 333 mg sodium;
    8 mg cholesterol; 4 g dietary fiber

Spinach and Bacon Sauté

2 teaspoons olive *or* vegetable oil
½ cup sliced onion
1 small garlic clove, minced
4 cups thoroughly washed and
    drained spinach leaves,* torn
    into bite-size pieces
4 sun-dried tomato halves (not
    packed in oil), chopped
2 slices crisp bacon, crumbled
1 tablespoon *each* balsamic *or*
    red wine vinegar and grated
    Parmesan cheese

In 10-inch skillet heat oil; add onion and garlic and cook over high heat, stirring frequently, until translucent, about 1 minute. Add spinach and tomatoes and stir to combine. Reduce heat to low, cover, and cook until spinach is wilted, about 1 minute. Add bacon and vinegar and stir until combined. Transfer to serving platter and sprinkle with cheese.

MAKES 2 SERVINGS

Each serving provides: 2½ Vegetable Exchanges;
    1 Fat Exchange; 60 Optional Calories
Per serving: 147 calories; 8 g protein; 9 g fat;
    11 g carbohydrate; 171 mg calcium; 254 mg sodium;
    8 mg cholesterol; 5 g dietary fiber

*Four cups fresh spinach yield about 1 cup cooked spinach.

To boost your iron intake, eat spinach, whole grains, iron-fortified cereals, enriched pasta, lean red meat, kidney beans, and dried fruit.

Butternut Squash Whip Ⓜ

¾ pound cubed seeded pared
   butternut squash
2 tablespoons *each* dried currants
   or dark raisins, water, and
   half-and-half (blend of milk and
   cream)
1 tablespoon whipped butter
1 teaspoon firmly packed light
   brown sugar

In 1-quart microwavable casserole arrange squash; cover with vented plastic wrap and microwave on High (100%) for 5 minutes, until squash is fork-tender. Let stand, covered, for 1 to 2 minutes.

   In microwavable cup or small bowl combine currants (or raisins) and water and microwave on High for 1 minute, until plumped; set aside. In separate microwavable cup or small bowl combine half-and-half, butter, and brown sugar and microwave on High for 30 seconds, until butter is melted.

   Transfer squash to large mixing bowl. Using electric mixer on low speed, beat squash until smooth, 1 to 2 minutes. Add half-and-half mixture and beat on high speed until squash is light and fluffy; stir in currant (or raisin) mixture.

MAKES 2 SERVINGS

Each serving provides: 1½ Bread Exchanges;
   ½ Fruit Exchange; 60 Optional Calories
Per serving with currants: 156 calories; 3 g protein; 5 g fat;
   29 g carbohydrate; 108 mg calcium; 44 mg sodium;
   13 mg cholesterol; 0.5 g dietary fiber (this figure does
   not include butternut squash; nutrition analysis not
   available)
With raisins: 158 calories; 3 g protein; 5 g fat;
   30 g carbohydrate; 105 mg calcium; 45 mg sodium;
   13 mg cholesterol; 0.5 g dietary fiber (this figure does
   not include butternut squash; nutrition analysis not
   available)

Italian Squash ©Ⓜ

½ cup canned Italian tomatoes
  (with liquid); drain, seed, and
  chop tomatoes, reserving liquid
1 teaspoon minced fresh parsley
1 garlic clove, minced
¼ teaspoon oregano leaves
⅛ teaspoon salt
1 medium yellow squash (about
  5 ounces), sliced (¼-inch-thick
  slices)

In 1-quart microwavable casserole combine tomatoes with liquid, parsley, garlic, oregano, and salt; add squash and stir to combine. Cover with vented plastic wrap and microwave on High (100%) for 5 minutes, stirring halfway through cooking. Let stand, covered, for 1 minute.

MAKES 2 SERVINGS

Each serving provides: 1½ Vegetable Exchanges
Per serving: 28 calories; 1 g protein; 0.3 g fat;
  6 g carbohydrate; 38 mg calcium; 238 mg sodium;
  0 mg cholesterol; 1 g dietary fiber

Minted Zucchini Ⓒ

1½ teaspoons whipped butter
1 teaspoon olive *or* vegetable oil
½ cup diced onion
2 cups julienne-cut zucchini
  (matchstick pieces)
1 tablespoon chopped fresh mint
  or ½ teaspoon mint flakes

In 9-inch skillet combine butter and oil and heat until butter is melted; add onion and sauté over high heat until translucent, about 1 minute. Add zucchini and stir to combine. Reduce heat to low, cover, and cook, stirring occasionally, until zucchini is tender, 2 to 3 minutes. Stir in mint and cook 30 seconds longer.

MAKES 2 SERVINGS

Each serving provides: 2½ Vegetable Exchanges;
  ½ Fat Exchange; 15 Optional Calories
Per serving: 65 calories; 2 g protein; 4 g fat;
  7 g carbohydrate; 31 mg calcium; 19 mg sodium;
  4 mg cholesterol; 1 g dietary fiber

Although zucchini is considered a summer squash, it is available year-round in many areas. For lowest cost and greatest freshness and flavor, however, late spring through summer is the peak season.

Creamy Diced Potatoes Ⓒ

If you have extra time, prepare the potatoes for this recipe in advance.

1 teaspoon margarine
2 tablespoons thinly sliced
   scallion (green portion only)
3 tablespoons half-and-half (blend
   of milk and cream)
2 tablespoons sour cream
6 ounces cooked diced pared
   all-purpose potatoes
½ teaspoon salt
⅛ teaspoon white pepper

In 9-inch nonstick skillet melt margarine; add scallion and sauté over medium heat until softened, about 1 minute. Add half-and-half and cook, stirring occasionally, until mixture begins to come to a boil, about 1 minute; stir in sour cream. Reduce heat to low; add potatoes, salt, and pepper and stir to combine. Cook, stirring frequently, until potatoes are heated through and mixture thickens, 1 to 2 minutes.

MAKES 2 SERVINGS

Each serving provides: 1 Bread Exchange;
   ⅛ Vegetable Exchange; ½ Fat Exchange;
   70 Optional Calories
Per serving: 152 calories; 3 g protein; 8 g fat;
   19 g carbohydrate; 55 mg calcium; 591 mg sodium;
   15 mg cholesterol; 2 g dietary fiber

Microwave Scalloped Potatoes Ⓒ Ⓜ

9 ounces thinly sliced all-purpose potatoes
Water
Salt
1 tablespoon whipped butter
2 teaspoons margarine
2½ teaspoons all-purpose flour
½ cup evaporated skimmed milk
½ packet (½ teaspoon) instant chicken broth and seasoning mix
Dash pepper
2 ounces Swiss cheese, shredded, divided
⅛ teaspoon paprika

In 1-quart microwavable casserole combine potatoes, 1 tablespoon water, and ¼ teaspoon salt; cover with vented plastic wrap and microwave on High (100%) for 5 minutes, stirring halfway through cooking. Let stand, covered, for 2 minutes.

In small microwavable mixing bowl combine butter and margarine; microwave on High, uncovered, for 30 seconds, until melted. Using a wire whisk, stir in flour; gradually stir in milk, ¼ cup water, the broth mix, ⅛ teaspoon salt, and pepper. Microwave on High, uncovered, for 2 minutes, stirring halfway through cooking. Stir in 1 ounce cheese; microwave on High, uncovered, for 15 seconds, until cheese melts. Pour cheese mixture evenly over potato slices; sprinkle with remaining 1 ounce cheese and the paprika. Microwave on Medium-High (70%), uncovered, for 1½ minutes, until cheese melts.

MAKES 2 SERVINGS

Each serving provides: 1 Protein Exchange;
    1½ Bread Exchanges; 1 Fat Exchange;
    ½ Milk Exchange; 40 Optional Calories
Per serving: 331 calories; 16 g protein; 15 g fat;
    34 g carbohydrate; 472 mg calcium; 891 mg sodium;
    36 mg cholesterol; 2 g dietary fiber

Old-Fashioned Coleslaw ☉

1 tablespoon plus 1 teaspoon
   margarine
1 tablespoon all-purpose flour
½ cup low-fat milk (1% milk fat)
1 egg
¼ cup apple cider vinegar
½ teaspoon *each* powdered
   mustard and granulated sugar
¼ teaspoon *each* celery seed and
   salt
⅛ teaspoon white pepper
8 cups shredded green cabbage
½ cup chopped celery
¼ cup *each* chopped onion, green
   bell pepper, and pimiento

In small saucepan melt margarine over medium-high heat; add flour and stir quickly to combine. Cook, stirring constantly, for 1 minute; stir in milk. Reduce heat to low and let simmer, stirring constantly, until mixture is smooth and thickened, 3 to 4 minutes.

Using a wire whisk, in small mixing bowl beat together egg, vinegar, mustard, sugar, celery seed, salt, and pepper. Gradually stir some of the milk mixture into the egg mixture; stir egg mixture into milk mixture in saucepan. Cook, stirring frequently, until flavors blend, 1 to 2 minutes *(do not overcook)*. Set aside and let cool.

In medium mixing bowl combine remaining ingredients; add dressing and toss to coat. Cover with plastic wrap and refrigerate until chilled and flavors blend, at least 1 hour.

MAKES 4 SERVINGS

Each serving provides: ¼ Protein Exchange;
   4½ Vegetable Exchanges; 1 Fat Exchange;
   25 Optional Calories
Per serving: 124 calories; 5 g protein; 6 g fat;
   14 g carbohydrate; 126 mg calcium; 254 mg sodium;
   70 mg cholesterol; 2 g dietary fiber

Kohlrabi Slaw ©

2 cups shredded pared kohlrabi
½ cup shredded carrot
2 tablespoons *each* chopped
    scallion (green onion) and plain
    low-fat yogurt
1 tablespoon chopped fresh
    Italian (flat-leaf) parsley
2 teaspoons reduced-calorie
    mayonnaise
½ teaspoon apple cider vinegar
Dash *each* salt and pepper

In salad bowl combine kohlrabi, carrot, and scallion; set aside. In small bowl combine remaining ingredients; pour over vegetable mixture and toss to coat thoroughly. Cover and refrigerate until chilled, about 30 minutes. Toss again just before serving.

MAKES 2 SERVINGS

Each serving provides: 2½ Vegetable Exchanges;
    ½ Fat Exchange; 10 Optional Calories
Per serving: 74 calories; 4 g protein; 2 g fat;
    13 g carbohydrate; 72 mg calcium; 151 mg sodium;
    3 mg cholesterol; 2 g dietary fiber

What's a cabbage turnip? It's another name for kohlrabi. Fresh kohlrabi is available from late spring through early fall, with a peak in midsummer. Select kohlrabi that have bulbs no more than about 3 inches in diameter. Larger kohlrabi tend to be tough and bitter-tasting.

Guacamole Salad

A colorful salad with a bit of chili pepper. *Olé!*

2 medium tomatoes, diced
1 cup sliced red onions
½ cup *each* red and yellow bell
    pepper strips
¼ medium avocado (about
    2 ounces), pared and diced
2 slices crisp bacon, crumbled
2 tablespoons *each* seeded and
    minced mild *or* hot chili pepper
    and freshly squeezed lime juice
1 tablespoon apple cider vinegar
1 teaspoon olive *or* vegetable oil
½ teaspoon salt
Dash pepper
2 cups torn lettuce

In large mixing bowl combine all ingredients except lettuce and toss to combine. To serve, line serving platter with lettuce and top with avocado mixture.

MAKES 2 SERVINGS

Each serving provides: 6⅛ Vegetable Exchanges;
    1½ Fat Exchanges; 45 Optional Calories
Per serving: 185 calories; 6 g protein; 10 g fat;
    23 g carbohydrate; 83 mg calcium; 670 mg sodium;
    5 mg cholesterol; 4 g dietary fiber

Jicama Salad

⅛ medium avocado (about
  1 ounce), pared and diced
2 tablespoons freshly squeezed
  lime juice, divided
4 cups shredded pared jicama
½ cup plain low-fat yogurt
2 tablespoons minced red onion
1 tablespoon plus 1 teaspoon
  reduced-calorie mayonnaise
1 tablespoon seeded and minced
  jalapeño pepper
½ teaspoon salt
⅛ teaspoon ground red pepper
8 lettuce leaves

In small bowl combine avocado and 1 table-spoon lime juice; set aside. In large mixing bowl combine remaining ingredients except lettuce and toss to thoroughly combine; add avocado mixture and stir to combine.

To serve, line salad bowl with lettuce leaves and top with jicama mixture.

MAKES 2 SERVINGS

Each serving provides: 5⅛ Vegetable Exchanges;
  1½ Fat Exchanges; ½ Milk Exchange
Per serving: 193 calories; 7 g protein; 6 g fat;
  30 g carbohydrate; 171 mg calcium; 684 mg sodium;
  7 mg cholesterol; 5 g dietary fiber

Greek-Style Potato Salad

9 ounces cooked small red potatoes, quartered
¼ cup *each* diced red bell pepper and scallions (green onions)
6 Calamata, Gaeta, *or* black olives, pitted and chopped
1 tablespoon *each* red wine vinegar, water, and chopped fresh dill *or* ½ teaspoon dillweed
2 teaspoons olive oil
¼ teaspoon *each* oregano leaves and pepper
1 ounce feta cheese, crumbled

In medium serving bowl combine potatoes, bell pepper, scallions, and olives. In cup or small bowl combine remaining ingredients except cheese and mix well. Pour over potato mixture and toss well to coat. Sprinkle with cheese.

MAKES 2 SERVINGS

Each serving provides: ½ Protein Exchange; 1½ Bread Exchanges; ½ Vegetable Exchange; 1½ Fat Exchanges
Per serving with Calamata *or* Gaeta olives: 214 calories; 5 g protein; 10 g fat; 26 g carbohydrate; 93 mg calcium; 406 mg sodium; 13 mg cholesterol; 3 g dietary fiber
With black olives: 209 calories; 5 g protein; 10 g fat; 26 g carbohydrate; 98 mg calcium; 251 mg sodium; 13 mg cholesterol; 3 g dietary fiber

Sweet Potato Salad Ⓜ

3 cups water
9 ounces cubed pared sweet
  potatoes
½ cup canned crushed pineapple
  (no sugar added)
2 tablespoons *each* diced celery
  and red onion
1 tablespoon minced fresh
  parsley
2 teaspoons peanut *or* vegetable
  oil
1 teaspoon raspberry *or* apple
  cider vinegar
Dash *each* ground cinnamon,
  ground nutmeg, salt, and white
  pepper

In 1½-quart microwavable casserole combine water and potatoes and microwave on High (100%) for 10 minutes, stirring once halfway through cooking. Drain potatoes, discarding cooking liquid and set aside.

In salad bowl combine remaining ingredients; fold in potatoes and serve immediately.

MAKES 2 SERVINGS

Each serving provides: 1½ Bread Exchanges;
  ¼ Vegetable Exchange; 1 Fat Exchange;
  ½ Fruit Exchange
Per serving: 218 calories; 3 g protein; 5 g fat;
  42 g carbohydrate; 46 mg calcium; 91 mg sodium;
  0 mg cholesterol; 3 g dietary fiber

Mixed Braised Salad with Goat Cheese

2 teaspoons olive *or* vegetable oil
1 cup *each* sliced onions, sliced
    mushrooms, and red bell
    pepper strips
1 small garlic clove, minced
½ ounce shelled walnuts, broken
    into pieces
2 slices crisp bacon, crumbled
2 tablespoons red wine vinegar
1 tablespoon *each* lemon zest*
    and freshly squeezed lemon
    juice
4 cups thoroughly washed and
    drained spinach leaves,† torn
    into bite-size pieces
1 cup *each* torn Boston, Bibb, red
    leaf lettuce, and green leaf
    lettuce†
1 ounce chèvre (French goat
    cheese), crumbled

In 10-inch skillet heat oil; add onions, mushrooms, bell pepper, and garlic and cook over medium heat, stirring occasionally, until vegetables are tender-crisp, about 10 minutes. Add nuts, bacon, vinegar, lemon zest, and lemon juice and stir to combine; cook, stirring frequently, until mixture comes to a boil, about 1 minute. Add spinach and lettuce and stir to combine; cover and cook until spinach and lettuce are wilted, 2 to 3 minutes.

To serve, transfer mixture to serving platter and top with cheese.

MAKES 2 SERVINGS

Each serving provides: 1 Protein Exchange;
    5 Vegetable Exchanges; 1½ Fat Exchanges;
    45 Optional Calories
Per serving: 274 calories; 12 g protein; 17 g fat;
    22 g carbohydrate; 246 mg calcium; 292 mg sodium;
    18 mg cholesterol; 8 g dietary fiber

Variation: Mixed Braised Salad with Feta Cheese — Substitute 1 ounce feta cheese for the chèvre.

Per serving: 260 calories; 12 g protein; 16 g fat;
    22 g carbohydrate; 294 mg calcium; 363 mg sodium;
    18 mg cholesterol; 7 g dietary fiber

*The zest of the lemon is the peel without any of the pith (white membrane). To remove zest from lemon, use a zester or vegetable peeler; wrap lemon in plastic wrap and refrigerate for use at another time.
†Four cups *each* fresh spinach and lettuce yield a total of about 2 cups cooked.

Asparagus and Strawberry Salad

An unusual combination that's worth a try.

1 medium Belgian endive (about
   3 ounces), separated into leaves
24 Boston *or* Bibb lettuce leaves
½ cup enoki *or* sliced white
   mushrooms
12 medium asparagus spears,
   blanched
1 cup strawberries, sliced
2 tablespoons lemon juice
1½ teaspoons honey
1 teaspoon vegetable oil
Dash *each* salt and white pepper

Onto half of each of 2 serving plates arrange half of the endive leaves. Top with lettuce leaves, mushrooms, and asparagus. Decoratively arrange half of the strawberries onto bottom portion of each plate.

   In cup or small bowl combine remaining ingredients; pour half of mixture over each salad.

MAKES 2 SERVINGS

Each serving provides: 3½ Vegetable Exchanges;
   ½ Fat Exchange; ½ Fruit Exchange;
   15 Optional Calories
Per serving: 110 calories; 5 g protein; 3 g fat;
   20 g carbohydrate; 99 mg calcium; 84 mg sodium;
   0 mg cholesterol; 5 g dietary fiber

Variation: Poppy, Asparagus, and Strawberry Salad — Add ¼ teaspoon poppy seed to honey mixture. Increase Optional Calories to 20.

Per serving: Increase calories to 112 and calcium to 104 mg

Bread, Pasta, and Grains

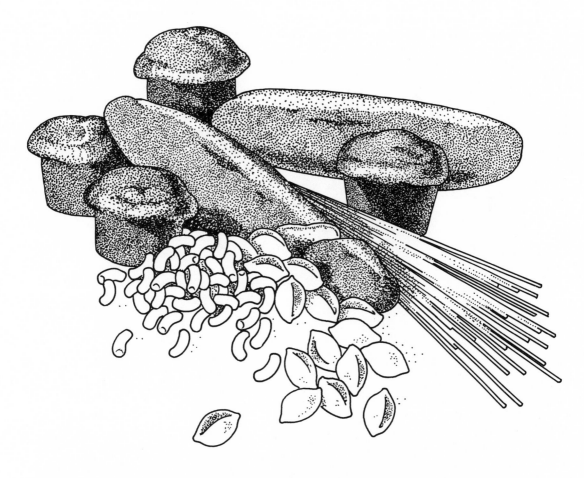

Today's nutrition experts recommend increasing your intake of complex carbohydrates — the kind found in bread, grains, and pasta — and our quick and delicious recipes fit right in with this trend. In this chapter you'll find tempting microwave side dishes like Spanish Rice and Couscous Pilaf. There are main-dish pasta recipes such as Pasta with Vegetable-Cheese Sauce, Salmon and Pasta Salad, and Italian Pasta Bake. And who can resist waking up to a morning meal of Breakfast Puffs or Blueberry Pancakes? With our wonderful recipes, you'll get your share of complex carbohydrates *and* great taste!

Breakfast Puffs

1 cup plus 2 tablespoons
   all-purpose flour
1 teaspoon *each* ground
   cinnamon, divided, and double-
   acting baking powder
¼ cup granulated sugar, divided
¼ cup less 1 teaspoon margarine
1 egg
⅓ cup skim *or* nonfat milk
½ ounce ground walnuts
1 tablespoon whipped butter,
   melted

Preheat oven to 350°F. In small mixing bowl combine flour, ½ teaspoon cinnamon, and the baking powder; set aside.

Using electric mixer at medium speed, in medium mixing bowl combine 3 tablespoons sugar, the margarine, and the egg and beat until creamy. Alternately add flour mixture and milk, beating until combined. Stir in walnuts.

Drop batter by tablespoonfuls onto non-stick baking sheet, forming 12 equal mounds, and leaving a space of about 2 inches between each. Brush each mound with an equal amount of melted butter. In cup or small bowl combine remaining tablespoon sugar and ½ teaspoon cinnamon and sprinkle an equal amount of sugar mixture over each mound. Bake until puffed and golden, 12 to 15 minutes. Remove puffs to wire rack and let cool.

MAKES 12 SERVINGS

Each serving provides: ½ Bread Exchange;
   1 Fat Exchange; 40 Optional Calories
Per serving: 112 calories; 2 g protein; 5 g fat;
   14 g carbohydrate; 35 mg calcium; 91 mg sodium;
   24 mg cholesterol; 0.5 g dietary fiber

Morning rush got you frazzled? If you prepare ahead and then freeze your home-baked favorites, all you have to do is pop them into the microwave or toaster-oven for a warm breakfast in minutes.

Banana-Pecan Farina

While cereal cooks, toast the shredded coconut.

1½ cups water
1½ ounces uncooked
   quick-cooking farina
Dash salt
1 medium banana (about
   6 ounces), peeled and sliced
½ ounce shelled pecans, broken
   into pieces
2 teaspoons *each* shredded
   coconut, toasted, and firmly
   packed light brown sugar
¼ cup skim *or* nonfat milk

In small saucepan bring water to a boil; gradually stir in farina and salt. Cook over medium heat, stirring constantly, until liquid is absorbed and mixture thickens, 2 to 3 minutes.

   To serve, divide cereal into 2 cereal bowls; top each portion with half of the banana slices, pecans, coconut, sugar, and milk.

MAKES 2 SERVINGS

Each serving provides: ½ Protein Exchange;
   1 Bread Exchange; ½ Fat Exchange; 1 Fruit Exchange;
   40 Optional Calories
Per serving: 213 calories; 5 g protein; 6 g fat;
   37 g carbohydrate; 155 mg calcium; 137 mg sodium;
   1 mg cholesterol; 1 g dietary fiber (this figure does not
   include farina and coconut; nutrition analyses not
   available)

Cinnamon-Apple Farina

1½ cups water
1½ ounces uncooked
   quick-cooking farina
2 tablespoons dried currants *or*
   dark raisins
½ teaspoon ground cinnamon
Dash salt
½ cup applesauce (no sugar
   added)
1 tablespoon maple syrup
2 teaspoons margarine
½ cup low-fat milk (1% milk fat)

In small saucepan bring water to a boil; gradually stir in farina, currants (or raisins), cinnamon, and salt. Cook over medium heat, stirring constantly, until liquid is absorbed and mixture thickens, 2 to 3 minutes. Stir in applesauce.

To serve, divide cereal into 2 cereal bowls; top each portion with half of the syrup, margarine, and milk.

MAKES 2 SERVINGS

Each serving provides: 1 Bread Exchange;
   1 Fat Exchange; 1 Fruit Exchange; ¼ Milk Exchange;
   35 Optional Calories
Per serving with currants: 215 calories; 5 g protein; 5 g fat;
   39 g carbohydrate; 210 mg calcium; 197 mg sodium;
   2 mg cholesterol; 1 g dietary fiber (this figure does not
   include farina; nutrition analysis not available)
With raisins: 217 calories; 5 g protein; 5 g fat;
   40 g carbohydrate; 207 mg calcium; 198 mg sodium;
   2 mg cholesterol; 1 g dietary fiber (this figure does not
   include farina; nutrition analysis not available)

Nutty Oatmeal with Raisins

1 cup water
1½ ounces uncooked quick-
   cooking oats
1 tablespoon *each* dark and
   golden raisins
Dash salt
1 ounce chopped walnuts
2 teaspoons shredded coconut
1 tablespoon half-and-half (blend
   of milk and cream)

In small saucepan bring water to a boil; gradually stir in oats, raisins, and salt. Cook over medium heat, stirring constantly, until liquid is absorbed and mixture thickens, about 1 minute.

To serve, divide cereal into 2 cereal bowls; top each portion with half of the nuts, coconut, and half-and-half.

MAKES 2 SERVINGS

Each serving provides: 1 Protein Exchange;
   1 Bread Exchange; 1 Fat Exchange; ½ Fruit Exchange;
   25 Optional Calories
Per serving: 218 calories; 6 g protein; 12 g fat;
   25 g carbohydrate; 37 mg calcium; 73 mg sodium;
   3 mg cholesterol; 2 g dietary fiber

Oatmeal with Dried Fruits ☉

1 cup water
1½ ounces uncooked quick-
   cooking oats
4 dried apricot halves, diced
2 tablespoons golden raisins
Dash salt
2 teaspoons honey
¼ cup low-fat milk (1% milk fat)

In small saucepan bring water to a boil; gradually stir in oats, apricots, raisins, and salt. Cook over medium heat, stirring constantly, until liquid is absorbed and mixture thickens, about 1 minute.

To serve, divide cereal into 2 cereal bowls; top each portion with half of the honey and milk.

MAKES 2 SERVINGS

Each serving provides: 1 Bread Exchange;
   1 Fruit Exchange; 35 Optional Calories
Per serving: 160 calories; 5 g protein; 2 g fat;
   33 g carbohydrate; 57 mg calcium; 84 mg sodium;
   1 mg cholesterol; 3 g dietary fiber

Blueberry Pancakes

You can prepare the batter for these delicious pancakes (excluding the blueberries) the night before and store it in the refrigerator. Stir in the berries just before cooking.

⅓ cup plus 2 teaspoons
   buttermilk baking mix
1 egg
2 tablespoons skim *or* nonfat milk
Dash ground cinnamon
½ cup fresh *or* frozen blueberries
   (no sugar added)
2 teaspoons whipped butter

In blender container combine all ingredients except blueberries and butter and process until smooth; stir in blueberries.

   Spray 10-inch nonstick skillet or griddle with nonstick cooking spray and heat over medium-high heat. Using 2 tablespoons of batter for each pancake, drop batter into hot skillet (or griddle), making 3 pancakes; using the back of a spoon, spread each pancake into a circle about 3 inches in diameter. Cook until bubbles appear on surface and pancakes are browned on bottom; using pancake turner, turn pancakes over and cook until other side is browned. Remove pancakes to serving platter and keep warm. Repeat procedure, spraying skillet (or griddle) with nonstick cooking spray and making 3 more pancakes.

   To serve, arrange pancakes on serving platter and top with whipped butter.

MAKES 2 SERVINGS, 3 PANCAKES EACH

Each serving provides: ½ Protein Exchange;
   1 Bread Exchange; ½ Fruit Exchange;
   40 Optional Calories
Per serving: 168 calories; 5 g protein; 7 g fat;
   20 g carbohydrate; 66 mg calcium; 326 mg sodium;
   142 mg cholesterol; 1 g dietary fiber

Ginger-Pear Pancake ⊙

½ small Bosc *or* Bartlett pear
　(about 2½ ounces), cored and
　thinly sliced
1 teaspoon lemon juice
⅓ cup plus 2 teaspoons
　buttermilk baking mix
1 teaspoon granulated sugar,
　divided
¼ teaspoon ground ginger
1 egg
2 tablespoons low-fat milk
　(1% milk fat)
1 teaspoon vanilla extract
½ teaspoon firmly packed light
　brown sugar
¼ teaspoon ground cinnamon
2 tablespoons reduced-calorie
　pancake syrup (60 calories per
　fluid ounce)

Preheat oven to 450°F. In small bowl combine pear slices and lemon juice; toss to coat and set aside.

In medium mixing bowl combine baking mix, ½ teaspoon granulated sugar, and the ginger; set aside. In small mixing bowl beat together egg, milk, and vanilla; stir into baking mix mixture, stirring until batter is smooth and thoroughly combined.

Spray 8-inch nonstick pie pan with nonstick cooking spray; pour batter evenly into pan. Decoratively arrange pear slices over batter. In cup or small bowl combine remaining ½ teaspoon granulated sugar, the brown sugar, and cinnamon; sprinkle over pear slices and batter. Bake until pancake is puffed and golden brown, 10 to 15 minutes.

To serve, cut pancake in half and top each portion with 1 tablespoon syrup.

MAKES 2 SERVINGS, ½ PANCAKE EACH

Each serving provides: ½ Protein Exchange;
　1 Bread Exchange; ¼ Fruit Exchange;
　70 Optional Calories
Per serving: 218 calories; 6 g protein; 6 g fat;
　34 g carbohydrate; 48 mg calcium; 355 mg sodium;
　138 mg cholesterol; 3 g dietary fiber

Vegetable Pancakes

½ cup plus 1 tablespoon
   buttermilk baking mix
¼ cup plain low-fat yogurt
1 egg
½ cup *each* finely diced onion and
   red bell pepper
1 tablespoon chopped fresh
   Italian (flat-leaf) parsley
Dash *each* salt and pepper
2 tablespoons sour cream

In blender container combine baking mix, yogurt, and egg and process until smooth; stir in remaining ingredients except sour cream.

Spray 10-inch nonstick skillet or griddle with nonstick cooking spray and heat over medium-high heat. Using 2 tablespoons of batter for each pancake, drop batter into hot skillet (or griddle), making 3 pancakes; using the back of a spoon, spread each pancake into a circle about 3 inches in diameter. Cook until bubbles appear on surface and pancakes are browned on bottom; using pancake turner, turn pancakes over and cook until other side is browned. Remove pancakes to serving platter and keep warm. Repeat procedure, spraying skillet (or griddle) with nonstick cooking spray and making 3 more pancakes. Top pancakes with sour cream.

MAKES 2 SERVINGS, 3 PANCAKES EACH

Each serving provides: ½ Protein Exchange;
   1½ Bread Exchanges; 1 Vegetable Exchange;
   ¼ Milk Exchange; 65 Optional Calories
Per serving: 242 calories; 8 g protein; 11 g fat;
   27 g carbohydrate; 155 mg calcium; 523 mg sodium;
   145 mg cholesterol; 1 g dietary fiber

Corn Chowder with Shrimp

1 tablespoon whipped butter
½ cup *each* red *or* green bell
    pepper strips, diced onion, and
    diagonally sliced celery
1 tablespoon seeded and minced
    jalapeño pepper
1 small garlic clove, minced
2 teaspoons all-purpose flour
1 cup skim *or* nonfat milk
½ cup bottled clam juice
1½ cups fresh *or* frozen whole
    kernel corn
5 ounces shelled and deveined
    medium shrimp
1 tablespoon chopped fresh
    cilantro (Chinese parsley) *or*
    fresh Italian (flat-leaf) parsley

In 2-quart saucepan melt butter over high heat; add bell pepper, onion, celery, jalapeño pepper, and garlic and sauté until vegetables are tender-crisp, about 2 minutes. Sprinkle with flour and stir quickly to combine; cook, stirring constantly, for 1 minute. Remove from heat and stir in milk and clam juice. Return saucepan to medium heat and cook until mixture thickens, 1 to 2 minutes *(do not boil)*. Add corn and shrimp and stir to combine; cook just until shrimp turn pink, about 3 minutes. Sprinkle with cilantro (or parsley) and serve.

MAKES 2 SERVINGS, ABOUT 2 CUPS EACH

Each serving provides: 2 Protein Exchanges;
    1½ Bread Exchanges; 1½ Vegetable Exchanges;
    ½ Milk Exchange; 45 Optional Calories
Per serving: 282 calories; 24 g protein; 6 g fat;
    37 g carbohydrate; 224 mg calcium; 373 mg sodium;
    118 mg cholesterol; 3 g dietary fiber

Barley with Mushrooms and Bacon © Ⓜ

1 teaspoon margarine
½ cup sliced mushrooms
¼ cup finely chopped onion
1½ ounces uncooked pearl barley
1½ cups water
1 packet instant beef broth and
    seasoning mix
1 slice crisp bacon, crumbled
⅛ teaspoon pepper

In 1-quart microwavable shallow casserole microwave margarine on High (100%) for 1 minute, until melted. Add mushrooms and onion and microwave on High for 1 minute, until softened. Add barley and stir to combine; microwave on High for 1 minute. Add water and broth mix and stir to dissolve broth mix; microwave on High for 15 minutes, until liquid is absorbed and barley is tender, stirring every 5 minutes. Stir in bacon and pepper.

MAKES 2 SERVINGS

Each serving provides: 1 Bread Exchange;
    ¾ Vegetable Exchange; ½ Fat Exchange;
    25 Optional Calories
Per serving: 126 calories; 4 g protein; 4 g fat;
    19 g carbohydrate; 13 mg calcium; 541 mg sodium;
    3 mg cholesterol; 3 g dietary fiber

For crisp bacon in a hurry, cook it in the microwave oven. One slice of bacon is ready in about a minute.

Asparagus and Strawberry Salad

Cheese Toasts
Fruit and Cheese Pizza
Black Bean Terrine
Mint Pesto with Pitas

Microwave Golden Baked Beans
Dijon Pork Chops

Ham with Port and Red Grapes
Harvest Turkey-Chestnut Salad

Mediterranean-Style Shrimp

Couscous Pilaf Ⓜ

Tired of potatoes? Give couscous a try. Here we've combined it with fruits and pignolias for a sweet side dish.

1 small Granny Smith apple (about ¼ pound), cored, pared, and diced
¼ cup *each* diced celery and diagonally cut thinly sliced scallions (green onions)
1 tablespoon golden raisins
2 dried apricot halves, diced
1 ounce pignolias (pine nuts), toasted
2 teaspoons whipped butter
¾ cup water
⅓ cup apricot *or* pear nectar
½ teaspoon curry powder
1½ ounces uncooked couscous (dry precooked semolina)
Garnish: mint sprig

In 1-quart microwavable casserole combine apple, celery, scallions, raisins, apricot, pignolias, and butter and stir to combine. Microwave on High (100%) for 2 minutes. Add water, nectar, and curry powder and microwave on High for 3 minutes, until liquid is reduced. Stir in couscous, cover with plastic wrap, and let stand until liquid is absorbed, about 5 minutes.

To serve, transfer to serving platter and garnish with mint.

MAKES 2 SERVINGS

Each serving provides: 1 Protein Exchange;
1 Bread Exchange; ½ Vegetable Exchange;
1 Fat Exchange; 1½ Fruit Exchanges;
15 Optional Calories
Per serving: 239 calories; 6 g protein; 9 g fat;
37 g carbohydrate; 21 mg calcium; 39 mg sodium;
5 mg cholesterol; 2 g dietary fiber (this figure does not include pignolias and couscous; nutrition analyses not available)

Kasha Varnishkes Ⓒ Ⓜ

½ cup *each* diced onion and
   sliced mushrooms
2 teaspoons margarine
2 cups water
1½ ounces uncooked bow-tie
   macaroni
2 packets instant chicken broth
   and seasoning mix
2 ounces uncooked coarse-grain
   buckwheat groats (kasha)

In 2-quart microwavable casserole combine vegetables and margarine and microwave on High (100%) for 2 minutes until vegetables are softened. Add water, macaroni, and broth mix and stir to combine; microwave on High for 8 minutes, stirring halfway through cooking. Stir in buckwheat groats, cover with vented plastic wrap, and microwave on High for 3 minutes, stirring after 2 minutes. Let stand for 5 minutes, until water is absorbed.

MAKES 2 SERVINGS

Each serving provides: 2 Bread Exchanges;
   1 Vegetable Exchange; 1 Fat Exchange;
   10 Optional Calories
Per serving: 233 calories; 8 g protein; 5 g fat;
   41 g carbohydrate; 50 mg calcium; 1,037 mg sodium;
   0 mg cholesterol; 1 g dietary fiber

Although the term "kasha" generally refers to buckwheat groats, it is really an eastern European name for a grain pilaf. Buckwheat groats come in coarse, medium, and fine grinds. Use coarse grain groats for hearty dishes and medium or fine groats in recipes requiring a more delicate texture.

Polenta with Mushroom-Cream Sauce

1½ cups water
¼ teaspoon salt
2¼ ounces uncooked instant polenta (quick-cooking yellow cornmeal)
2 teaspoons margarine, divided
1 tablespoon whipped butter
¼ cup thinly sliced shiitake *or* white mushrooms
1½ teaspoons finely chopped shallot *or* onion
1 tablespoon all-purpose flour
½ cup low-fat milk (2% milk fat)
¼ cup canned ready-to-serve chicken broth
Dash pepper
2 teaspoons grated Parmesan cheese

Spray 7-inch flameproof pie plate with non-stick cooking spray; set aside. In 1½-quart saucepan combine water and salt and cook over high heat until mixture comes to a full boil; stirring constantly with a wooden spoon, add polenta in a steady stream. Stir in 1 teaspoon margarine. Reduce heat to medium-high and cook, stirring constantly, until water is absorbed, about 4 minutes. Pour polenta into prepared pie plate; set aside.

In 1-quart saucepan melt remaining teaspoon margarine and the butter; add mushrooms and shallot (or onion) and sauté over medium heat until mushrooms are softened, about 3 minutes. Sprinkle flour over mushroom mixture and stir quickly to combine; cook, stirring constantly, for 1 minute. Using a wire whisk, gradually stir in milk and broth; cook over high heat, stirring constantly, until mixture comes to a boil and is thickened, about 1 minute. Stir in pepper. Pour mushroom mixture over polenta in pie plate; sprinkle with Parmesan cheese. Broil until cheese is golden, about 1 minute.

MAKES 2 SERVINGS

Each serving provides: 1½ Bread Exchanges;
¼ Vegetable Exchange; 1 Fat Exchange;
¼ Milk Exchange; 65 Optional Calories
Per serving: 352 calories; 9 g protein; 9 g fat;
57 g carbohydrate; 107 mg calcium; 533 mg sodium;
14 mg cholesterol; 4 g dietary fiber

Sausage and Apple "Stuffing"

1 small apple (about ¼ pound),
  cored and diced
1 teaspoon *each* lemon juice and
  margarine
¼ cup *each* chopped onion and
  celery
3 ounces cooked veal sausage,
  crumbled
6 small canned chestnuts
  (no sugar added)
½ cup water
1½ ounces croutons
1 packet instant chicken broth
  and seasoning mix
⅛ teaspoon rubbed sage
Dash pepper

Preheat oven to 425°F. In cup or small bowl combine apple and lemon juice and toss to coat. In 10-inch nonstick skillet melt margarine; add apple, onion, and celery and sauté over medium-high heat, stirring frequently, until apple and vegetables are lightly browned, 2 to 3 minutes. Add sausage and chestnuts and cook, stirring occasionally, until mixture is heated through, 1 to 2 minutes. Transfer to medium mixing bowl; add remaining ingredients and mix well.

Spray flameproof 1-quart shallow casserole with nonstick cooking spray; spread sausage mixture evenly in casserole and bake for 15 minutes. Turn oven control to broil and broil until sausage mixture is crisp and browned, 2 to 3 minutes.

MAKES 2 SERVINGS

Each serving provides: 1½ Protein Exchanges;
  2 Bread Exchanges; ½ Vegetable Exchange;
  ½ Fat Exchange; ½ Fruit Exchange; 5 Optional Calories
Per serving: 195 calories; 13 g protein; 8 g fat;
  16 g carbohydrate; 26 mg calcium; 1,146 mg sodium
  (estimated); 43 mg cholesterol; 1 g dietary fiber (this
  figure does not include chestnuts; nutrition analysis not
  available)

Variation: Veal and Apple "Stuffing" — Substitute 3 ounces cooked ground veal for the veal sausage.

Per serving: Reduce sodium to 617 mg

Southwestern Corn Bread "Stuffing" Ⓜ

To brown the prepared "stuffing," transfer it to a flameproof casserole and broil for 1 to 2 minutes.

¼ cup *each* chopped onion, celery, and red bell pepper
2 tablespoons seeded and chopped mild *or* hot chili pepper
1 day-old corn muffin (2 ounces), cubed
¼ cup water
1 teaspoon poultry seasoning
1 packet instant chicken broth and seasoning mix
Dash pepper

Spray 1-quart microwavable shallow casserole with nonstick cooking spray; add onion, celery, and peppers and microwave on High (100%) for 1 minute, until vegetables are softened. Add remaining ingredients and stir until thoroughly combined; spread mixture evenly over bottom of casserole. Cover with wax paper and microwave on High for 5 minutes, until liquid is absorbed.

MAKES 2 SERVINGS

Each serving provides: 1 Bread Exchange;
   ¾ Vegetable Exchange; ½ Fat Exchange;
   5 Optional Calories
Per serving: 111 calories; 3 g protein; 3 g fat;
   18 g carbohydrate; 49 mg calcium; 646 mg sodium;
   15 mg cholesterol; 1 g dietary fiber

Broccoli-Cheddar Cups ⊙

These broccoli and Cheddar cheese-topped biscuits are yummy not only hot from the oven but also when eaten cold.

10-ounce package ready-to-bake refrigerated buttermilk flaky biscuits (10 biscuits)

2 cups chopped broccoli, cooked and well drained

5 ounces Cheddar cheese, shredded

1 large plum tomato, diced

¼ cup minced scallions (green onions)

1 tablespoon plus 2 teaspoons margarine, melted

Preheat oven to 400°F. Between 2 sheets of wax paper roll each biscuit into a circle about 4 inches in diameter. Into each of ten 2½-inch-diameter nonstick muffin pan cups place 1 biscuit; press each biscuit into bottom and up sides of cup to form a crust. Set aside.

In small mixing bowl thoroughly combine remaining ingredients and spoon an equal amount of mixture into each biscuit-lined cup. Partially fill remaining cups with water (this will prevent pan from burning and/or warping) and bake until biscuits are golden, about 10 minutes. Remove pan from oven and carefully drain off water (remember, it will be boiling hot).

MAKES 10 SERVINGS

Each serving provides: ½ Protein Exchange;
    1 Bread Exchange; ½ Vegetable Exchange;
    ½ Fat Exchange
Per serving: 166 calories; 6 g protein; 10 g fat;
    14 g carbohydrate; 113 mg calcium; 411 mg sodium;
    15 mg cholesterol; 0.4 g dietary fiber (this figure does
    not include biscuits; nutrition analysis not available)

Greek Biscuits ◉

These delightful biscuits can be served as an hors d'oeuvre or as a change from the usual lunchtime sandwich.

5 ounces feta cheese, crumbled
2 tablespoons *each* chopped fresh dill and scallion (green onion)
6 pimiento-stuffed green olives, chopped
1 tablespoon lemon juice
10-ounce package ready-to-bake refrigerated buttermilk flaky biscuits (10 biscuits)*

Preheat oven to 400°F. In small mixing bowl combine all ingredients except biscuits; set aside.

Spray ten 2½-inch-diameter muffin pan cups with nonstick cooking spray. Separate each biscuit into 2 thin layers of dough and arrange 1 layer in bottom of each sprayed cup, reserving remaining layers. Arrange ¹/₁₀ of cheese mixture over each biscuit in cup, then top each with a remaining biscuit layer; press around edge of each biscuit to seal. Partially fill remaining cups with water (this will prevent pan from burning and/or warping). Bake until biscuits are golden brown, 8 to 10 minutes. Remove pan from oven and carefully drain off water (remember, it will be boiling hot). Remove biscuits to wire rack and let cool.

MAKES 5 SERVINGS, 2 BISCUITS EACH

Each serving provides: 1 Protein Exchange;
  2 Bread Exchanges; 10 Optional Calories
Per serving: 251 calories; 7 g protein; 14 g fat;
  27 g carbohydrate; 149 mg calcium; 995 mg sodium;
  25 mg cholesterol; 0.2 g dietary fiber (this figure does
  not include biscuits; nutrition analysis not available)

*Keep biscuits refrigerated until ready to use. Separate dough into layers as soon as biscuits are removed from refrigerator; they will be difficult to work with if allowed to come to room temperature.

Oatmeal Drop Biscuits ⊙

1½ cups all-purpose flour
3 ounces uncooked quick-
   cooking oats
2 tablespoons firmly packed dark
   brown sugar
1 tablespoon grated orange peel
   (optional)
2 teaspoons double-acting baking
   powder
½ teaspoon *each* baking soda and
   ground cinnamon
Dash salt
¼ cup margarine
2 tablespoons sweet whipped
   butter
¾ cup buttermilk
⅓ cup plus 2 teaspoons dark
   raisins, plumped

Preheat oven to 425°F. In large mixing bowl combine flour, oats, sugar, orange peel (if desired), baking powder, baking soda, cinnamon, and salt. With pastry blender, or 2 knives used scissors-fashion, cut in margarine and butter until mixture resembles coarse meal. Add buttermilk and raisins and stir to form thick batter (mixture will be lumpy).

Drop batter by heaping tablespoonfuls onto nonstick baking sheet, forming 12 biscuits and leaving about 2 inches between each. Bake until biscuits are golden brown, 17 to 20 minutes. Using a spatula, remove biscuits to wire rack to cool.

MAKES 12 SERVINGS, 1 BISCUIT EACH

Each serving provides: 1 Bread Exchange;
   1 Fat Exchange; ¼ Fruit Exchange; 25 Optional Calories
Per serving: 155 calories; 3 g protein; 5 g fat;
   23 g carbohydrate; 66 mg calcium; 188 mg sodium;
   3 mg cholesterol; 1 g dietary fiber

Blueberry-Corn Muffins

Prepare ahead and freeze. Thaw muffins overnight at room temperature or heat in microwave oven or toaster-oven and serve warm.

5¼ ounces (1 cup less 2 table-
    spoons) uncooked yellow
    cornmeal
1 cup less 1 tablespoon all-
    purpose flour
¼ cup granulated sugar
1 tablespoon plus 1 teaspoon
    double-acting baking powder
1 cup skim *or* nonfat milk
¼ cup vegetable oil
1 egg
1½ cups fresh *or* frozen
    blueberries (no sugar added)
1 tablespoon *each* whipped
    butter, melted, and firmly
    packed light brown sugar,
    sifted

Preheat oven to 400°F. In medium mixing bowl combine cornmeal, flour, granulated sugar, and baking powder. In small mixing bowl beat together milk, oil, and egg until blended; add to dry ingredients and stir until blended *(do not beat or overmix)*. Fold in blueberries.

Spray twelve 2½-inch muffin pan cups with nonstick cooking spray. Fill each with an equal amount of batter (each will be about ¾ full). Bake in middle of center oven rack for 15 minutes. Brush top of each muffin with an equal amount of melted butter and sprinkle with an equal amount of brown sugar. Return to oven and bake for 5 minutes (until muffins are golden brown and a toothpick, inserted in center, comes out clean). Set pan on wire rack and let cool.

MAKES 12 SERVINGS, 1 MUFFIN EACH

Each serving provides: 1 Bread Exchange;
   1 Fat Exchange; ¼ Fruit Exchange; 45 Optional Calories
Per serving: 170 calories; 3 g protein; 6 g fat;
   26 g carbohydrate; 102 mg calcium; 165 mg sodium;
   25 mg cholesterol; 1 g dietary fiber (this figure does not
   include cornmeal; nutrition analysis not available)

Orange-Gingerbread Muffins

Prepare these delicious muffins ahead and freeze them. When you're ready to serve them, just thaw at room temperature; to enjoy warm muffins, heat them in the microwave oven or toaster-oven before serving.

2¼ cups all-purpose flour
¼ cup firmly packed brown sugar
1 tablespoon grated orange peel
1½ teaspoons baking soda
½ teaspoon *each* ground ginger
  and ground cinnamon
⅛ teaspoon ground cloves
¾ cup water
2 eggs, lightly beaten
¼ cup dark molasses
¼ cup *each* margarine and
  whipped butter, melted and
  cooled

Preheat oven to 375°F. In large mixing bowl combine flour, sugar, orange peel, baking soda, and spices; set aside.

In small mixing bowl thoroughly combine remaining ingredients; add to flour mixture and stir until mixture is moistened (*do not beat or overmix*).

Spray twelve 2½-inch-diameter muffin pan cups with nonstick cooking spray and fill each with an equal amount of batter (each will be about ¾ full). Bake in middle of center oven rack for 15 minutes (until muffins are brown and a toothpick, inserted in center, comes out clean). Invert muffins onto wire rack and let cool.

MAKES 12 SERVINGS, 1 MUFFIN EACH

Each serving provides: 1 Bread Exchange;
  1 Fat Exchange; 70 Optional Calories
Per serving: 182 calories; 4 g protein; 7 g fat;
  26 g carbohydrate; 63 mg calcium; 187 mg sodium;
  51 mg cholesterol; 1 g dietary fiber

Vegetarian Chili with Corn Muffin ☻

This shortcut chili uses canned baked beans to save you time in the kitchen.

1 teaspoon olive *or* vegetable oil
¼ cup *each* diced onion and
    green bell pepper
1 tablespoon seeded and minced
    mild *or* hot chili pepper
2 garlic cloves, minced
8 ounces (1 cup) canned baked
    beans (without meat)
¼ cup drained canned Italian
    tomatoes, seeded and chopped
1 tablespoon chopped fresh
    cilantro (Chinese parsley) *or*
    fresh Italian (flat-leaf) parsley
1 corn muffin (2 ounces), cut into
    quarters and toasted
1 ounce Monterey Jack *or*
    Cheddar cheese, shredded,
    divided

In small skillet heat oil; add onion, bell pepper, chili pepper, and garlic and cook over medium heat, stirring constantly, until tender, about 1 minute. Add beans, tomatoes, and cilantro (or parsley) and stir to combine. Cook until mixture is heated through, 1 to 2 minutes.

To serve, onto each of 2 plates arrange 2 corn muffin quarters; top each portion with half of the bean mixture and then with half of the cheese.

MAKES 2 SERVINGS

Each serving provides: ½ Protein Exchange;
    2 Bread Exchanges; ¾ Vegetable Exchange;
    1 Fat Exchange; 45 Optional Calories
Per serving with Monterey Jack cheese: 290 calories;
    12 g protein; 10 g fat; 42 g carbohydrate; 213 mg calcium;
    713 mg sodium; 27 mg cholesterol; 4 g dietary fiber
With Cheddar cheese: 294 calories; 12 g protein; 10 g fat;
    42 g carbohydrate; 209 mg calcium; 725 mg sodium;
    30 mg cholesterol; 4 g dietary fiber

Steamed Shrimp Dumplings Ⓜ

4 cups water
3 tablespoons chopped scallion
  (green onion), divided
1 tablespoon *each* minced pared
  gingerroot, divided, reduced-
  sodium soy sauce, and rice
  vinegar
1 large garlic clove, minced,
  divided
1 teaspoon Chinese sesame oil
½ teaspoon granulated sugar
5 ounces shelled and deveined
  shrimp
10 wonton skins (wrappers),
  3 x 3-inch squares

In 12 x 8-inch microwavable baking dish microwave water on High (100%) for 10 minutes, until boiling.

In cup or small bowl combine 1 tablespoon scallion, 2 teaspoons gingerroot, the soy sauce, vinegar, 2 teaspoons garlic, the oil, and sugar; stir to combine.

In work bowl of food processor combine shrimp, remaining 2 tablespoons scallion, remaining 1 teaspoon gingerroot, and remaining garlic and process, using on-off motion, until mixture forms a paste, 1 to 2 minutes. On work surface spread out wonton skins. Spoon an equal amount of shrimp mixture (about 1 heaping teaspoonful) onto center of each wonton skin. Lightly moisten inside edges of 1 wonton skin with water; bring edges together, forming a dumpling and enclosing filling. Repeat procedure, making 9 more dumplings.

Arrange dumplings on microwavable rack that is large enough to hold 10 dumplings in a single layer and set rack on baking dish of boiling water. Loosely cover rack with plastic wrap and microwave on Medium (50%) for 4 minutes. Brush each dumpling with an equal amount of soy sauce mixture, reserving remaining mixture; re-cover and microwave on Medium for 4 minutes. Serve with remaining soy sauce mixture for dipping.

MAKES 2 SERVINGS, 5 DUMPLINGS EACH

Each serving provides: 2 Protein Exchanges;
  1 Bread Exchange; ⅛ Vegetable Exchange;
  ½ Fat Exchange; 5 Optional Calories
Per serving: 223 calories; 19 g protein; 4 g fat;
  27 g carbohydrate; 56 mg calcium; 407 mg sodium;
  108 mg cholesterol; 1 g dietary fiber

"Pissaladière"

Our version of French pizza.

1 tablespoon chopped onion
1 garlic clove, chopped
3 drained canned anchovy fillets,
   chopped
3 large pitted black olives,
   chopped
2 tablespoons *each* tomato puree
   and dry red table wine
1 teaspoon chopped fresh parsley
⅛ teaspoon oregano leaves
4 ready-to-bake refrigerated
   buttermilk flaky biscuits
   (1 ounce each)
2 teaspoons grated Parmesan
   cheese

Preheat oven to 450°F. Spray small nonstick skillet with nonstick cooking spray and heat; add onion and garlic and cook over high heat, stirring frequently, for 30 seconds. Add anchovies and olives and cook for 30 seconds; add tomato puree, wine, parsley, and oregano. Reduce heat to medium and cook, stirring frequently, for 1½ minutes. Remove from heat and set aside.

Spray four 2½-inch-diameter muffin pan cups with nonstick cooking spray; arrange 1 biscuit in each sprayed cup. Top each with ¼ of the tomato mixture and then sprinkle each with ½ teaspoon cheese. Partially fill remaining cups with water (this will prevent pan from burning and/or warping). Bake for 8 minutes until edges of biscuits are golden brown. Remove pan from oven and carefully drain off water (remember, it will be boiling hot). Let biscuits cool in pan for 2 minutes.

MAKES 4 SERVINGS

Each serving provides: 1 Bread Exchange;
   25 Optional Calories
Per serving: 111 calories; 3 g protein; 5 g fat;
   14 g carbohydrate; 27 mg calcium; 475 mg sodium;
   2 mg cholesterol; 0.3 g dietary fiber (this figure does not
   include biscuits; nutrition analysis not available)

Fruit and Cheese Pizza

2 pitas (2 ounces each)
1 tablespoon whipped butter,
  melted
½ teaspoon granulated sugar
1 small nectarine (about 5 ounces)
  or medium peach (about
  ¼ pound), pitted and sliced
1 medium kiwi fruit (about
  3 ounces), pared, cut in half
  lengthwise, and sliced
2 ounces Gorgonzola cheese,
  crumbled

On baking sheet arrange pitas in a single
layer; brush each with half of the melted
butter and then sprinkle each with half of
the sugar. Broil until sugar melts and pitas
are toasted, about 1 minute. Decoratively
arrange half of the nectarine (or peach) and
kiwi fruit slices on each pita, then top each
with half of the cheese. Broil until cheese
is melted, about 1 minute.

MAKES 2 SERVINGS, 1 PIZZA EACH

Each serving provides: 1 Protein Exchange;
    2 Bread Exchanges; 1 Fruit Exchange;
    30 Optional Calories
Per serving with nectarine: 358 calories; 12 g protein;
    12 g fat; 52 g carbohydrate; 174 mg calcium;
    790 mg sodium; 29 mg cholesterol; 3 g dietary fiber
With peach: 345 calories; 12 g protein; 12 g fat;
    49 g carbohydrate; 173 mg calcium; 790 mg sodium;
    29 mg cholesterol; 3 g dietary fiber

Sausage Bread ©

There is no yeast in this bread—just refrigerated all-ready pizza crust dough—which makes this recipe oh-so-easy!

2½ teaspoons olive *or* vegetable oil, divided
13 ounces veal sausage, removed from casing
1 cup *each* diced onions and green *or* red bell peppers
1 small garlic clove, minced
1 teaspoon fennel seed (optional)
Dash *each* salt and pepper
1 refrigerated all-ready pizza crust dough (10 ounces)

Preheat oven to 425°F. In 10-inch skillet heat 2 teaspoons oil; add sausage, onions, bell peppers, and garlic and cook, breaking up large pieces of sausage with a wooden spoon, until sausage is crumbly and no longer pink, and vegetables are soft, about 2 to 3 minutes. If desired, stir in fennel; stir in salt and pepper. Set aside and let cool.

On work surface, press pizza dough into a 12 x 10-inch rectangle. Spread sausage mixture over entire surface of dough, pressing mixture into dough. Starting from wide end, roll dough jelly-roll fashion to enclose filling; pinch each narrow end to seal and tuck ends underneath loaf.

Transfer loaf, seam-side down, to 9 x 5 x 3-inch nonstick loaf pan and bake until golden brown, about 15 minutes. Using pastry brush, brush remaining ½ teaspoon oil over bread and bake 5 minutes longer. Remove pan from oven and let cool for 5 minutes. To serve, cut into 10 equal slices.

MAKES 5 SERVINGS, 2 SLICES EACH

Each serving provides: 2 Protein Exchanges;
    2 Bread Exchanges; ¾ Vegetable Exchange;
    ½ Fat Exchange
Per serving: 314 calories; 21 g protein; 11 g fat;
    29 g carbohydrate; 17 mg calcium; 1,033 mg sodium
    (estimated); 57 mg cholesterol; 1 g dietary fiber (this
    figure does not include pizza dough; nutrition analysis
    not available)

Ham and Brie 'wiches Ⓜ

2 ounces Italian bread, diagonally
  cut into 4 equal slices
1 teaspoon *each* whipped butter,
  Dijon-style mustard, and honey
1 ounce *each* prosciutto (Italian-
  style ham) and Brie cheese (rind
  removed), each cut into 4 equal
  slices
2 teaspoons chopped chives

On baking sheet arrange bread slices in a
single layer and broil, turning once, until
golden, about 30 seconds on each side. Set
aside. In 1-cup microwavable liquid measure
combine butter, mustard, and honey and
microwave on High (100%) for 30 seconds,
until butter is melted; stir to combine.

Using a pastry brush, brush one side of
each slice of bread with ⅛ of the butter mixture. Top each slice of bread with ¼ ounce
prosciutto and ¼ ounce cheese; then brush
each with an equal amount of the remaining
butter mixture. Broil until cheese melts,
about 1 minute. Sprinkle each slice of bread
with ½ teaspoon chives.

MAKES 2 SERVINGS, 2 SLICES EACH

Each serving provides: 1 Protein Exchange;
  1 Bread Exchange; 20 Optional Calories
Per serving: 174 calories; 8 g protein; 7 g fat;
  20 g carbohydrate; 33 mg calcium; 526 mg sodium;
  25 mg cholesterol; 1 g dietary fiber

Italian Pasta Bake Ⓜ

To skim a few minutes from your preparation time, purchase mozzarella cheese that is already shredded.

¼ cup diced onion
1 teaspoon olive *or* vegetable oil
1 large garlic clove, minced
1½ cups canned Italian tomatoes, pureed
2 tablespoons chopped fresh basil *or* 1 teaspoon basil leaves
1½ cups cooked ziti macaroni
3 ounces cooked veal sausage, crumbled
¼ cup part-skim ricotta cheese
1 tablespoon grated Parmesan cheese
1 ounce mozzarella cheese, shredded

In 1-quart microwavable casserole combine onion, oil, and garlic and stir to thoroughly coat; microwave on High (100%) for 1 minute, until onion is tender. Stir in tomatoes and basil; cover with wax paper and microwave on High for 10 minutes, stirring every 2 minutes.

Transfer ¾ cup of tomato mixture to medium mixing bowl; add ziti, sausage, ricotta cheese, and Parmesan cheese and mix well. Spray 1-quart microwavable casserole with nonstick cooking spray; spread ziti mixture evenly in casserole. Spread remaining tomato mixture evenly over ziti mixture and then sprinkle with mozzarella cheese. Microwave on High for 5 minutes, rotating casserole halfway through cooking, until ziti mixture is heated through and cheese is melted.

MAKES 2 SERVINGS

Each serving provides: 2½ Protein Exchanges; 1½ Bread Exchanges; 1¾ Vegetable Exchanges; ½ Fat Exchange; 15 Optional Calories
Per serving: 378 calories; 25 g protein; 15 g fat; 36 g carbohydrate; 276 mg calcium; 984 mg sodium (estimated); 66 mg cholesterol; 3 g dietary fiber

Linguine with Vegetables

To accompany this colorful pasta side dish, toss together an extra-special spinach salad that includes diced ham or cooked shrimp.

2 teaspoons olive *or* vegetable oil
2 small garlic cloves, sliced
1 tablespoon whipped butter
½ cup *each* sliced mushrooms, sliced red onion, and low-fat milk (1% milk fat)
1 teaspoon tomato paste
1 cup *each* frozen whole baby carrots and sugar snap peas *or* Chinese pea pods (snow peas)
1½ cups cooked linguine (hot)
2 ounces grated Parmesan cheese

In 10-inch nonstick skillet heat oil; add garlic and sauté over high heat until golden, 30 seconds to 1 minute. Using a slotted spoon, remove and discard garlic.

In same skillet melt butter; add mushrooms and onion and sauté over high heat until tender-crisp, 1 to 2 minutes. In 1-cup liquid measure combine milk and tomato paste and stir to combine; stir into mushroom-onion mixture and bring to a boil. Reduce heat to low; add carrots and snap peas (or Chinese pea pods), cover, and let simmer until vegetables are heated through, about 5 minutes. Add linguine and cheese and, using 2 forks, toss to combine.

MAKES 2 SERVINGS

Each serving provides: 1 Protein Exchange;
 1½ Bread Exchanges; 3 Vegetable Exchanges;
 1 Fat Exchange; ¼ Milk Exchange; 30 Optional Calories
Per serving: 430 calories; 22 g protein; 17 g fat;
 48 g carbohydrate; 551 mg calcium; 663 mg sodium;
 33 mg cholesterol; 3 g dietary fiber (this figure does not
 include baby carrots; nutrition analysis not available)

Pasta Puttanesca Ⓜ

A classic Neapolitan dish that combines wine, tomatoes, olives, and pasta.

1 tablespoon dry red table wine
1 teaspoon *each* olive oil and
   minced shallot *or* onion
1 garlic clove, minced
½ cup drained canned Italian
   tomatoes, seeded and chopped
6 Gaeta olives, pitted and cut into
   quarters
2 drained canned anchovy fillets,
   cut into ½-inch pieces
1½ teaspoons rinsed drained
   capers
Dash oregano leaves
2 cups cooked linguine (hot)
1½ teaspoons chopped fresh
   Italian (flat-leaf) parsley

In small microwavable bowl combine wine, oil, shallot (or onion), and garlic; microwave on High (100%) for 30 seconds. Add remaining ingredients except linguine and parsley; microwave on Medium-High (70%) for 4 minutes, stirring halfway through cooking.

   To serve, arrange linguine in serving bowl; top with tomato-olive mixture and, using 2 forks, toss to combine. Sprinkle with parsley.

MAKES 2 SERVINGS

Each serving provides: 2 Bread Exchanges;
   ½ Vegetable Exchange; 1 Fat Exchange;
   15 Optional Calories
Per serving: 229 calories; 7 g protein; 6 g fat;
   36 g carbohydrate; 48 mg calcium; 508 mg sodium;
   2 mg cholesterol; 3 g dietary fiber

Variation: Parmesan Pasta Puttanesca —
Before serving, sprinkle with 2 teaspoons grated Parmesan cheese. Increase Optional Calories to 25.

Per serving: 237 calories; 7 g protein; 6 g fat;
   36 g carbohydrate; 71 mg calcium; 570 mg sodium;
   4 mg cholesterol; 3 g dietary fiber

Pasta with Broccoli Rabe ⏲

Enjoy the slightly bitter flavor of broccoli rabe in this Italian-style side dish.

2 teaspoons olive *or* vegetable oil
2 garlic cloves, minced
1 cup trimmed sliced broccoli rabe (base stems removed and cut into 2-inch pieces)
¼ cup *each* drained canned Italian tomatoes, seeded and diced, and canned ready-to-serve chicken broth
1½ cups cooked fettuccine, linguine, *or* spaghetti (hot)
2 tablespoons grated Parmesan cheese
⅛ teaspoon *each* salt and pepper

In 10-inch nonstick skillet heat oil; add garlic and sauté, stirring frequently, for 1 minute. Add broccoli rabe, tomatoes, and broth and stir to combine; cover and cook, stirring occasionally, until broccoli rabe is tender, 3 to 4 minutes. Add remaining ingredients and, using 2 forks, toss to combine.

MAKES 2 SERVINGS

Each serving provides: 1½ Bread Exchanges; 1¼ Vegetable Exchanges; 1 Fat Exchange; 35 Optional Calories
Per serving with fettuccine: 234 calories; 9 g protein; 8 g fat; 32 g carbohydrate; 123 mg calcium; 431 mg sodium; 41 mg cholesterol; 2 g dietary fiber
With linguine *or* spaghetti: 200 calories; 7 g protein; 7 g fat; 28 g carbohydrate; 120 mg calcium; 430 mg sodium; 4 mg cholesterol; 2 g dietary fiber

Always read a recipe through completely before beginning to cook so you can see exactly what you'll need to do. If the recipe calls for cooked pasta, put the water on to boil before you do anything else.

Pasta with Vegetable-Cheese Sauce

Spinach fettuccine, sun-dried tomatoes, and French goat cheese make this recipe a gourmet's delight.

2 teaspoons olive *or* vegetable oil
½ cup *each* thinly sliced onion and carrot
1 small garlic clove, minced
1 teaspoon all-purpose flour
½ packet (about ½ teaspoon) instant chicken broth and seasoning mix
1 cup *each* water, broccoli florets, and cauliflower florets
¼ pound chèvre (French goat cheese)
8 sun-dried tomato halves (not packed in oil), sliced
1½ cups cooked spinach fettuccine (hot)

In 10-inch skillet heat oil; add onion, carrot, and garlic and cook over medium-high heat, stirring frequently, until onion is translucent, about 2 minutes. Sprinkle flour and broth mix over vegetables and stir quickly to combine; cook, stirring constantly, for 1 minute. Add water and stir to combine; cook over high heat until mixture comes to a boil. Reduce heat to low; add broccoli and cauliflower and stir to combine. Cover and let simmer until florets are tender-crisp, about 5 minutes. Stir in cheese and tomatoes and cook, stirring constantly, until cheese melts, about 1 minute.

To serve, on serving platter arrange fettuccine and top with vegetable mixture.

MAKES 2 SERVINGS

Each serving provides: 2 Protein Exchanges;
    1½ Bread Exchanges; 5 Vegetable Exchanges;
    1 Fat Exchange; 10 Optional Calories
Per serving: 470 calories; 21 g protein; 23 g fat;
    48 g carbohydrate; 170 mg calcium; 646 mg sodium;
    82 mg cholesterol; 8 g dietary fiber (this figure does not
    include broccoli florets; nutrition analysis not available)

Variation: Pasta with Vegetable-Ricotta Sauce —Substitute ½ cup part-skim ricotta cheese for the chèvre. Decrease Protein Exchange to 1 Exchange.

Per serving: 342 calories; 17 g protein; 11 g fat;
    47 g carbohydrate; 240 mg calcium; 368 mg sodium;
    48 mg cholesterol; 8 g dietary fiber (this figure does not
    include broccoli florets; nutrition analysis not available)

Minted Orzo with Nuts and Currants

1 teaspoon margarine
½ ounce pignolias (pine nuts)
¼ cup canned ready-to-serve
   chicken broth
2 tablespoons dried currants
1½ ounces uncooked orzo (rice-
   shaped macaroni), cooked
   according to package
   directions and drained
1 tablespoon chopped fresh mint
¼ teaspoon salt
⅛ teaspoon pepper

In 10-inch nonstick skillet melt margarine; add pignolias and cook over medium heat, stirring frequently, until lightly browned, 2 to 3 minutes. Stir in broth and currants; cook until liquid is reduced by half and currants are plumped, 1 to 2 minutes. Add remaining ingredients and stir to combine; cook, stirring frequently, until orzo is heated through and flavors blend, 2 to 3 minutes.

MAKES 2 SERVINGS

Each serving provides: ½ Protein Exchange;
   1 Bread Exchange; 1 Fat Exchange; ½ Fruit Exchange;
   5 Optional Calories
Per serving: 162 calories; 5 g protein; 6 g fat;
   24 g carbohydrate; 19 mg calcium; 419 mg sodium;
   0 mg cholesterol; 1 g dietary fiber (this figure does not
   include pignolias; nutrition analysis not available)

Variation: Minted Orzo with Nuts and Raisins — Substitute 2 tablespoons dark raisins for the currants.

Per serving: 164 calories; 5 g protein; 6 g fat;
   25 g carbohydrate; 16 mg calcium; 420 mg sodium;
   0 mg cholesterol; 1 g dietary fiber (this figure does not
   include pignolias; nutrition analysis not available)

Orzo Pilaf

1 tablespoon whipped butter
1 teaspoon olive *or* vegetable oil
½ cup diced shiitake *or*
  white mushrooms
1 garlic clove, minced
¼ cup canned ready-to-serve
  chicken broth
1 tablespoon chopped fresh
  parsley
1½ ounces uncooked orzo
  (rice-shaped macaroni), cooked
  according to package
  directions and drained
⅛ teaspoon salt
Dash pepper
1 tablespoon grated Parmesan
  cheese

In 10-inch nonstick skillet combine butter and oil and heat until butter is melted; add mushrooms and garlic and sauté over medium-high heat, stirring frequently, until mushrooms are softened, 1 to 2 minutes. Stir in broth and parsley and cook, stirring occasionally, until liquid is reduced by half, 2 to 3 minutes. Stir in orzo, salt, and pepper and cook, stirring frequently, until orzo is heated through, 1 to 2 minutes. Add Parmesan cheese and stir to thoroughly combine.

MAKES 2 SERVINGS

Each serving provides: 1 Bread Exchange;
  ½ Vegetable Exchange; ½ Fat Exchange;
  45 Optional Calories
Per serving: 147 calories; 4 g protein; 6 g fat;
  18 g carbohydrate; 48 mg calcium; 342 mg sodium;
  10 mg cholesterol; 1 g dietary fiber

Variation: Rice Pilaf — Substitute 1 cup cooked long-grain rice for the orzo.

Per serving: 175 calories; 3 g protein; 6 g fat;
  26 g carbohydrate; 49 mg calcium; 340 mg sodium;
  10 mg cholesterol; 1 g dietary fiber

Asian Noodle Salad

1½ cups cooked cellophane
    noodles
1 cup (about 4 ounces) drained
    canned whole baby corn ears
½ cup drained canned straw *or*
    button mushrooms
¼ cup *each* broccoli florets, sliced
    carrots, Chinese pea pods
    (snow peas), stem ends and
    string removed, and green *or*
    wax beans, blanched
¼ cup *each* red *or* yellow bell
    pepper strips and diagonally
    sliced scallions (green onions)
2 teaspoons *each* rice vinegar and
    teriyaki sauce
1½ teaspoons peanut *or*
    vegetable oil
½ teaspoon Chinese sesame oil
⅛ teaspoon grated pared
    gingerroot
1 small garlic clove, mashed

In medium salad bowl combine noodles and vegetables. Using a fork, in cup or small bowl combine remaining ingredients and stir to combine. Pour dressing over noodle-vegetable mixture and toss to coat.

MAKES 2 SERVINGS

Each serving provides: 2 Bread Exchanges;
    2 Vegetable Exchanges; 1 Fat Exchange
Per serving: 216 calories; 5 g protein; 5 g fat;
    39 g carbohydrate; 45 mg calcium; 360 mg sodium;
    0 mg cholesterol; 3 g dietary fiber (this figure does not
    include broccoli florets; nutrition analysis not available)

Cold India Pasta ©

½ cup plain low-fat yogurt
2 tablespoons plus 2 teaspoons
   instant nonfat dry milk powder
1 tablespoon rice vinegar
¼ teaspoon ground cumin
⅛ teaspoon pepper
1½ cups cooked rigatoni *or* ziti
   macaroni
¼ cup *each* finely diced radishes
   and celery
1½ teaspoons minced scallion
   (green onion)
1 teaspoon *each* chopped fresh
   mint and cilantro (Chinese
   parsley) *or* Italian (flat-leaf)
   parsley

Using a wire whisk, in medium mixing bowl combine yogurt, milk powder, vinegar, cumin, and pepper and stir to thoroughly combine. Add remaining ingredients and stir to coat. Cover with plastic wrap and refrigerate until ready to serve.

MAKES 2 SERVINGS

Each serving provides: 1½ Bread Exchanges;
   ½ Vegetable Exchange; ¾ Milk Exchange
Per serving: 180 calories; 9 g protein; 1 g fat;
   33 g carbohydrate; 195 mg calcium; 89 mg sodium;
   4 mg cholesterol; 2 g dietary fiber

Pasta Slaw

While the spaghetti is cooking, you'll have time to prepare the vegetables and dressing.

1 cup cooked thin spaghetti (hot)
1 cup *each* finely shredded green cabbage and carrots
½ cup *each* diced red bell pepper and red onion
1 small garlic clove, minced
1 tablespoon *each* chopped fresh parsley, lemon juice, and balsamic, red wine, *or* apple cider vinegar
2 teaspoons olive *or* vegetable oil
¼ teaspoon *each* oregano leaves, salt, and pepper

In medium salad bowl combine spaghetti, vegetables, and garlic. Using a fork, in cup or small bowl combine remaining ingredients and stir to combine. Pour dressing over spaghetti-vegetable mixture and toss to coat.

MAKES 2 SERVINGS

Each serving provides: 1 Bread Exchange;
    3 Vegetable Exchanges; 1 Fat Exchange
Per serving: 175 calories; 4 g protein; 5 g fat;
    29 g carbohydrate; 59 mg calcium; 301 mg sodium;
    0 mg cholesterol; 3 g dietary fiber

Salmon and Pasta Salad

If tuna is more to your liking, drained canned tuna can be substituted for the salmon.

¼ cup plain low-fat yogurt
1 tablespoon plus 1 teaspoon reduced-calorie mayonnaise
1 tablespoon lemon juice
1 teaspoon chopped fresh basil *or* ¼ teaspoon basil leaves
Dash *each* oregano leaves, salt, and pepper
1 cup cooked ditalini *or* small shell macaroni (hot)
4 ounces drained canned salmon, flaked
½ cup *each* sliced celery, diced red bell pepper, and diced red onion

In medium mixing bowl combine yogurt, mayonnaise, lemon juice, basil, oregano, salt, and pepper and stir to combine. Add remaining ingredients and toss to coat. Serve immediately or cover and refrigerate until ready to serve. Stir again just before serving.

MAKES 2 SERVINGS

Each serving provides: 2 Protein Exchanges; 1 Bread Exchange; 1½ Vegetable Exchanges; 1 Fat Exchange; ¼ Milk Exchange
Per serving: 229 calories; 17 g protein; 7 g fat; 25 g carbohydrate; 227 mg calcium; 467 mg sodium; 27 mg cholesterol; 1 g dietary fiber

Microwave Noodle Pudding Ⓜ

Serve warm or chilled.

½ medium banana (about
   3 ounces), peeled and sliced
½ cup evaporated skimmed milk
⅓ cup *each* instant nonfat dry
   milk powder and water
1 egg
2 tablespoons granulated sugar
¼ teaspoon ground cinnamon
2 cups cooked bow-tie noodles
6 dried apricot halves, diced,
   divided
3 tablespoons dark raisins,
   divided

In blender container combine banana, milk, milk powder, water, egg, sugar, and cinnamon; process on high speed until banana is pureed and mixture is thoroughly combined, about 1½ minutes, scraping down sides of container as necessary.

Spray 2-quart microwavable casserole with nonstick cooking spray; add noodles and all but 1 tablespoon each of the apricots and raisins and toss to combine. Pour banana mixture over noodle-fruit mixture. Cover casserole with vented plastic wrap and microwave on Medium-High (70%) for 3 minutes, stirring halfway through cooking. Stir noodle mixture again, re-cover with vented plastic wrap, and microwave on Low (30%) for 5 minutes. Let stand for 2 minutes, until set. Sprinkle remaining apricots and raisins over pudding.

MAKES 4 SERVINGS

Each serving provides: ¼ Protein Exchange;
   1 Bread Exchange; 1 Fruit Exchange;
   ½ Milk Exchange; 30 Optional Calories
Per serving: 235 calories; 10 g protein; 3 g fat;
   44 g carbohydrate; 185 mg calcium; 88 mg sodium;
   96 mg cholesterol; 3 g dietary fiber

Chili Pepper and Rice Casserole ⓒⓂ

1 cup cooked long-grain rice
1 ounce Monterey Jack cheese
   with jalapeño peppers, divided
2 tablespoons *each* sour cream,
   chopped tomato, and seeded
   and diced drained canned
   green chili pepper
1 tablespoon chopped fresh
   parsley

In medium mixing bowl combine rice, $\frac{1}{2}$ ounce cheese, the sour cream, tomato, pepper, and parsley; mix well. Spray 2-cup microwavable casserole with nonstick cooking spray; spread rice mixture evenly in casserole, then sprinkle with remaining $\frac{1}{2}$ ounce cheese. Microwave on High (100%) for 5 minutes, rotating casserole $\frac{1}{2}$ turn halfway through cooking, until rice is heated through and cheese is melted.

MAKES 2 SERVINGS

Each serving provides: $\frac{1}{2}$ Protein Exchange;
   1 Bread Exchange; $\frac{1}{4}$ Vegetable Exchange;
   35 Optional Calories
Per serving: 202 calories; 6 g protein; 8 g fat;
   27 g carbohydrate; 128 mg calcium; 155 mg sodium;
   21 mg cholesterol; 1 g dietary fiber

Fruited Rice with Cinnamon Ⓜ

To prevent dried fruit from sticking to knife while dicing, spray knife blade with nonstick cooking spray.

1 teaspoon margarine
½ ounce sliced almonds
¼ cup *each* diced onion and canned ready-to-serve chicken broth
4 dried apricot halves, diced
2 tablespoons golden raisins
2 cups cooked long-grain rice
¼ teaspoon ground cinnamon
⅛ teaspoon *each* salt and white pepper

In 1-quart microwavable shallow casserole heat margarine on High (100%) for 30 seconds, until melted. Add almonds and onion and microwave on High for 1 minute, stirring once halfway through cooking, until onion is softened. Add broth, apricots, and raisins and microwave on High for 2 minutes. Add rice and stir to combine; microwave on High for 2 minutes, until rice is heated through. Stir in cinnamon, salt, and pepper.

MAKES 4 SERVINGS

Each serving provides: ¼ Protein Exchange; 1 Bread Exchange; ⅛ Vegetable Exchange; ½ Fat Exchange; ½ Fruit Exchange; 3 Optional Calories
Per serving: 161 calories; 3 g protein; 3 g fat; 30 g carbohydrate; 27 mg calcium; 144 mg sodium; 0 mg cholesterol; 2 g dietary fiber

Dried fruits are good sources of potassium and iron, as well as fiber. But since they also are high in calories, you'll find the recommended serving size is smaller than that for the fresh fruit.

Pork-Fried Rice ©

2 teaspoons peanut *or* vegetable
   oil
1 cup *each* diagonally sliced
   scallions (green onions),
   diagonally sliced celery, and
   sliced mushrooms
1½ cups cooked instant rice
1 ounce cooked pork, shredded
1 tablespoon reduced-sodium soy
   sauce
1 egg, lightly beaten

In 9-inch nonstick skillet heat oil; add vegetables and cook over high heat, stirring frequently, until tender-crisp, 3 to 4 minutes. Add rice, pork, and soy sauce and cook, stirring constantly, until rice is lightly browned, 2 to 3 minutes. Stir in egg and, continuing to stir, cook until egg is set, about 1 minute.

MAKES 2 SERVINGS

Each serving provides: 1 Protein Exchange;
   1½ Bread Exchanges; 3 Vegetable Exchanges;
   1 Fat Exchange
Per serving: 283 calories; 12 g protein; 9 g fat;
   38 g carbohydrate; 74 mg calcium; 400 mg sodium;
   150 mg cholesterol; 4 g dietary fiber

Variation: Chicken-Fried Rice—Substitute 1 ounce shredded cooked chicken for the pork.

Per serving: 277 calories; 12 g protein; 9 g fat;
   38 g carbohydrate; 75 mg calcium; 403 mg sodium;
   150 mg cholesterol; 4 g dietary fiber

Spanish Rice Ⓒ Ⓜ

½ cup *each* diced onion and
  green bell pepper
2 teaspoons olive *or* vegetable oil
1 small garlic clove, minced
1 cup canned Italian tomatoes
  (with liquid); drain and chop
  tomatoes, reserving liquid
2 ounces uncooked instant rice
Dash *each* crushed red pepper,
  salt, and pepper

In 1-quart microwavable casserole combine onion, bell pepper, oil, and garlic and stir to coat. Microwave on High (100%) for 3 minutes, until vegetables are softened, stirring once after 1 minute. Add tomatoes, reserved tomato liquid, and rice and stir to combine; cover with vented plastic wrap and microwave on High for 10 minutes, until rice is tender, stirring once after 5 minutes. Remove from oven, stir in seasonings, and let stand for 1 minute, until flavors blend.

MAKES 2 SERVINGS

Each serving provides: 1 Bread Exchange;
  2 Vegetable Exchanges; 1 Fat Exchange
Per serving: 192 calories; 4 g protein; 5 g fat;
  33 g carbohydrate; 47 mg calcium; 264 mg sodium;
  0 mg cholesterol; 2 g dietary fiber

Tomato Risotto with Shrimp Ⓜ

Risotto must be made with short-grain rice. Arborio rice is the short-grain rice of northern Italy.

¼ cup chopped onion
1 teaspoon olive *or* vegetable oil
1 garlic clove, minced
3 ounces uncooked short-grain rice (arborio rice)
1½ cups water
¼ cup drained canned Italian tomatoes, seeded and diced
1 packet instant chicken broth and seasoning mix
5 ounces shelled and deveined small shrimp, quartered
1 tablespoon *each* grated Parmesan cheese and whipped butter
1 teaspoon chopped fresh Italian (flat-leaf) parsley
Dash pepper
½ teaspoon grated lemon peel
Garnish: Italian (flat-leaf) parsley sprig

In 1-quart microwavable shallow casserole combine onion, oil, and garlic and stir to thoroughly coat; microwave on High (100%) for 1 minute, until onion is tender. Add rice and stir to combine; microwave on High for 30 seconds. Add water, tomatoes, and broth mix and stir to combine; microwave on High for 10 minutes, until thickened, stirring every 2 minutes. Add shrimp and microwave on High for 4 minutes, until shrimp turn pink, stirring halfway through cooking. Add cheese, butter, chopped parsley, and pepper and stir well to combine.

To serve, transfer shrimp mixture to serving platter and top with lemon peel; garnish with parsley sprig.

MAKES 2 SERVINGS

Each serving provides: 2 Protein Exchanges;
    1½ Bread Exchanges; ½ Vegetable Exchange;
    ½ Fat Exchange; 45 Optional Calories
Per serving: 306 calories; 19 g protein; 7 g fat;
    39 g carbohydrate; 100 mg calcium; 728 mg sodium;
    117 mg cholesterol; 1 g dietary fiber

Sauces and Dressings

When it comes to today's life-style, "quick" and "easy" are the two key words that come to mind. In this chapter you'll find quick and easy recipes for all kinds of sauces, dressings, and dips. Try Mint Pesto with Pitas or Fresh Tomato Coulis; Caviar Dip or Pecan Vinaigrette. Each is fresh, delicious, and can go a long way toward turning a simple dish into an elegant meal.

Microwave Apple Butter ⓒⓜ

You can keep this delicious mixture for up to 1 week in the refrigerator.

2 pounds McIntosh apples, cored, pared, and quartered
¼ cup maple syrup
¼ teaspoon ground cinnamon

In 3-quart microwavable casserole combine all ingredients; cover with vented plastic wrap and microwave on High (100%) for 15 minutes, until apples are tender.

Transfer apple mixture to blender container and process until smooth. Return to casserole and microwave on High for 5 minutes, until mixture thickens. Set aside and let cool, about 20 minutes. Transfer to jar with tight-fitting cover and refrigerate until ready to use.

MAKES 8 SERVINGS,
ABOUT 2 TABLESPOONS EACH

Each serving provides: 1 Fruit Exchange;
  30 Optional Calories
Per serving: 80 calories; 0.1 g protein; 0.3 g fat;
  21 g carbohydrate; 15 mg calcium; 1 mg sodium;
  0 mg cholesterol; 2 g dietary fiber

Caviar Dip

½ cup plain low-fat yogurt
¼ cup thawed frozen dairy
   whipped topping
2 tablespoons minced red onion
1 tablespoon sour cream
1 ounce rinsed drained red *or*
   golden caviar

In small bowl combine all ingredients and mix well. Cover with plastic wrap and refrigerate until ready to serve. Just before serving, stir well.

MAKES 4 SERVINGS, ABOUT ¼ CUP EACH

Each serving provides: ¼ Protein Exchange;
   ¼ Milk Exchange; 20 Optional Calories
Per serving: 57 calories; 3 g protein; 3 g fat;
   4 g carbohydrate; 57 mg calcium; 133 mg sodium;
   45 mg cholesterol; trace dietary fiber

Concerned about the sodium level of caviar? Put the caviar in a fine mesh tea strainer and rinse it before you add it to a recipe. This will reduce its salty flavor.

Chunky Salsa Dip ⊙

Serve with taco shell pieces for dipping.

½ cup chopped scallions (green
  onions)
1 large plum tomato, chopped
2 tablespoons *each* sour cream
  and lime juice (no sugar added)
1 tablespoon plus 1 teaspoon
  reduced-calorie mayonnaise
½ teaspoon salt
4 to 6 drops hot sauce
Dash ground red pepper

In small bowl combine all ingredients and
mix well. Cover with plastic wrap and
refrigerate until ready to serve. Just
before serving, stir well.

MAKES 4 SERVINGS, ABOUT ¼ CUP EACH

Each serving provides: ½ Vegetable Exchange;
  ½ Fat Exchange; 15 Optional Calories
Per serving: 36 calories; 1 g protein; 3 g fat;
  2 g carbohydrate; 20 mg calcium; 321 mg sodium;
  5 mg cholesterol; 0.5 g dietary fiber

Seafood Dip ☉

Delicious served with assorted vegetables for dipping.

¼ pound thawed frozen imitation
    fish
¼ cup fresh dill
3 tablespoons whipped cream
    cheese
1 tablespoon plus 1 teaspoon
    reduced-calorie mayonnaise
1 tablespoon *each* pickle relish,
    lemon juice, and
    Worcestershire sauce

In work bowl of food processor combine all ingredients and process until smooth, about 1 minute, scraping down sides of container as necessary. Transfer mixture to small serving bowl; cover with plastic wrap and refrigerate until ready to serve. Just before serving, stir well.

MAKES 4 SERVINGS, ABOUT ¼ CUP EACH

Each serving provides: 1 Protein Exchange;
   ½ Fat Exchange; 35 Optional Calories
Per serving: 77 calories; 5 g protein; 4 g fat;
   5 g carbohydrate; 22 mg calcium; 175 mg sodium;
   17 mg cholesterol; dietary fiber data not available

Crunchy Salad Dressing ⊙

½ cup plain low-fat yogurt
2 tablespoons sour cream
2 teaspoons *each* reduced-calorie mayonnaise and red wine vinegar
1 tablespoon *each* finely diced green bell pepper, finely diced red onion, pickle relish, and minced fresh parsley *or* dill
½ packet (½ teaspoon) instant chicken *or* beef broth and seasoning mix

Using a wire whisk, in small mixing bowl combine yogurt, sour cream, mayonnaise, and vinegar and stir to combine; stir in remaining ingredients. Cover with plastic wrap and refrigerate until ready to use.

MAKES 4 SERVINGS, ABOUT 3 TABLESPOONS EACH

Each serving provides: ¼ Fat Exchange; ¼ Milk Exchange; 25 Optional Calories
Per serving: 48 calories; 2 g protein; 3 g fat; 4 g carbohydrate; 63 mg calcium; 194 mg sodium; 6 mg cholesterol; 0.1 g dietary fiber

Cucumber-Dill Dressing ©

¾ cup buttermilk
¼ cup sour cream
2 tablespoons chopped fresh dill
1 teaspoon freshly squeezed
   lemon juice
½ teaspoon *each* granulated
   sugar and salt
⅛ teaspoon white pepper
½ cup minced seeded pared
   cucumber

Using a wire whisk, in medium mixing bowl combine all ingredients except cucumber, stirring until smooth. Stir in cucumber. Cover with plastic wrap and refrigerate until flavors blend, at least 30 minutes. Stir again before serving.

MAKES 4 SERVINGS, ABOUT ⅓ CUP EACH

Each serving provides: ¼ Vegetable Exchange;
   ¼ Milk Exchange; 35 Optional Calories
Per serving: 55 calories; 2 g protein; 3 g fat;
   4 g carbohydrate; 82 mg calcium; 331 mg sodium;
   8 mg cholesterol; 0.1 g dietary fiber

Citrus Salsa ⊙

Serve over broiled chicken or fish.

½ cup orange and grapefruit
    sections (no sugar added), diced
2 tablespoons *each* minced red
    onion and green bell pepper
1 tablespoon *each* chopped fresh
    cilantro (Chinese parsley) *or*
    Italian (flat-leaf) parsley and
    lime juice (no sugar added)
2 teaspoons olive oil
1 teaspoon seeded and minced
    jalapeño pepper
½ teaspoon salt
Dash ground red pepper

In small bowl combine all ingredients and mix well. Cover with plastic wrap and refrigerate until ready to serve. Just before serving, stir well.

MAKES 2 SERVINGS, ABOUT ⅓ CUP EACH

Each serving provides: ¼ Vegetable Exchange;
    1 Fat Exchange; ½ Fruit Exchange
Per serving: 67 calories; 1 g protein; 5 g fat;
    7 g carbohydrate; 21 mg calcium; 549 mg sodium;
    0 mg cholesterol; 1 g dietary fiber

Fresh Tomato Coulis Ⓜ

Serve this thick tomato mixture over pasta, rice, poultry, or seafood.

¼ cup minced shallots *or onion*
1 tablespoon plus 1 teaspoon
   olive oil
12 large plum tomatoes, blanched,
   peeled, seeded, and chopped
2 bay leaves
¼ teaspoon thyme leaves
2 tablespoons *each* minced fresh
   Italian (flat-leaf) parsley and
   fresh basil
Dash *each* salt and pepper

In 1½-quart microwavable casserole combine shallots (or onion) and oil and stir to coat; microwave on High (100%) for 30 seconds. Add tomatoes, bay leaves, and thyme and stir to combine; microwave on High for 4 minutes, stirring once halfway through cooking. Remove and discard bay leaves. Add parsley, basil, salt, and pepper and stir to combine. Let stand for 1 minute, until flavors blend.

MAKES 4 SERVINGS, ABOUT ⅔ CUP EACH

Each serving provides: 3⅛ Vegetable Exchanges;
   1 Fat Exchange
Per serving: 83 calories; 2 g protein; 5 g fat;
   10 g carbohydrate; 34 mg calcium; 48 mg sodium;
   0 mg cholesterol; 1 g dietary fiber

Your body will absorb iron better in the presence of vitamin C, so it's a good idea to eat iron-rich foods along with vitamin C-rich foods. Some suggestions: meatballs and spaghetti sauce; a roast beef sandwich with an orange for dessert.

Herbed Green Sauce ☻

Few recipes are as versatile as this basil-flavored sauce. Serve it over chilled poached chicken or salmon, toss it with pasta for a delicious side dish, or use it as a salad dressing.

⅔ cup cottage cheese
½ cup evaporated skimmed milk
3 tablespoons whipped cream
   cheese
2 tablespoons plus 2 teaspoons
   reduced-calorie mayonnaise
2 tablespoons lemon juice
½ garlic clove
¼ teaspoon salt
⅛ teaspoon ground white pepper
½ cup firmly packed basil leaves

In blender container combine all ingredients except basil and process on high speed for 2 minutes, scraping down sides of container as necessary. Add basil and process until smooth. Transfer to bowl, cover with plastic wrap, and refrigerate until ready to use.

MAKES 8 SERVINGS, ABOUT ¼ CUP EACH

Each serving provides: ¼ Protein Exchange;
   ½ Fat Exchange; 25 Optional Calories
Per serving: 61 calories; 4 g protein; 3 g fat;
   4 g carbohydrate; 90 mg calcium; 209 mg sodium;
   9 mg cholesterol; dietary fiber data not available

Mint Pesto with Pitas

The pesto, a creamy mixture of fresh mint, raisins, and walnuts, can be stored in a covered container in your refrigerator for up to 2 weeks. Try it tossed with cooked pasta or rice or as a dip with crudités rather than pitas.

1 cup firmly packed fresh mint (reserve 1 mint sprig for garnish)
¼ cup golden raisins
½ ounce walnut halves (reserve 1 walnut half for garnish)
3 tablespoons whipped cream cheese
1 tablespoon olive *or* vegetable oil
1 small shallot
4 pitas (1 ounce each), cut into pieces

In work bowl of food processor combine all ingredients except reserved mint sprig, walnut half, and the pitas and process until smooth, about 1 minute, scraping down sides of container as necessary.

To serve, transfer mixture to serving bowl and garnish with reserved mint sprig and walnut. Serve with pitas for dipping.

MAKES 4 SERVINGS,
ABOUT 3 TABLESPOONS PESTO EACH

Each serving provides: ¼ Protein Exchange;
    1 Bread Exchange; 1 Fat Exchange; ½ Fruit Exchange;
    25 Optional Calories
Per serving: 173 calories; 4 g protein; 6 g fat;
    27 g carbohydrate; 25 mg calcium; 209 mg sodium;
    7 mg cholesterol; 1 g dietary fiber (this figure does not
    include mint; nutrition analysis not available)

Raisin-Onion Sauce Ⓜ

Serve this warm versatile sauce over poultry or ham, or refrigerate and serve as a salad dressing.

½ cup diced onion
¼ cup golden raisins
1 tablespoon plus 1 teaspoon
   vegetable oil
¼ cup water
1 tablespoon *each* rice vinegar,
   Dijon-style mustard, and honey

In small microwavable mixing bowl combine onion, raisins, and oil and stir to combine; cover with vented plastic wrap and microwave on High (100%) for 4 minutes, until raisins are plumped, stirring once halfway through cooking. Transfer mixture to blender container; add remaining ingredients and process until smooth. Return mixture to microwavable bowl; cover with vented plastic wrap and microwave on High for 2 minutes, until flavors blend.

MAKES 4 SERVINGS, ABOUT ¼ CUP EACH

Each serving provides: ¼ Vegetable Exchange;
   1 Fat Exchange; ½ Fruit Exchange; 15 Optional Calories
Per serving: 95 calories; 1 g protein; 5 g fat;
   14 g carbohydrate; 10 mg calcium; 115 mg sodium;
   0 mg cholesterol; 1 g dietary fiber

Avocado Relish

A colorful addition to broiled chicken or fish.

½ medium avocado (about
    ¼ pound), pared and finely diced
2 tablespoons lime juice (no sugar
    added)
¼ cup *each* diced red onion, red
    bell pepper, and green bell
    pepper
2 large plum tomatoes, diced
1 tablespoon *each* chopped fresh
    cilantro (Chinese parsley) *or*
    Italian (flat-leaf) parsley, and
    seeded mild *or* hot chili pepper
2 small garlic cloves, chopped
2 teaspoons olive *or* vegetable oil
Dash *each* salt and pepper

In small bowl combine avocado and lime juice; set aside. In separate small bowl combine remaining ingredients and mix well; carefully fold in avocado mixture. Cover with plastic wrap and refrigerate until flavors blend, at least 30 minutes. Just before serving, stir well.

MAKES 4 SERVINGS, ABOUT ½ CUP EACH

Each serving provides: 1 Vegetable Exchange;
    1½ Fat Exchanges
Per serving: 76 calories; 1 g protein; 6 g fat;
    6 g carbohydrate; 12 mg calcium; 40 mg sodium;
    0 mg cholesterol; 1 g dietary fiber

Pecan Vinaigrette

⅓ cup water
2 tablespoons thawed frozen
   concentrated orange juice
   (no sugar added)
2 teaspoons *each* rice vinegar,
   teriyaki sauce, and vegetable oil
1 teaspoon *each* honey and
   Dijon-style mustard
1 ounce shelled pecans, toasted
   and finely ground

In blender container combine all ingredients except pecans and process until combined. Transfer mixture to small serving bowl; add pecans and stir to combine. Cover with plastic wrap and refrigerate until ready to serve. Just before serving, stir well.

MAKES 4 SERVINGS, ABOUT ¼ CUP EACH

Each serving provides: ½ Protein Exchange;
   1 Fat Exchange; ¼ Fruit Exchange; 5 Optional Calories
Per serving: 91 calories; 1 g protein; 7 g fat;
   7 g carbohydrate; 6 mg calcium; 154 mg sodium;
   0 mg cholesterol; 1 g dietary fiber

Snacks and Beverages

Dieting doesn't mean giving up snacks, and our recipes prove it! As long as you plan them, snacks can add zip to your weight-loss program. Snack foods are also convenient for those people who prefer to "graze," eating several small meals a day. Use the microwave oven to make Sugar-Spiced Pecans, Santa Fe Peanuts, and Honey-Sesame Popcorn, three crunchy and satisfying super-speedy snacks everyone will love. And for a beverage change-of-pace, try Sparkling Tea Punch, Cranberry Cooler, or Kir Spritzer. They're simple to make and so refreshing!

Honey-Sesame Popcorn Ⓒ Ⓜ

1 tablespoon whipped butter
2 teaspoons *each* honey and
   sesame seed, toasted
4 cups prepared plain popcorn

In small microwavable cup or bowl combine butter and honey and microwave on High (100%) for 1 minute, until melted. Stir in sesame seed. In medium mixing bowl arrange popcorn; pour honey mixture evenly over popcorn and toss to coat.

MAKES 2 SERVINGS

Each serving provides: 1 Bread Exchange;
   65 Optional Calories
Per serving: 110 calories; 2 g protein; 5 g fat;
   16 g carbohydrate; 32 mg calcium; 30 mg sodium;
   8 mg cholesterol; dietary fiber data not available

Store honey in a tightly closed jar in a cool, dark, dry place. If the jar lid isn't tight, the honey may develop a moldy crust.

Marshmallow-Popcorn Snack ⓒⓜ

½ ounce miniature marshmallows
2 tablespoons whipped butter
1 teaspoon margarine
2 cups prepared plain popcorn
½ ounce salted dry-roasted
     peanuts, chopped

In small microwavable mixing bowl combine marshmallows, butter, and margarine and microwave on Medium (50%) for 2 minutes, until mixture is smooth and creamy, stirring halfway through cooking.

In medium mixing bowl combine popcorn and peanuts and toss to combine; pour marshmallow mixture evenly over popcorn mixture and stir well to thoroughly coat. Spray 7⅜ x 3⅝ x 2¼-inch nonstick loaf pan with nonstick cooking spray; transfer marshmallow-popcorn mixture to loaf pan and firmly pat into bottom of pan. Cover marshmallow-popcorn mixture with sheet of wax paper and refrigerate until firm, 20 to 30 minutes. Remove marshmallow-popcorn mixture from loaf pan and cut in half crosswise.

MAKES 2 SERVINGS

Each serving provides: ½ Protein Exchange;
     ½ Bread Exchange; 1 Fat Exchange;
     75 Optional Calories
Per serving: 154 calories; 3 g protein; 11 g fat;
     12 g carbohydrate; 4 mg calcium; 146 mg sodium;
     16 mg cholesterol; dietary fiber data not available

Santa Fe Peanuts Ⓜ

1 ounce salted dry-roasted
  peanuts
1 teaspoon peanut *or* vegetable oil
¼ teaspoon *each* chili powder
  and hot sauce

In 1-quart microwavable shallow casserole combine all ingredients and stir to thoroughly coat. Microwave on High (100%) for 2 minutes, stirring halfway through cooking. Set aside and let cool for 5 minutes.

MAKES 2 SERVINGS

Each serving provides: 1 Protein Exchange;
    1½ Fat Exchanges
Per serving: 101 calories; 4 g protein; 9 g fat;
    3 g carbohydrate; 1 mg calcium; 144 mg sodium;
    0 mg cholesterol; dietary fiber data not available

Spiced Chick-Pea Snack ☻

4 ounces rinsed well-drained canned chick-peas
¼ teaspoon *each* garlic powder, ground cumin, and curry powder
⅛ teaspoon *each* salt and pepper

Preheat oven to 350°F. Pat chick-peas dry with paper towels; set aside. In small mixing bowl combine garlic powder, cumin, curry powder, salt, and pepper; add chick-peas and turn to thoroughly coat with seasonings.

Spray nonstick baking sheet with nonstick cooking spray and arrange chick-peas on sheet. Bake for 15 minutes, stirring every 5 minutes until dry. Store in airtight container until ready to serve.

MAKES 2 SERVINGS, ABOUT ⅓ CUP EACH

Each serving provides: 1 Bread Exchange
Per serving: 72 calories; 4 g protein; 1 g fat;
    12 g carbohydrate; 25 mg calcium; 324 mg sodium
    (estimated); 0 mg cholesterol; 1 g dietary fiber

Sugar-Spiced Pecans Ⓜ

1 tablespoon *each* whipped butter
    and confectioners' sugar
¼ teaspoon ground cinnamon
⅛ teaspoon ground nutmeg
Dash ground cloves
1 ounce pecan halves

In 1-quart microwavable shallow casserole combine butter, sugar, cinnamon, nutmeg, and cloves and microwave on High (100%) for 1 minute, until melted. Add pecans and stir to coat; microwave on High for 2 minutes, until pecans are glazed. Transfer nuts to sheet of wax paper; set aside and let cool, until sugar mixture hardens, 5 to 10 minutes.

MAKES 2 SERVINGS

Each serving provides: 1 Protein Exchange;
   1 Fat Exchange; 55 Optional Calories
Per serving: 136 calories; 1 g protein; 13 g fat;
   7 g carbohydrate; 10 mg calcium; 30 mg sodium;
   8 mg cholesterol; 1 g dietary fiber

Cold Avocado Soup

¾ medium avocado (about
    6 ounces), pared and diced
1 cup water, divided
½ cup plain low-fat yogurt
3 tablespoons sour cream
1 tablespoon lemon juice
1 packet instant onion broth and
    seasoning mix
Dash *each* white pepper and hot
    sauce
½ cup diced tomato

In blender container combine avocado, ¼ cup water, the yogurt, sour cream, lemon juice, and broth mix; using on-off motion, process on medium speed until pureed, scraping down sides of container as necessary. Remove center of blender cover and, with blender running, gradually add remaining ¾ cup water. Add pepper and hot sauce and process on high speed until combined. Transfer to soup tureen; cover and refrigerate until chilled, at least 30 minutes.

To serve, ladle soup into 4 soup bowls and top each portion with 2 tablespoons tomato.

MAKES 4 SERVINGS, ABOUT ¾ CUP EACH

Each serving provides: ¼ Vegetable Exchange;
    1½ Fat Exchanges; ¼ Milk Exchange;
    30 Optional Calories
Per serving: 97 calories; 3 g protein; 7 g fat;
    6 g carbohydrate; 70 mg calcium; 224 mg sodium;
    6 mg cholesterol; 1 g dietary fiber

Cheese Toasts

2 ounces French bread, cut
    diagonally into 12 equal slices
2 teaspoons olive *or* vegetable oil
2 small plum tomatoes, seeded
    and finely chopped
¼ cup chopped fresh basil
2 drained canned anchovy fillets,
    mashed
¼ teaspoon oregano leaves
Dash *each* garlic powder and
    pepper
2 ounces Gruyère *or* Swiss
    cheese, shredded
Garnish: basil leaves

Using a pastry brush, brush both sides of each slice of bread with an equal amount of oil and arrange slices in a single layer on nonstick baking sheet. Broil, turning once, until golden, about 30 seconds on each side.

In small mixing bowl combine remaining ingredients except cheese and garnish; spoon ¹/₁₂ of tomato mixture onto each slice of bread. Using a fork, press mixture evenly over surface of bread; top each with ¹/₁₂ of the cheese. Broil until cheese melts, about 1 minute. Transfer to serving platter and garnish with basil leaves.

MAKES 2 SERVINGS, 6 SLICES EACH

Each serving provides: 1 Protein Exchange;
    1 Bread Exchange; ½ Vegetable Exchange;
    1 Fat Exchange; 5 Optional Calories
Per serving with Gruyère cheese: 260 calories;
    13 g protein; 15 g fat; 19 g carbohydrate; 361 mg calcium;
    410 mg sodium; 34 mg cholesterol; 1 g dietary fiber
With Swiss cheese: 249 calories; 12 g protein; 14 g fat;
    20 g carbohydrate; 347 mg calcium; 388 mg sodium;
    29 mg cholesterol; 1 g dietary fiber

Herbed Toast ©

1 tablespoon plus 1 teaspoon
   reduced-calorie margarine (tub)
1 tablespoon *each* chopped fresh
   basil and parsley
2 slices Italian *or* French bread
   (1½ ounces each)
2 teaspoons grated Parmesan
   cheese

In small mixing bowl combine margarine, basil, and parsley and mix until thoroughly combined. Onto each slice of bread spread half of the margarine mixture; sprinkle 1 teaspoon cheese on each slice of bread.

   On nonstick baking sheet arrange bread slices, herb-side up and broil until cheese is golden, about 1 minute.

MAKES 2 SERVINGS

Each serving provides: 1½ Bread Exchanges;
   1 Fat Exchange; 10 Optional Calories
Per serving with Italian bread: 160 calories; 5 g protein;
   5 g fat; 25 g carbohydrate; 45 mg calcium;
   361 mg sodium; 2 mg cholesterol; 1 g dietary fiber
With French bread: 166 calories; 5 g protein; 6 g fat;
   24 g carbohydrate; 56 mg calcium; 358 mg sodium;
   3 mg cholesterol; 1 g dietary fiber

Confused about the difference between herbs and spices? An herb is usually a leaf or stem of a plant; a spice is usually the seeds, bark, or root. Spices come from tropical climates whereas herbs do not.

Onion Board ⊙

1½ teaspoons margarine
1 teaspoon vegetable oil
2 cups finely diced onions
1 refrigerated all-ready pizza
   crust dough (10 ounces)
1 teaspoon poppy seed

Preheat oven to 425°F. In 9-inch nonstick skillet combine margarine and oil and heat until margarine is melted; add onions and sauté over high heat until golden, about 2 minutes. Set aside. Line 15 x 10 x ¼-inch nonstick jelly-roll pan with pizza crust dough, pressing dough to edges of pan. Spread onion mixture evenly over surface of dough, leaving ½-inch edge on all four sides of dough; sprinkle poppy seed over onion mixture. Bake until dough is golden brown, about 20 minutes. Cut into 20 equal slices.

MAKES 10 SERVINGS, 2 SLICES EACH

Each serving provides: 1 Bread Exchange;
   ½ Vegetable Exchange; ¼ Fat Exchange;
   2 Optional Calories
Per serving: 94 calories; 3 g protein; 2 g fat;
   15 g carbohydrate; 12 mg calcium; 143 mg sodium;
   0 mg cholesterol; 0.3 g dietary fiber (this figure does not
   include pizza dough; nutrition analysis not available)

Apple-Yogurt Treat

Pack in a resealable plastic container for a brown-bag snack.

1 cup plain low-fat yogurt
1 small Granny Smith apple
   (about ¼ pound), cored, pared,
   and cubed
½ ounce blanched shelled whole
   almonds, chopped
2 tablespoons dark raisins
2 teaspoons granulated sugar

In small mixing bowl combine all ingredients; stir to combine. Cover with plastic wrap and refrigerate until ready to serve.

MAKES 2 SERVINGS

Each serving provides: ½ Protein Exchange;
   ½ Fat Exchange; 1 Fruit Exchange; 1 Milk Exchange;
   20 Optional Calories
Per serving: 185 calories; 8 g protein; 6 g fat;
   28 g carbohydrate; 231 mg calcium; 81 mg sodium;
   7 mg cholesterol; 1 g dietary fiber (this figure does not
   include almonds; nutrition analysis not available)

Not all bacteria cause disease or produce bad results. If it weren't for the friendly bacteria that cause milk to ferment, we'd miss out on a delicious dairy food... yogurt.

Cranberry Cooler ⊙

For an attractive presentation, garnish each cooler with a mint sprig.

½ cup low-calorie cranberry juice
⅓ cup apricot nectar
¼ cup orange juice (no sugar added)
1 cup crushed ice
⅔ cup club soda *or* seltzer

In 2-cup liquid measure or small pitcher combine cranberry juice, nectar, and orange juice and stir well. Divide ice into each of two 10-ounce glasses. Pour half of the cranberry mixture and half of the club soda (or seltzer) into each glass.

MAKES 2 SERVINGS, ABOUT ¾ CUP EACH

Each serving provides: 1 Fruit Exchange
Per serving: 48 calories; 0.4 g protein; trace fat;
   12 g carbohydrate; 15 mg calcium; 20 mg sodium;
   0 mg cholesterol; 0.3 g dietary fiber (this figure does not
   include cranberry juice; nutrition analysis not available)

What's the difference between seltzer and club soda? Seltzer is filtered tap water that has been carbonated. Club soda is also filtered tap water with carbonation, to which minerals and salts have been added.

Coffee Diablo ☕

**2 tablespoons plus 1½ teaspoons
  ground automatic drip coffee**
**1 tablespoon *each* freshly grated
  orange peel and firmly packed
  light *or* dark brown sugar**
1 cinnamon stick (2 inches)
Dash ground cloves
1¼ cups water

Arrange ground coffee in paper filter; set in automatic drip coffee maker. In coffee maker glass carafe arrange orange peel, sugar, cinnamon stick, and cloves. Pour water into coffee maker and brew. Let brewed coffee stand in glass carafe until flavors blend, 2 to 3 minutes. Stir coffee; pour through a sieve into each of two coffee cups, discarding solids.

MAKES 2 SERVINGS

Each serving provides: 30 Optional Calories
Per serving: 35 calories; 0.2 g protein; trace fat;
    9 g carbohydrate; 28 mg calcium; 6 mg sodium;
    0 mg cholesterol; dietary fiber data not available

Prolong the freshness of ground coffee by keeping it in the refrigerator for up to three weeks or in the freezer for several months.

Kir Spritzer

8 ice cubes
½ cup *each* chilled dry
** champagne and seltzer**
1 tablespoon black currant liqueur
¼ cup raspberries

In 2-cup liquid measure or small pitcher combine ice, champagne, and seltzer; stir in liqueur. Pour mixture through a strainer into 2 chilled 8-ounce glasses; add 2 tablespoons raspberries to each portion.

MAKES 2 SERVINGS

Each serving provides: ¼ Fruit Exchange;
    75 Optional Calories
Per serving: 68 calories; 0.2 g protein; 0.1 g fat;
    4 g carbohydrate; 9 mg calcium; 3 mg sodium;
    0 mg cholesterol; 1 g dietary fiber

Sparkling Tea Punch ⓒ

4 cups brewed herb tea, chilled
2²/₃ cups carbonated unfermented
    apple cider *or* carbonated
    apple juice, chilled (no sugar
    added)
2 tablespoons superfine sugar*
½ teaspoon ground cinnamon
1¹/₃ cups club soda *or* seltzer,
    chilled
8 lemon slices

In punch bowl combine tea, cider (or juice), sugar, and cinnamon and stir to dissolve sugar. Pour in club soda (or seltzer); add lemon slices.

MAKES 8 SERVINGS, ABOUT 1 CUP EACH

Each serving provides: 1 Fruit Exchange;
    15 Optional Calories
Per serving: 52 calories; trace protein; 0.1 g fat;
    13 g carbohydrate; 9 mg calcium; 14 mg sodium;
    0 mg cholesterol; dietary fiber data not available

*If superfine sugar is not available, process granulated sugar in blender until superfine.

Tea has a tendency to absorb moisture and odors, so keep it in a tightly closed container and store it in a cool, dry place.

Spiced Wine ⓒⓜ

2/3 cup apple juice (no sugar
    added)
1/3 cup pear nectar
1/4 cup *each* dry white table wine
    and water
2-inch strip lemon zest*
2 cinnamon sticks (2 inches each)
2 whole cloves
2 lemon slices

In 2-cup microwavable liquid measure or small pitcher combine all ingredients except lemon slices. Microwave on High (100%) for 2 minutes, until mixture is heated through. Pour mixture through sieve into each of two 8-ounce cups, reserving cinnamon sticks and discarding cloves and lemon zest. Add 1 reserved cinnamon stick and 1 lemon slice to each cup.

MAKES 2 SERVINGS, ABOUT ¾ CUP EACH

Each serving provides: 1½ Fruit Exchanges;
    25 Optional Calories
Per serving: 88 calories; 0.2 g protein; 0.1 g fat;
    18 g carbohydrate; 27 mg calcium; 6 mg sodium;
    0 mg cholesterol; 0.3 g dietary fiber (this figure does not
    include apple juice; nutrition analysis not available)

Variation: Chilled Spiced Wine — Chill wine mixture. Into each of two 12-ounce glasses pour half of the wine mixture. Add ½ cup crushed ice, ¼ cup club soda, 1 reserved cinnamon stick, and 1 lemon slice to each glass.

*The zest of the lemon is the peel without any of the pith (white membrane). To remove zest from lemon, use a zester or vegetable peeler; wrap lemon in plastic wrap and refrigerate for use at another time.

Desserts

Does your mouth water at the thought of White Chocolate, Fruit, and Cream or Quick Apple Tart? How about Chocolate Sundae Cupcakes or Pineapple Right-Side-Up Cakes? These are only a few of the tantalizing treats we've dreamed up just for you. If you always thought great desserts required hours of preparation, think again! You'll be amazed at how quick and easy these recipes are. We've even included a few microwave recipes so you can whip up a dessert in no time flat — Ladyfinger Pudding and Microwave Chocolate Custard are as delicious as they are quick. With all these guilt-free goodies to sample, you'll never again feel pressured to pass up dessert.

Banana-Yogurt Orleans Ⓜ

1 tablespoon whipped butter
1 teaspoon margarine
¼ cup freshly squeezed orange juice
1 tablespoon dark rum
2 teaspoons firmly packed light brown sugar
⅛ teaspoon ground cinnamon
1 medium banana (about 6 ounces), peeled and diagonally sliced
1 cup plain low-fat yogurt
½ teaspoon vanilla extract
2 teaspoons grated orange zest*

In 1-quart microwavable shallow casserole combine butter and margarine and microwave on High (100%) for 30 seconds, until melted. Stir in orange juice, rum, sugar, and cinnamon and stir to dissolve sugar. Microwave on High for 2 minutes until mixture is reduced by ¼. Add banana and turn to coat; microwave on High for 30 seconds, until banana is heated through (do not overcook).

In small mixing bowl combine yogurt and vanilla. Into each of 2 dessert dishes spoon half of the yogurt; top each portion with half of the banana mixture and 1 teaspoon orange zest.

MAKES 2 SERVINGS

Each serving provides: ½ Fat Exchange;
  1¼ Fruit Exchanges; 1 Milk Exchange;
  65 Optional Calories
Per serving: 220 calories; 7 g protein; 7 g fat;
  30 g carbohydrate; 225 mg calcium; 133 mg sodium;
  15 mg cholesterol; 1 g dietary fiber

*The zest of the orange is the peel without any of the pith (white membrane). To remove zest from orange, use a zester or vegetable peeler; wrap orange in plastic wrap and refrigerate for use at another time.

Minted Three-Berry Ice

Keep this refreshing summertime dessert on hand in your freezer, but watch out that the kids don't reach for it instead of ice cream.

1 cup *each* strawberries and raspberries
1 tablespoon *each* granulated sugar and mint leaves
1 teaspoon freshly squeezed lemon juice
½ cup blueberries
Garnish: 4 mint sprigs

In work bowl of food processor combine all ingredients except blueberries and mint sprigs and process, using on-off motion, until mixture is chunky *(do not puree)*. Transfer to 8 x 8 x 2-inch nonstick pan; stir in blueberries. Cover with plastic wrap and freeze for at least 2 hours or overnight.

To serve, into each of 4 dessert dishes spoon ¼ of the berry mixture; garnish each portion with a mint sprig.

MAKES 4 SERVINGS

Each serving provides: 1 Fruit Exchange;
    15 Optional Calories
Per serving: 49 calories; 1 g protein; 0.4 g fat;
    12 g carbohydrate; 14 mg calcium; 2 mg sodium;
    0 mg cholesterol; 3 g dietary fiber

Citrus fruits aren't the only way to get vitamin C. You'll also find this important vitamin in strawberries, cantaloupe, broccoli, tomatoes, cabbage, and peppers.

Cherry Fruit Soup Ⓜ

Serve this classic fruit soup warm from the microwave oven or refrigerate it and enjoy it chilled.

1 cup low-calorie cranberry juice
2 teaspoons *each* cornstarch and freshly squeezed lemon juice
1 teaspoon *each* granulated sugar and vanilla extract
Dash *each* ground allspice and ground cinnamon
15 large pitted fresh *or* thawed frozen cherries (no sugar added), cut into halves
1 tablespoon cherry-flavored liqueur
2 teaspoons half-and-half (blend of milk and cream)

In small microwavable mixing bowl combine all ingredients except cherries, liqueur, and half-and-half and stir to dissolve cornstarch. Microwave on High (100%) for 3 minutes, stirring halfway through cooking, until mixture thickens slightly. Add cherries and liqueur and stir to combine; microwave on High for 1 minute, until thoroughly heated. Let stand for 2 minutes, until flavors blend.

To serve, ladle soup into 2 soup bowls and pour 1 teaspoon half-and-half over each portion of soup; using a toothpick swirl half-and-half to create a decorative pattern.

MAKES 2 SERVINGS, ABOUT 1 CUP EACH

Each serving provides: 1¼ Fruit Exchanges;
    55 Optional Calories
Per serving: 113 calories; 1 g protein; 1 g fat;
    22 g carbohydrate; 25 mg calcium; 6 mg sodium;
    2 mg cholesterol; 1 g dietary fiber (this figure does not
    include cranberry juice; nutrition analysis not available)

Bananas and Berries au Chocolat ☺

⅓ cup plus 2 teaspoons thawed
    frozen dairy whipped topping
2 teaspoons chocolate syrup
½ medium banana (about
    3 ounces), peeled and thinly
    sliced
½ teaspoon freshly squeezed
    lemon juice
1 cup strawberries, halved
⅛ ounce (about 1 tablespoon)
    grated milk chocolate

In small mixing bowl combine whipped topping and syrup; stir to combine and set aside.

In separate small mixing bowl combine banana and lemon juice and toss to coat to prevent discoloring; add strawberries and toss to combine.

Into each of two dessert dishes spoon half of the fruit mixture; top each portion with half of the whipped topping mixture and then with half of the chocolate.

MAKES 2 SERVINGS

Each serving provides: 1 Fruit Exchange;
    65 Optional Calories
Per serving: 109 calories; 1 g protein; 4 g fat;
    20 g carbohydrate; 18 mg calcium; 24 mg sodium;
    0.4 mg cholesterol; 2 g dietary fiber (this figure does not
    include chocolate; nutrition analysis not available)

Variation: Bananas and Berries au Chocolat Blanc — Substitute ⅛ ounce white chocolate for the milk chocolate.

Per serving: Reduce calcium to 13 mg

For best results, always rinse strawberries before removing hulls so that berries do not absorb moisture.

Broiled Persimmon with Pecans

1 medium persimmon (about
  ¼ pound), cut in half lengthwise
¼ ounce chopped pecans
1 teaspoon firmly packed light
  brown sugar
1 tablespoon *each* sour cream
  and thawed frozen dairy
  whipped topping
Dash ground nutmeg

In flameproof 1¼-cup au gratin dish or
4 x 4 x 2-inch baking dish arrange persimmon
halves, cut-side up; set aside. In cup or small
bowl combine pecans and sugar; sprinkle
pecan mixture over persimmon halves,
reserving 1 teaspoon. Broil until sugar car-
melizes and pecans are lightly toasted, 2 to 3
minutes *(do not overcook)*. Set aside.

In cup or small bowl combine sour cream,
whipped topping, and nutmeg; top each
persimmon half with half of the sour cream
mixture and then sprinkle with half of the
reserved pecan mixture.

MAKES 2 SERVINGS

Each serving provides: ¼ Protein Exchange;
  ¼ Fat Exchange; 1 Fruit Exchange;
  35 Optional Calories
Per serving: 114 calories; 1 g protein; 5 g fat;
  20 g carbohydrate; 25 mg calcium; 7 mg sodium;
  3 mg cholesterol; 0.2 g dietary fiber (this figure does not
  include persimmon; nutrition analysis not available)

*The persimmon season runs from
October through the beginning of
January, with a peak in November.
Place unripe persimmons in a
pierced paper bag and leave in a
cool, dry place to ripen. Store the
ripe fruit in a resealable plastic bag
in the refrigerator and use within a
day or two.*

Figs with Pistachio Cream

1 tablespoon plus 1½ teaspoons
  whipped cream cheese
¼ ounce shelled pistachio nuts,
  ground
2 large fresh figs

In small mixing bowl combine cheese and nuts; stir to blend and set aside. Starting at stem-end, cut each fig lengthwise into quarters, being careful not to cut through base of fig. Gently open quarters and arrange on serving plate. Spoon half of the cheese-nut mixture into center of each fig.

MAKES 2 SERVINGS

Each serving provides: ¼ Protein Exchange;
  ¼ Fat Exchange; 1 Fruit Exchange; 25 Optional Calories
Per serving: 92 calories; 2 g protein; 4 g fat;
  13 g carbohydrate; 32 mg calcium; 27 mg sodium;
  7 mg cholesterol; dietary fiber data not available

Fresh figs, which are in season from early July through late October, are highly perishable. Store them in a resealable plastic bag in the refrigerator and use them within 36 hours.

Maple-Walnut Fruit Compote Ⓜ

Apples and pears are a happy combination in this tasty compote.

1/3 cup apple juice (no sugar
   added)
2 teaspoons maple syrup
1 teaspoon freshly squeezed
   lemon juice
1/2 teaspoon cornstarch
1 small McIntosh *or* Granny
   Smith apple (about 1/4 pound),
   cored and diced
1 small Bartlett pear (about
   5 ounces), cored and diced
1/2 ounce chopped walnuts
2 tablespoons thawed frozen
   dairy whipped topping

In 1-quart microwavable casserole combine apple juice, syrup, lemon juice, and cornstarch and stir to dissolve cornstarch. Add apple and pear and stir to combine. Cover with vented plastic wrap and microwave on High (100%) for 4 minutes, rotating dish 1/2 turn halfway through cooking.

To serve, into each of 2 dessert dishes spoon half of the fruit mixture; top each with half of the walnuts and whipped topping.

MAKES 2 SERVINGS

Each serving provides: 1/2 Protein Exchange;
   1/2 Fat Exchange; 1 1/2 Fruit Exchanges;
   35 Optional Calories
Per serving: 164 calories; 1 g protein; 6 g fat;
   30 g carbohydrate; 27 mg calcium; 8 mg sodium;
   0 mg cholesterol; 3 g dietary fiber

Peach and Almond Cream

1 cup plain low-fat yogurt
1 medium peach (about ¼ pound),
  blanched, pared, pitted, and
  chopped
¼ cup thawed frozen dairy
  whipped topping
½ ounce shelled almonds, toasted
  and ground
1½ teaspoons almond-flavored
  liqueur
1 amaretti cookie (¼ ounce),
  made into crumbs

In small mixing bowl combine all ingredients except cookie crumbs. Into each of two dessert or champagne glasses spoon half of the yogurt mixture. Top each portion with half of the cookie crumbs and serve.

MAKES 2 SERVINGS

Each serving provides: ½ Protein Exchange;
  ½ Fat Exchange; ½ Fruit Exchange; 1 Milk Exchange;
  55 Optional Calories
Per serving: 183 calories; 8 g protein; 8 g fat;
  20 g carbohydrate; 231 mg calcium; 99 mg sodium;
  8 mg cholesterol; 0.3 g dietary fiber (this figure does not
  include almonds and amaretti cookie; nutrition analyses
  not available)

Rum-Raisin Stuffed Pears Ⓜ

¼ ounce chopped pecans (about 6 halves)

1 tablespoon golden raisins, chopped

1½ teaspoons *each* firmly packed light brown sugar and whipped butter, melted

1 small Bosc *or* Bartlett pear (about 5 ounces), cut in half lengthwise, cored, and pared

1 teaspoon freshly squeezed lemon juice

2 tablespoons plus 2 teaspoons pear nectar

1 tablespoon dark rum

½ teaspoon cornstarch

¼ teaspoon vanilla extract

In small mixing bowl combine pecans, raisins, and sugar; stir in butter, mixing well. In 1-quart microwavable casserole arrange pear halves, cored-side up. Sprinkle pear halves evenly with lemon juice; spoon half of the pecan mixture into cored section of each pear half; set aside.

In cup or small bowl combine remaining ingredients and stir to dissolve cornstarch; pour into casserole. Cover casserole with vented plastic wrap and microwave on High (100%) for 4 minutes, until pear halves are fork-tender and sauce has thickened, rotating casserole ½ turn halfway through cooking.

MAKES 2 SERVINGS

Each serving provides: ¼ Protein Exchange;
  ¼ Fat Exchange; 1 Fruit Exchange; 50 Optional Calories
Per serving: 133 calories; 1 g protein; 4 g fat;
  21 g carbohydrate; 15 mg calcium; 17 mg sodium;
  4 mg cholesterol; 2 g dietary fiber

Sautéed Bourbon Fruits

2 teaspoons reduced-calorie
  margarine (tub)
1 small Bartlett pear (about
  5 ounces), cored and sliced
1 small Red Delicious apple
  (about ¼ pound), cored and
  sliced
⅓ cup pear nectar
2 tablespoons bourbon
½ teaspoon cornstarch
2 tablespoons thawed frozen
  dairy whipped topping
1 gingersnap cookie, made into
  crumbs

In 12-inch nonstick skillet melt margarine; add pear and apple slices and sauté over medium-high heat until fruits are tender and lightly browned, 2 to 3 minutes.

In 1-cup liquid measure combine nectar, bourbon, and cornstarch and stir to dissolve cornstarch; add to fruits in skillet and cook, stirring constantly, until mixture thickens, about 1 minute.

To serve, into each of two dessert dishes spoon half of the fruit mixture; top each portion with half of the whipped topping and half of the cookie crumbs.

MAKES 2 SERVINGS

Each serving provides: ½ Fat Exchange;
  1½ Fruit Exchanges; 65 Optional Calories
Per serving: 173 calories; 1 g protein; 4 g fat;
  28 g carbohydrate; 15 mg calcium; 67 mg sodium;
  1 mg cholesterol; 3 g dietary fiber

Bourbon adds a special touch to fruit desserts and other sweets. Why is this American corn whiskey called bourbon? It gets its name from its birthplace, Bourbon County, Kentucky.

Strawberry-Banana Whip ☻

This dessert takes only a few short minutes to prepare but will need about 1½ hours to chill. We suggest you prepare it in the evening and refrigerate it overnight.

1 envelope (four ½-cup servings) low-calorie strawberry-banana-flavored gelatin (8 calories per ½ cup)
¾ cup boiling water
1 cup ice cubes
½ medium banana (about 3 ounces), peeled
½ cup *each* plain low-fat yogurt and strawberries, cut into halves

In medium heatproof bowl sprinkle gelatin over boiling water and stir until dissolved; stir in ice cubes. Transfer to blender container; add banana and yogurt and process on low speed until pureed.

Into each of four 6-ounce dessert glasses pour ¼ of banana mixture. Cover and refrigerate until set, about 1½ hours.

To serve, top each portion with ¼ of the berries.

MAKES 4 SERVINGS

Each serving provides: ¼ Fruit Exchange; ¼ Milk Exchange; 15 Optional Calories
Per serving: 45 calories; 3 g protein; 1 g fat; 7 g carbohydrate; 55 mg calcium; 80 mg sodium; 2 mg cholesterol; 1 g dietary fiber

By law, products labeled "low-calorie" must contain 40 calories or less per serving.

Summer Fruits with Custard Sauce

Our version of this recipe uses blueberries and a nectarine, but other fruit such as strawberries, peaches, or baked apple work just as well.

½ cup skim *or* nonfat milk
1 tablespoon plus 1½ teaspoons all-purpose flour
1 tablespoon granulated sugar
2 eggs
2 teaspoons margarine
½ teaspoon almond extract
½ cup blueberries
1 small nectarine (about 5 ounces), blanched, pared, pitted, and thinly sliced

Using a wire whisk, in small saucepan combine milk, flour, and sugar and stir to dissolve flour; cook over medium-low heat, stirring constantly, until mixture is smooth and thickened, 1 to 2 minutes.

In small mixing bowl lightly beat eggs. Gradually stir in half of the milk mixture; slowly stir egg-milk mixture back into milk mixture in saucepan. Cook over low heat, stirring constantly, until bubbles begin to form around edge of pan, 2 to 3 minutes (do not boil). Transfer to small mixing bowl; stir in margarine and extract. Cover and refrigerate until chilled, at least 30 minutes.

To serve, into each of 2 dessert dishes arrange half of the blueberries and nectarine slices; top each with half of the custard mixture.

MAKES 2 SERVINGS

Each serving provides: 1 Protein Exchange;
¼ Bread Exchange; 1 Fat Exchange; 1 Fruit Exchange;
¼ Milk Exchange; 30 Optional Calories
Per serving: 235 calories; 10 g protein; 10 g fat;
27 g carbohydrate; 111 mg calcium; 148 mg sodium;
275 mg cholesterol; 2 g dietary fiber

Cappuccino Mousse

2 teaspoons unflavored gelatin
½ cup plus 2 tablespoons low-fat
   milk (1% milk fat)
1 ounce semisweet chocolate,
   grated (reserve 1 teaspoon for
   garnish)
1½ teaspoons instant espresso
   coffee powder
1 teaspoon vanilla extract
10 ice cubes
Cold water
6 egg whites
1 tablespoon granulated sugar
¾ cup thawed frozen dairy
   whipped topping, divided

In 1-quart saucepan sprinkle gelatin over milk and let stand for 1 minute to soften; cook over medium heat, stirring constantly, until gelatin is completely dissolved, about 1 minute. Add chocolate, espresso powder, and vanilla; cook, stirring constantly, until chocolate is melted.

In large mixing bowl combine ice cubes and enough cold water to cover. Transfer chocolate mixture to medium mixing bowl. Set bowl of chocolate mixture in bowl of ice water and let stand, stirring frequently with a rubber scraper, until mixture is cool to the touch and the consistency of egg whites, about 2 minutes.

Using an electric mixer on medium speed, in large mixing bowl beat egg whites and sugar until soft peaks form; set aside.

Remove bowl of chocolate mixture from ice water. Using a rubber scraper, stir ¼ cup of the whipped topping into the chocolate mixture; fold in ¼ cup whipped topping. Fold in the beaten egg whites, one third at a time.

Into eight 6-ounce dessert dishes spoon an equal amount of the mousse mixture. Refrigerate overnight or at least 2 hours.

To serve, top each portion with 1½ teaspoons of the remaining whipped topping and ⅛ teaspoon of the reserved chocolate.

MAKES 8 SERVINGS

Each serving provides: ¼ Protein Exchange;
   55 Optional Calories
Per serving: 67 calories; 4 g protein; 3 g fat;
   6 g carbohydrate; 26 mg calcium; 58 mg sodium;
   1 mg cholesterol; dietary fiber data not available

White Chocolate, Fruit, and Cream

2 cups strawberries (reserve
   2 berries, with hulls attached,
   for garnish)
⅓ cup plus 2 teaspoons thawed
   frozen dairy whipped topping
½ ounce white chocolate, melted

In work bowl of food processor process strawberries until pureed, scraping down sides of container when necessary. Transfer to 8 x 8 x 2-inch nonstick pan; fold in whipped topping. Stir in chocolate until blended. Cover with plastic wrap and freeze until partially frozen, about 30 minutes. Stir mixture from edges toward center; cover and freeze until smooth and creamy, about 1 hour.

To serve, into each of two dessert or champagne glasses scoop half of the strawberry mixture. Top each portion with a reserved strawberry.

MAKES 2 SERVINGS

Each serving provides: 1 Fruit Exchange;
   75 Optional Calories
Per serving: 120 calories; 1 g protein; 6 g fat;
   18 g carbohydrate; 21 mg calcium; 22 mg sodium;
   1 mg cholesterol; 3 g dietary fiber (this figure does not
   include white chocolate; nutrition analysis not available)

Chocolate melts like magic in the microwave oven. Microwave on Medium (50%) and in a matter of a minute or two it's done. Be sure to stir melting chocolate frequently.

Microwave Chocolate Custard ⓒⓜ

1 cup low-fat milk (2% milk fat)
⅓ cup instant nonfat dry milk
  powder
2 tablespoons chocolate syrup
1 tablespoon *each* granulated
  sugar and unsweetened cocoa
1 egg
¼ cup thawed frozen dairy
  whipped topping

Using a wire whisk, in medium microwavable mixing bowl combine milks, chocolate syrup, sugar, and cocoa. Microwave on High (100%) for 2 minutes.

Using a wire whisk, in separate medium mixing bowl lightly beat egg; continuing to stir, gradually add milk mixture. Spray four 6-ounce microwavable custard cups with nonstick cooking spray and pour ¼ custard mixture into each cup. Set cups in 8 x 8 x 2-inch microwavable baking dish and pour hot water into dish until water is at the same level as custard mixture in cups. Microwave on Medium (50%) for 18 minutes, rotating baking dish ¼ turn every 4½ minutes (until a knife, inserted in center, comes out clean). Let stand for 5 minutes. Remove cups from water bath; cover with plastic wrap and refrigerate until chilled, about 1 hour.

To serve, onto each of 4 serving plates invert each custard; top each with 1 tablespoon whipped topping.

MAKES 4 SERVINGS

Each serving provides: ¼ Protein Exchange;
  ½ Milk Exchange; 70 Optional Calories
Per serving: 118 calories; 6 g protein; 4 g fat;
  16 g carbohydrate; 153 mg calcium; 93 mg sodium;
  74 mg cholesterol; 0.4 g dietary fiber (this figure does
  not include chocolate syrup; nutrition analysis not
  available)

Most puddings and custards require time to chill. If you prepare them before you sit down to dinner, they'll be ready in time for dessert.

Apple-Spice Pudding ☺

2 cups skim *or* nonfat milk
1 envelope (four ½-cup servings)
    reduced-calorie vanilla instant
    pudding mix
⅓ cup apple juice (no sugar
    added)
1 teaspoon *each* firmly packed
    light brown sugar and lemon
    juice
½ teaspoon ground cinnamon
½ pound apples, cored, pared,
    and minced
2 tablespoons golden raisins
¼ cup thawed frozen dairy
    whipped topping
Ground nutmeg

Using milk, prepare pudding according
to package directions; set aside.

In 9-inch nonstick skillet combine apple
juice, sugar, lemon juice, and cinnamon and
bring mixture to a boil; add apples and raisins
and cook over high heat, stirring frequently,
until apples are tender and liquid is reduced,
2 to 3 minutes. Add to prepared pudding and
stir to thoroughly combine.

Into each of 4 dessert dishes spoon ¼ of
the pudding mixture; cover each with plastic
wrap and refrigerate until pudding is set,
at least 30 minutes.

To serve, top each portion with 1 tablespoon whipped topping and sprinkle each
with a dash nutmeg.

MAKES 4 SERVINGS

Each serving provides: 1 Fruit Exchange;
    1 Milk Exchange; 20 Optional Calories
Per serving: 138 calories; 5 g protein; 1 g fat;
    28 g carbohydrate; 163 mg calcium; 401 mg sodium;
    2 mg cholesterol; 2 g dietary fiber (this figure does not
    include pudding mix; nutrition analysis not available)

Chocolate-Cheese Pudding ⊙

Although this rich chocolate dessert is ready in minutes, it will need to chill for a couple of hours before serving.

1 envelope unflavored gelatin
1 cup *each* low-fat milk (2% milk fat) and part-skim ricotta cheese
3 tablespoons chocolate syrup
½ teaspoon vanilla extract
2 graham crackers (2½-inch squares), made into fine crumbs
1 tablespoon plus 1 teaspoon thawed frozen dairy whipped topping
2 maraschino cherries, cut into halves

In small saucepan sprinkle gelatin over milk and let stand to soften, about 1 minute. Cook over medium-low heat, stirring constantly, until gelatin is completely dissolved, about 2 minutes (*do not boil*). Set aside and let cool slightly, about 2 minutes.

In blender container combine ricotta cheese, chocolate syrup, and vanilla and process on medium speed until pureed, about 1 minute, scraping down sides of container as necessary. Reduce speed to low; gradually add milk-gelatin mixture and process until combined. Pour into four 6-ounce custard cups; cover with plastic wrap and refrigerate until set, at least 2 hours.

To serve, sprinkle each pudding with ¼ of the graham cracker crumbs, then top each with 1 teaspoon whipped topping and a maraschino cherry half.

MAKES 4 SERVINGS

Each serving provides: 1 Protein Exchange;
    ¼ Bread Exchange; ¼ Milk Exchange;
    65 Optional Calories
Per serving: 173 calories; 11 g protein; 7 g fat;
    18 g carbohydrate; 245 mg calcium; 148 mg sodium;
    24 mg cholesterol; 0.1 g dietary fiber (this figure does
    not include chocolate syrup; nutrition analysis not
    available)

Calcium doesn't just build strong bones and teeth. Our bodies also need this important mineral for regulating the heartbeat, clotting the blood, and transmitting nerve impulses.

Chocolate-Layered Pudding

2 cups skim *or* nonfat milk
1 envelope (four ½-cup servings)
    reduced-calorie vanilla instant
    pudding mix
6 chocolate wafers (1½ ounces),
    made into crumbs (reserve
    1 tablespoon cookie crumbs for
    garnish)
1 ounce unsalted dry-roasted
    almonds, finely ground (reserve
    4 whole almonds for garnish)
1 tablespoon whipped butter,
    melted
¼ cup thawed frozen dairy
    whipped topping

Using milk, prepare pudding according to package directions; set aside.

In small mixing bowl combine cookie crumbs, the almonds, and butter and mix well. Using half of the crumb mixture into each of four 6-ounce dessert dishes or parfait glasses sprinkle an equal amount of mixture; top each with ¼ cup of the prepared pudding. Sprinkle an equal amount of remaining crumb mixture over each portion and then top each with ¼ cup pudding. Cover each portion with plastic wrap and refrigerate until pudding is set, at least 30 minutes.

To serve, top each portion with 1 tablespoon whipped topping, ¼ of the reserved cookie crumbs, and 1 reserved almond.

MAKES 4 SERVINGS

Each serving provides: ½ Protein Exchange;
    ½ Fat Exchange; 1 Milk Exchange; 80 Optional Calories
Per serving: 187 calories; 6 g protein; 8 g fat;
    22 g carbohydrate; 169 mg calcium; 489 mg sodium;
    6 mg cholesterol; 1 g dietary fiber (this figure does not
    include pudding mix and chocolate wafers; nutrition
    analyses not available)

Ladyfinger Pudding ©Ⓜ

1 cup low-fat milk (1% milk fat)
¼ cup evaporated skimmed milk
2 tablespoons plus 2 teaspoons
   instant nonfat dry milk powder
1 teaspoon vanilla extract
½ teaspoon confectioners' sugar
¼ teaspoon grated lemon peel
Dash ground nutmeg
2 eggs
3 ladyfingers (¼ ounce each), cut
   into ½-inch cubes

In medium microwavable mixing bowl combine milks, milk powder, vanilla, sugar, lemon peel, and nutmeg and stir to dissolve milk powder. Microwave on High (100%) for 2 minutes, until heated through. Using a wire whisk, in separate medium mixing bowl lightly beat eggs; gradually beat in milk mixture.

Spray two 10-ounce microwavable custard cups with nonstick cooking spray. Arrange half of the ladyfinger cubes in each cup, then pour half of the egg mixture over cubes, being sure they are thoroughly moistened. Set cups in microwavable 8 x 8 x 2-inch baking dish and pour water into dish to a depth of about 1 inch. Microwave on Medium (50%) for 17 minutes (until a knife, inserted in center, comes out clean). Let stand for 1 minute. Remove cups from water bath and let cool for 5 minutes. Cover with plastic wrap and refrigerate until chilled, about 30 minutes.

MAKES 2 SERVINGS

Each serving provides: 1 Protein Exchange;
   1 Milk Exchange; 70 Optional Calories
Per serving: 224 calories; 15 g protein; 8 g fat;
   21 g carbohydrate; 345 mg calcium; 205 mg sodium;
   319 mg cholesterol; dietary fiber data not available

Calcium is best absorbed by the body when vitamin D is present. That's why milk is vitamin D-fortified.

Mint-Chocolate Pudding

2 cups skim *or* nonfat milk
1 envelope (four ½-cup servings)
   reduced-calorie chocolate
   instant pudding mix
¼ teaspoon peppermint extract
4 graham crackers (2½-inch
   squares), made into crumbs
   (reserve 1 tablespoon graham
   cracker crumbs for garnish)
1 ounce unsalted dry-roasted
   shelled almonds, finely ground
1 tablespoon whipped butter,
   melted
¼ cup thawed frozen dairy
   whipped topping
1 ounce chocolate-mint wafer
   candies, chopped

Using milk, prepare pudding according to package directions; stir in extract and set aside.

In small mixing bowl combine graham cracker crumbs, almonds, and butter and mix well. Using ⅔ of the crumb mixture, into each of four 6-ounce dessert glasses sprinkle an equal amount of mixture; top each with ¼ of the prepared pudding. Sprinkle an equal amount of remaining crumb mixture over each portion of pudding. Cover each portion with plastic wrap and refrigerate until pudding is set, about 30 minutes.

To serve, top each portion with ¼ of the whipped topping and chocolate.

MAKES 4 SERVINGS

Each serving provides: ½ Protein Exchange;
   ½ Bread Exchange; ½ Fat Exchange; 1 Milk Exchange;
   65 Optional Calories
Per serving: 203 calories; 7 g protein; 9 g fat;
   26 g carbohydrate; 175 mg calcium; 382 mg sodium;
   6 mg cholesterol; 1 g dietary fiber (this figure does not
   include pudding mix; nutrition analysis not available)

Ozark Apple Pudding

Granny Smith or Golden Delicious apples are the perfect choice for this yummy pudding.

3 tablespoons all-purpose flour
1¼ teaspoons double-acting baking powder
Dash salt
1 egg
¼ cup granulated sugar
1 teaspoon vanilla extract
½ pound apples, cored, pared, and chopped
1 ounce chopped pecans

Preheat oven to 350°F. On sheet of wax paper or a paper plate sift together flour, baking powder, and salt; set aside.

Using electric mixer on high speed, in small mixing bowl beat together egg and sugar until mixture is thick and lemon colored; beat in vanilla. Add flour mixture and, using mixer on low speed, beat until thoroughly combined, about 1 minute. Stir in apples and pecans.

Spray 8-inch pie plate with nonstick cooking spray; spread apple mixture evenly in pie plate and bake for 20 to 25 minutes (until a toothpick, inserted in center, comes out clean). Let cool for 5 minutes.

MAKES 4 SERVINGS

Each serving provides: ¾ Protein Exchange;
¼ Bread Exchange; ½ Fat Exchange;
½ Fruit Exchange; 60 Optional Calories
Per serving: 169 calories; 3 g protein; 6 g fat;
26 g carbohydrate; 79 mg calcium; 183 mg sodium;
69 mg cholesterol; 2 g dietary fiber

Serving Suggestion: Top each portion of pudding with 1 tablespoon thawed frozen dairy whipped topping. Increase Optional Calories to 75.

Per serving: 181 calories; 3 g protein; 7 g fat;
27 g carbohydrate; 79 mg calcium; 188 mg sodium;
69 mg cholesterol; 2 g dietary fiber

Tapioca Pudding Ⓒ Ⓜ

A childhood favorite!

1 cup low-fat milk (1% milk fat)
½ cup evaporated skimmed milk
2 tablespoons uncooked quick-
    cooking pearl tapioca
1 tablespoon plus 1 teaspoon
    granulated sugar
1 egg, separated
1 teaspoon vanilla extract

In medium microwavable mixing bowl combine milks, tapioca, and sugar and stir to dissolve sugar. Cover with vented plastic wrap and microwave on High (100%) for 3 minutes, until slightly thickened. Uncover and microwave on High for 4 minutes, until thickened.

Using a wire whisk, in separate medium microwavable mixing bowl lightly beat egg yolk; gradually beat in milk mixture. Stir in vanilla. Microwave on Medium (50%), uncovered, for 2 minutes, stirring every 30 seconds.

Using electric mixer on high speed, in medium mixing bowl beat egg white until stiff but not dry; gently stir milk mixture into beaten egg white until thoroughly combined.

Into each of four 6-ounce custard cups pour ¼ of pudding mixture (about ½ cup). Set aside and let cool for 10 minutes. Cover with plastic wrap and refrigerate overnight or at least 2 hours, until pudding is chilled and set.

MAKES 4 SERVINGS

Each serving provides: ¼ Protein Exchange;
    ½ Milk Exchange; 40 Optional Calories
Per serving: 107 calories; 6 g protein; 2 g fat;
    15 g carbohydrate; 175 mg calcium; 85 mg sodium;
    72 mg cholesterol; 0.1 g dietary fiber

Cinnamon Tea Biscuits ☻

1 cup plus 2 tablespoons
    all-purpose flour
¼ teaspoon *each* baking soda and
    cream of tartar
¼ cup plus 2 teaspoons
    granulated sugar, divided
2 tablespoons reduced-calorie
    margarine (tub)
1 tablespoon sweet whipped
    butter
1 egg
½ teaspoon vanilla extract
¼ teaspoon ground cinnamon

Preheat oven to 375°F. On sheet of wax paper or a paper plate sift together flour, baking soda, and cream of tartar; set aside.

Using electric mixer on high speed, in large mixing bowl cream ¼ cup sugar, the margarine, and butter; add egg and vanilla and beat until light and fluffy, about 1 minute. Using electric mixer on low speed, gradually beat in flour mixture. Cover with plastic wrap and refrigerate for 30 minutes.

Spray cookie sheet with nonstick cooking spray. Using half of dough, divide dough into 9 equal portions and, using hands, shape each portion into a ball. On sheet of wax paper combine remaining 2 teaspoons sugar and the cinnamon; lightly roll dough balls in half of the sugar mixture, reserving remaining mixture. Arrange balls on cookie sheet, leaving a space of about 1 inch between each. Bake until biscuits are lightly browned and firm to the touch, 8 to 10 minutes. Transfer to wire rack and let cool. Repeat procedure with remaining dough and sugar mixture, making 9 more biscuits.

MAKES 6 SERVINGS, 3 BISCUITS EACH

Each serving provides: 1 Bread Exchange;
    ½ Fat Exchange; 65 Optional Calories
Per serving: 163 calories; 3 g protein; 4 g fat;
    28 g carbohydrate; 10 mg calcium; 95 mg sodium;
    48 mg cholesterol; 1 g dietary fiber

Both cinnamon and its relative, cassia, come from the inner bark of evergreen trees. Most of the "cinnamon" sold in this part of the world is really cassia. To be assured of potent dried spices and herbs, label containers with the date purchased, store them in a cool dark place, and keep no longer than 6 months.

Banana-Raisin-Walnut Muffins

1 cup plus 2 tablespoons
  all-purpose flour
½ cup instant nonfat dry milk
  powder
¼ cup firmly packed light brown
  sugar
2 teaspoons double-acting baking
  powder
½ teaspoon baking soda
¼ teaspoon ground nutmeg
1 cup plus 2 tablespoons
  buttermilk
1 egg, lightly beaten
¼ cup less 2 teaspoons vegetable
  oil
2 tablespoons sweet whipped
  butter, melted
1 very ripe banana (about
  6 ounces), peeled and mashed
½ cup golden raisins, plumped
1 ounce chopped walnuts

Preheat oven to 400°F. Line twelve 2½-inch-diameter muffin-pan cups with paper baking cups; set aside.

In medium mixing bowl combine flour, milk powder, sugar, baking powder, baking soda, and nutmeg; stir to combine and set aside. In small mixing bowl combine buttermilk, egg, oil, and butter and stir until blended; stir into dry ingredients. Add banana, raisins, and walnuts and stir to combine (mixture will be lumpy). Fill each baking cup with an equal amount of batter and bake for 15 minutes (until golden brown and a toothpick, inserted in center, comes out dry). Transfer muffins from pan to wire rack and let cool.

MAKES 12 SERVINGS, 1 MUFFIN EACH

Each serving provides: ¼ Protein Exchange;
  ½ Bread Exchange; 1 Fat Exchange; ½ Fruit Exchange;
  ¼ Milk Exchange; 30 Optional Calories
Per serving: 170 calories; 4 g protein; 7 g fat;
  24 g carbohydrate; 111 mg calcium; 163 mg sodium;
  27 mg cholesterol; 1 g dietary fiber

*Mash a banana with ease by using
a pastry blender rather than a fork.*

Maple-Walnut Loaf

10-ounce package ready-to-bake
  refrigerated buttermilk flaky
  biscuits (10 biscuits)*
2½ ounces shelled walnuts,
  broken into pieces and divided
1 tablespoon maple syrup,
  divided
¼ teaspoon ground cinnamon,
  divided

Preheat oven to 400°F. Spray 9 x 5 x 3-inch loaf pan with nonstick cooking spray. Carefully separate each biscuit into 3 thin layers of dough. Press 15 biscuit layers over bottom of pan; top with half of the walnuts, syrup, and cinnamon. Arrange remaining 15 biscuit layers over walnut mixture in pan, then top with remaining walnuts, syrup, and cinnamon. Bake until biscuits are golden, about 10 minutes. Let loaf cool in pan for 5 minutes. Transfer loaf to wire rack and let cool completely.

MAKES 5 SERVINGS

Each serving provides: 1 Protein Exchange;
  2 Bread Exchanges; 1 Fat Exchange;
  10 Optional Calories
Per serving: 272 calories; 5 g protein; 16 g fat;
  30 g carbohydrate; 19 mg calcium; 593 mg sodium;
  0 mg cholesterol; 1 g dietary fiber (this figure does not
  include biscuits; nutrition analysis not available)

*Keep biscuits refrigerated until ready to use. Separate
  dough into layers as soon as biscuits are removed from
  refrigerator; they will be difficult to work with if allowed
  to come to room temperature.

Oatmeal-Raisin Cookies ⓖ

Children and adults alike will enjoy these old-fashioned cookies.

⅓ cup plus 2 teaspoons
   all-purpose flour
1½ ounces uncooked quick oats
2 tablespoons dark raisins,
   chopped
⅛ teaspoon *each* baking soda
   and ground cinnamon
2 tablespoons *each* firmly packed
   light brown sugar and sweet
   whipped butter, softened
1 tablespoon plus 1 teaspoon
   each granulated sugar and
   margarine
1 egg
1 teaspoon vanilla extract

Preheat oven to 350°F. In small mixing bowl combine flour, oats, raisins, baking soda, and cinnamon; set aside.

Using electric mixer on medium speed, in medium mixing bowl beat together brown sugar, butter, granulated sugar, and margarine until light and fluffy; add egg and vanilla and continue beating until combined. Stir in oat mixture.

Spray nonstick cookie sheet with nonstick cooking spray and drop dough by tablespoonfuls onto sprayed sheet, forming 12 cookies and leaving a space of about 2 inches between each. Bake until cookies are lightly browned and crisp, 8 to 10 minutes.

MAKES 4 SERVINGS, 3 COOKIES EACH

Each serving provides: ¼ Protein Exchange;
   1 Bread Exchange; 1 Fat Exchange; ¼ Fruit Exchange;
   75 Optional Calories
Per serving: 222 calories; 5 g protein; 9 g fat;
   31 g carbohydrate; 26 mg calcium; 91 mg sodium;
   76 mg cholesterol; 1 g dietary fiber

Peach-Berry Cobbler

Since fresh fruits are abundant in the summer, it's the perfect time to try this golden cobbler.

2 tablespoons plus 2 teaspoons peach nectar
1 teaspoon *each* cornstarch and granulated sugar
⅛ teaspoon *each* ground cinnamon and ground nutmeg
½ pound peaches, blanched, peeled, pitted, and thinly sliced
¼ cup blueberries
⅓ cup plus 2 teaspoons *each* buttermilk baking mix and buttermilk
1 egg white

Preheat oven to 425°F. Using a wire whisk, in medium mixing bowl combine nectar, cornstarch, sugar, cinnamon, and nutmeg and stir to dissolve cornstarch. Add peaches and blueberries and stir to coat; set aside.

In small mixing bowl combine baking mix and buttermilk, stirring until smooth; set aside. Using electric mixer on high speed, in separate small mixing bowl beat egg white until stiff but not dry; gently fold into buttermilk mixture.

Spray two 1½-cup casseroles with nonstick cooking spray; spoon half of the fruit mixture into each casserole. Then spread half of the buttermilk mixture over the fruit mixture in each casserole. Bake until top is lightly browned, 15 to 20 minutes. Set casseroles on wire rack and let cool for 5 minutes.

MAKES 2 SERVINGS

Each serving provides: 1 Bread Exchange;
   1½ Fruit Exchanges; ¼ Milk Exchange;
   45 Optional Calories
Per serving: 201 calories; 6 g protein; 4 g fat;
   37 g carbohydrate; 70 mg calcium; 388 mg sodium;
   2 mg cholesterol; 1 g dietary fiber

Quick Apple Tart ⊙

This easy-to-make tart is at its very best when eaten warm from the oven.

1 small Golden Delicious apple
  (about ¼ pound), cored, pared,
  and thinly sliced
2 teaspoons lemon juice
1 ready-to-bake refrigerated
  buttermilk flaky biscuit
  (1 ounce)
1 teaspoon confectioners' sugar,
  sifted, divided
Dash *each* ground nutmeg and
  ground cinnamon

Preheat oven to 400°F. In small bowl combine apple slices and lemon juice and turn to coat; set aside. On nonstick cookie sheet roll biscuit into a circle about 6 inches in diameter; using the tines of a fork, prick surface of biscuit. Decoratively arrange apple slices over biscuit. Sprinkle with ½ teaspoon sugar and the spices. Bake until golden, about 15 minutes. Let cool slightly; sprinkle with remaining ½ teaspoon sugar and serve.

MAKES 1 SERVING

Each serving provides: 1 Bread Exchange;
  1 Fruit Exchange; 20 Optional Calories
Per serving: 154 calories; 2 g protein; 4 g fat;
  30 g carbohydrate; 7 mg calcium; 298 mg sodium;
  0 mg cholesterol; 2 g dietary fiber (this figure does not
  include buttermilk biscuit; nutrition analysis not
  available)

Chocolate Sundae Cupcakes ⊙

¾ cup cake flour
3 tablespoons unsweetened cocoa
¾ teaspoon baking soda
2 eggs, separated
¼ cup *each* granulated sugar and
    vegetable oil
½ cup buttermilk
¼ cup thawed frozen dairy
    whipped topping
1 tablespoon plus 1 teaspoon
    chocolate syrup
4 maraschino cherries, cut into
    halves

*Read ingredient lists on labels care-
fully to spot the sodium content.
These terms should alert you to the
presence of sodium: soda (as in
baking soda), sodium (as in mono-
sodium glutamate), or salt (as in
garlic salt).*

Preheat oven to 350°F. On sheet of wax paper or a paper plate sift together flour, cocoa, and baking soda; set aside. Using electric mixer on high speed, in large mixing bowl beat together egg yolks and sugar until thick and lemon colored; gradually beat in oil. Add flour mixture alternately with butter-milk, beating after each addition, until combined; set aside.

Using clean beaters, in small mixing bowl beat egg whites on high speed until stiff but not dry. Gently fold beaten whites into flour mixture. Spray eight 2½-inch-diameter muffin-pan cups with nonstick cooking spray; fill each cup with an equal amount of batter (about ¼ cup) and partially fill remaining cups with water (this will prevent pan from burning and/or warping). Bake in middle of center oven rack for 15 to 20 minutes (until a toothpick, inserted in center, comes out clean). Remove pan from oven and carefully drain off water (remember, it will be boiling hot). Remove cupcakes from pan and set on wire rack to cool.

To serve, top each cupcake with ⅛ of the whipped topping and syrup, then top each with ½ maraschino cherry.

MAKES 8 SERVINGS

Each serving provides: ¼ Protein Exchange;
    ½ Bread Exchange; 1½ Fat Exchanges;
    65 Optional Calories
Per serving: 170 calories; 3 g protein; 9 g fat;
    20 g carbohydrate; 30 mg calcium; 116 mg sodium;
    69 mg cholesterol; 1 g dietary fiber (this figure does not
    include chocolate syrup; nutrition analysis not available)

Date and Nut Cakes

8 dried dates, pitted and finely
   diced
2 tablespoons granulated sugar
1 ounce chopped walnuts *or*
   pecans
4 graham crackers (2½-inch
   squares), made into crumbs
2 eggs, separated
Dash cream of tartar

Preheat oven to 375°F. In small mixing bowl combine dates and sugar and toss to coat; add nuts and graham cracker crumbs and stir to combine. Set aside.

Using electric mixer on medium speed, in medium mixing bowl beat egg yolks until thick and lemon colored; add to date mixture and stir to combine. Set aside. Using clean beaters, combine egg whites and cream of tartar and beat on medium speed until stiff peaks form; fold into date-egg yolk mixture.

Spray four 2½-inch-diameter muffin pan cups with nonstick cooking spray; spoon ¼ of batter into each sprayed cup and partially fill remaining cups with water (this will prevent pan from burning and/or warping). Bake in middle of center oven rack for 12 minutes (until cakes are golden brown and a toothpick, inserted in center, comes out clean). Remove pan from oven and carefully drain off water (remember, it will be boiling hot). Let cakes cool in pan for 1 minute. Remove cakes from pan and set on wire rack to cool.

MAKES 4 SERVINGS, 1 CAKE EACH

Each serving provides: 1 Protein Exchange;
   ½ Bread Exchange; ½ Fat Exchange; 1 Fruit Exchange;
   30 Optional Calories
Per serving: 185 calories; 4 g protein; 8 g fat;
   25 g carbohydrate; 25 mg calcium; 83 mg sodium;
   137 mg cholesterol; 2 g dietary fiber

Pineapple-Orange Cake ⓜ

2 graham crackers (2½-inch
   squares), made into crumbs
1 cup less 1 tablespoon
   all-purpose flour
1¼ teaspoons double-acting
   baking powder
½ teaspoon grated orange peel
   (optional)
Dash salt
½ cup granulated sugar
¼ cup sweet whipped butter
¼ cup less 1 teaspoon margarine
2 eggs
½ cup orange juice (no sugar
   added)
4 slices drained canned pineapple
   (no sugar added)
2 tablespoons reduced-calorie
   orange marmalade (16 calories
   per 2 teaspoons), melted
½ ounce sliced almonds, toasted

Spray 9-inch microwavable pie plate with nonstick cooking spray. Cut a sheet of wax paper into a 7-inch-diameter circle and set in pie plate; spray with nonstick cooking spray. Sprinkle graham cracker crumbs in pie plate and set aside.

In small mixing bowl combine flour, baking powder, orange peel (if desired), and the salt; set aside. Using electric mixer on medium speed, in large mixing bowl beat together sugar, butter, and margarine until light and fluffy, about 1 minute. Add eggs, 1 at a time, beating after each addition until thoroughly combined. Alternately add flour mixture and orange juice, beating after each addition until blended. Transfer batter to prepared pie plate, spreading top of batter until smooth. Microwave on Medium (50%) for 12 minutes, rotating pie plate ¼ turn every 4 minutes. Microwave on High (100%) for 30 seconds. Set pie plate on wire rack and let cool slightly, about 5 minutes.

Invert cake onto serving platter; remove and discard wax paper. Decoratively arrange pineapple slices on top of cake, brush slices with marmalade, and then top cake with almonds.

MAKES 12 SERVINGS

Each serving provides: ¼ Protein Exchange;
   ½ Bread Exchange; 1 Fat Exchange; ¼ Fruit Exchange;
   60 Optional Calories
Per serving: 161 calories; 3 g protein; 7 g fat;
   22 g carbohydrate; 38 mg calcium; 136 mg sodium;
   51 mg cholesterol; 0.5 g dietary fiber

Pineapple Right-Side-Up Cakes

1 cup plus 2 tablespoons
  all-purpose flour
2½ teaspoons double-acting
  baking powder
½ cup buttermilk
½ teaspoon vanilla extract
⅓ cup plus 2 teaspoons
  granulated sugar
¼ cup sweet whipped butter
1 egg
¼ cup less 2 teaspoons margarine
6 slices drained canned pineapple
  (no sugar added), each slice cut
  into quarters
6 maraschino cherries, cut into
  halves
1 ounce ground walnuts
2 tablespoons firmly packed light
  brown sugar

Preheat oven to 350°F. Line twelve 2½-inch-diameter muffin pan cups with paper baking cups; set aside. In small mixing bowl combine flour and baking powder; stir to combine and set aside. In separate small mixing bowl combine buttermilk and vanilla; stir to combine and set aside.

Using electric mixer on high speed, in medium mixing bowl beat together sugar, butter, egg, and margarine until thick and lemon colored, about 1 minute. Alternately add milk and flour mixtures, beating after each addition. Fill each baking cup with an equal amount of batter (each will be about ⅔ full). Top each with 2 pieces of pineapple and a cherry half. In cup or small bowl combine nuts and sugar; sprinkle 1/12 of mixture over each muffin cup. Bake for 15 to 20 minutes (until cakes are golden and a toothpick, inserted in center, comes out clean). Transfer cakes from pan to wire rack and let cool.

MAKES 12 SERVINGS, 1 CAKE EACH

Each serving provides: ¼ Protein Exchange;
    ½ Bread Exchange; 1 Fat Exchange; ¼ Fruit Exchange;
    65 Optional Calories
Per serving: 166 calories; 3 g protein; 7 g fat;
    23 g carbohydrate; 70 mg calcium; 164 mg sodium;
    28 mg cholesterol; 1 g dietary fiber

Southern Squash Pie Ⓜ

8 cinnamon graham crackers
  (2½-inch squares), made into
  crumbs, divided
1 tablespoon plus 1 teaspoon
  margarine, melted
2 eggs
1 package (8 ounces) frozen
  cooked squash puree, thawed
1 cup evaporated skimmed milk
2 tablespoons plus 2 teaspoons
  instant nonfat dry milk powder
2 tablespoons *each* firmly packed
  light brown sugar, divided, and
  half-and-half (blend of milk and
  cream)
1 teaspoon vanilla extract
½ teaspoon ground cinnamon
Dash ground nutmeg
½ ounce chopped pecans

In small mixing bowl combine all but 1 tablespoon graham cracker crumbs and the margarine and mix thoroughly; using the back of a spoon, press crumb mixture over bottom and up sides of 9-inch microwavable pie plate. Cover crust with paper plate or paper towel and microwave on High (100%) for 1½ minutes, rotating plate ½ turn halfway through cooking. Set aside.

Using a wire whisk, in medium mixing bowl beat eggs; stir in squash, milk, milk powder, 1 tablespoon sugar, the half-and-half, vanilla, cinnamon, and nutmeg. Pour squash mixture into prepared crust and microwave, uncovered, on Medium (50%) for 14 minutes, rotating pie plate ½ turn halfway through cooking.

In cup or small bowl combine reserved tablespoon graham cracker crumbs, sugar, and the pecans and sprinkle evenly over pie. Microwave, uncovered, on Medium for 1 minute. Let stand for 5 minutes. Cover pie with plastic wrap and refrigerate until chilled, at least 30 minutes.

MAKES 6 SERVINGS

Each serving provides: ½ Protein Exchange;
    1 Bread Exchange; ¾ Fat Exchange; ¼ Milk Exchange;
    45 Optional Calories
Per serving: 182 calories; 7 g protein; 8 g fat;
    22 g carbohydrate; 182 mg calcium; 179 mg sodium;
    95 mg cholesterol; 0.5 g dietary fiber

Chocolate-Mint Sauce ⓒⓜ

Serve warm or chilled. This sauce will keep in the refrigerator for up to 1 week.

½ cup evaporated skimmed milk
1 teaspoon cornstarch
1½ ounces semisweet chocolate
 chips
2 teaspoons margarine
½ teaspoon peppermint extract

In small microwavable mixing bowl combine milk and cornstarch and stir to dissolve cornstarch. Microwave on High (100%) for 1 minute. Add chocolate and margarine and microwave on High for 1 minute, until chocolate is melted and mixture thickens, stirring every 30 seconds. Stir in extract. Transfer to jar with tight-fitting cover and refrigerate until ready to serve.

**MAKES 4 SERVINGS,
ABOUT 3 TABLESPOONS EACH**

Each serving provides: ½ Fat Exchange;
 ¼ Milk Exchange; 60 Optional Calories
Per serving: 101 calories; 3 g protein; 6 g fat;
 10 g carbohydrate; 96 mg calcium; 59 mg sodium;
 1 mg cholesterol; dietary fiber data not available

Eggnog Sauce Ⓜ

This rum-spiked sauce can be stored in the refrigerator for up to 3 days. Serve it over fresh figs, berries, or ice milk.

½ cup evaporated skimmed milk
1 tablespoon *each* granulated
  sugar and dark rum
1 teaspoon cornstarch
1 egg
¼ teaspoon vanilla extract
⅛ teaspoon ground nutmeg

In small microwavable mixing bowl combine milk, sugar, rum, and cornstarch, and stir to dissolve cornstarch. Microwave on High (100%) for 1½ minutes, stirring every 30 seconds.

Using a wire whisk, in separate small microwavable mixing bowl beat egg; slowly stir milk mixture into egg. Stir in vanilla and nutmeg; microwave on Medium (50%) for 1½ minutes, until slightly thickened, stirring every 15 seconds *(do not overcook)*. Set aside and let cool slightly. Serve immediately or transfer to jar with tight-fitting cover and refrigerate until ready to serve.

**MAKES 4 SERVINGS,
ABOUT 3 TABLESPOONS EACH**

Each serving provides: ¼ Protein Exchange;
  ¼ Milk Exchange; 25 Optional Calories
Per serving: 68 calories; 4 g protein; 1 g fat;
  8 g carbohydrate; 100 mg calcium; 54 mg sodium;
  70 mg cholesterol; 0 g dietary fiber

Multi-Berry Sauce

Serve over ice milk or ice cream for a "berry" special dessert.

¾ cup *each* frozen raspberries and blueberries (no sugar added)
10 frozen pitted cherries (no sugar added)
2 teaspoons granulated sugar

In 1-quart saucepan (not aluminum) combine all ingredients and cook over medium-low heat until fruits are thawed and sugar is dissolved, about 5 minutes. Reduce heat to low and let simmer for 5 minutes. Transfer sauce to bowl; cover with plastic wrap and refrigerate until chilled.

MAKES 4 SERVINGS, ABOUT ¼ CUP EACH

Each serving provides: 1 Fruit Exchange;
   10 Optional Calories
Per serving: 47 calories; 1 g protein; 0.4 g fat;
   11 g carbohydrate; 9 mg calcium; 2 mg sodium;
   0 mg cholesterol; 2 g dietary fiber

Variation: Fresh Multi-Berry Sauce — Substitute fresh raspberries, blueberries, and cherries for the frozen fruit. Add 1 tablespoon water to saucepan, along with sugar, and cook for *6 minutes.*

8 Weeks of Menu Planners

Are you looking for new and exciting menu ideas for yourself and your family? Do you find you're just too busy to plan a week of menus? Are you concerned about the amount of sodium and cholesterol in your diet? Or are you a lacto-ovo vegetarian?

If you answered "yes" to one or more of these questions, you'll love our special Menu Planner section. It contains eight recipe-keyed, seven-day Menu Planners: two for anyone following the Weight Watchers program, two for vegetarian meals, two for sodium-reduced meals, and two for cholesterol-reduced meals. And all of the Menu Planners include recipes from throughout this book.

Our Vegetarian Menu Planners are based on the Weight Watchers Vegetarian Plan, a lacto-ovo diet that includes milk, milk products, and eggs, but no meat, poultry, or fish. The Sodium-Reduced Menu Planners are designed to help you lower your sodium intake by restricting daily sodium levels to no more than 1,600 milligrams. Our Cholesterol-Reduced Menu Planners contain no more than 140 milligrams of cholesterol per day. All the Menu Planners feature delicious and satisfying meals for your dining pleasure.

Bold type on the Menu Planners indicates that the item is a recipe from this book; menus are based on one serving of each recipe.

Keep in mind that the weights indicated in the Menu Planners for poultry, meat, and fish are net cooked (or drained canned) weights (without skin and bones).

The menus in this book were designed for women. Since the daily food requirements differ slightly for men and youths, the menus should be adjusted as follows:

Men and Youths: Daily add 2 Protein Exchanges, 2 Bread Exchanges, 1 Fat Exchange, and 1 to 2 Fruit Exchanges.

Youths only: Daily add 1 Milk Exchange.

MENU PLANNER #1

Day 1

BREAKFAST
¾ cup Orange-Grapefruit Juice
¾ ounce Cold Cereal
¾ cup Skim Milk
Coffee or Tea

LUNCH
Italian Tuna-Pasta Salad (2 ounces tuna with ½ cup each cooked small shell macaroni, broccoli florets, and sliced celery, 3 cherry tomatoes, cut into halves, and 1½ teaspoons Italian dressing mixed with 2 teaspoons red wine vinegar on 4 lettuce leaves)
1 small Pear
Coffee, Tea, or Mineral Water

DINNER
1 serving Chicken-Corn Bread Pies (page 115)
½ cup Cooked Spinach
Tomato-Sprout Salad (4 tomato wedges with ½ cup alfalfa sprouts and 1½ teaspoons blue cheese dressing mixed with 2 tablespoons plain low-fat yogurt and ¼ teaspoon mustard on 1 cup torn lettuce)
½ cup Reduced-Calorie Chocolate Pudding topped with 1 tablespoon Whipped Topping
Coffee or Tea

SNACK
Cherry Yogurt (½ cup plain low-fat yogurt mixed with 5 large cherries, pitted)

Optional Calories: 78

Day 2

BREAKFAST
½ medium Grapefruit sprinkled with ½ teaspoon Confectioners' Sugar
Bagel 'n' Lox (½ small bagel with 1 tablespoon cream cheese and 1 ounce smoked salmon)
½ cup Skim Milk
Coffee or Tea

LUNCH
Turkey and Coleslaw on Rye (2 ounces sliced turkey with ¼ cup coleslaw, 3 tomato slices, and 2 lettuce leaves on 2 slices reduced-calorie rye bread)
6 each Cucumber Spears and Green Bell Pepper Strips
Coffee, Tea, or Mineral Water

DINNER
1 serving Marinated Lamb Chops with Ginger (page 156)
1 cup Cooked Sliced Green Beans
1-ounce Roll
1 teaspoon Margarine
1½ cups Tossed Salad with 1½ teaspoons Thousand Island Dressing mixed with 2 tablespoons Plain Low-Fat Yogurt and ¼ teaspoon Mustard
½ cup Canned Pineapple Chunks sprinkled with 1 teaspoon Shredded Coconut
Coffee or Tea

SNACK
1 serving Strawberry-Banana Whip (page 329); 1 cup Skim Milk

Optional Calories: 90

Day 3

BREAKFAST
½ medium Banana, sliced
½ cup Cooked Cereal
¾ cup Skim Milk
Coffee or Tea

LUNCH
2 ounces Brie Cheese
1½ ounces Flatbreads
½ cup Broccoli Florets and 6 Carrot Sticks
1 small Pear
Coffee, Tea, or Mineral Water

DINNER
1 serving Sweet 'n' Spicy Chicken (page 103)
3-ounce Baked Potato, split and topped with 2 tablespoons Plain Low-Fat Yogurt and 2 teaspoons Chopped Chives
½ cup Cooked Sliced Zucchini
Mushroom, Celery, and Carrot Salad (½ cup each sliced mushrooms, sliced celery, and shredded carrot with 1 tablespoon French dressing mixed with 2 teaspoons lemon juice and ¼ teaspoon mustard on 4 lettuce leaves)
1 cup Cantaloupe Balls
Coffee or Tea

SNACK
½ cup Fruit Salad; 1 serving Reduced-Calorie Chocolate Dairy Drink

Optional Calories: 35

Day 4

BREAKFAST

1 cup Strawberries
Vegetable Omelet (1 egg with 2 tablespoons each chopped onion and green bell pepper)
1 slice Reduced-Calorie Wheat Bread, toasted
1 teaspoon Reduced-Calorie Margarine
¾ cup Skim Milk
Coffee or Tea

LUNCH

Roast Beef on a Bagel (2 ounces sliced roast beef with 2 lettuce leaves, ¼ cup sliced cucumber, and 2 teaspoons reduced-calorie mayonnaise on 1 small bagel)
½ cup Cauliflower Florets and 6 Celery Sticks
10 large Cherries
Coffee, Tea, or Mineral Water

DINNER

1 serving Zucchini-Buttermilk Soup (page 207)
3 ounces Broiled Swordfish Steak with Lemon Wedges
½ cup Cooked Brussels Sprouts
Tomato and Red Pepper Salad (6 each tomato wedges and red bell pepper strips with 1½ teaspoons Italian dressing mixed with 2 teaspoons red wine vinegar on 1 cup shredded lettuce)
½ cup Applesauce with dash Cinnamon
Coffee or Tea

SNACK

1 medium Chocolate Chip Cookie (½ ounce); 1 serving Reduced-Calorie Hot Cocoa

Optional Calories: 80

Day 5

BREAKFAST

1 cup Cantaloupe Chunks
¾ ounce Cold Cereal
1 cup Skim Milk
Coffee or Tea

LUNCH

1 slice Cheese Pizza (⅛ of 14-inch pie)
1½ cups Tossed Salad with 1 teaspoon Olive Oil plus Red Wine Vinegar and Herbs
Coffee, Tea, or Mineral Water

DINNER

3 ounces Roast Chicken
1 serving Barley with Mushrooms and Bacon (page 248)
Maple-Flavored Carrots (½ cup cooked sliced carrots drizzled with ½ teaspoon maple syrup)
1½ cups Mixed Green Salad with 1½ teaspoons Blue Cheese Dressing mixed with 2 tablespoons Plain Low-Fat Yogurt and ¼ teaspoon Mustard
½ cup Canned Pineapple Chunks
Coffee or Tea

SNACK

1 Graham Cracker; ¾ cup Skim Milk

Optional Calories: 35

Day 6

BREAKFAST

¾ cup Orange-Grapefruit Juice
1 serving BLT Egg Muffin (page 28)
1 cup Skim Milk
Coffee or Tea

LUNCH

Open-Face Turkey Salad Sandwich (2 ounces diced turkey with 2 tablespoons chopped celery, 2 teaspoons reduced-calorie mayonnaise, and 2 each tomato slices and lettuce leaves on 1 slice reduced-calorie wheat bread)
½ cup Broccoli Florets and 6 Carrot Sticks
Coffee, Tea, or Mineral Water

DINNER

1 serving Pasta with Spinach and Shrimp (page 64)
½ cup Cooked Sliced Zucchini with ¼ cup each Cooked Pearl Onions and Diced Red Bell Pepper
Cauliflower-Mushroom Salad (½ cup each cauliflower florets and sliced mushrooms with 1½ teaspoons Italian dressing mixed with 2 teaspoons red wine vinegar on 1 cup torn lettuce)
Coffee or Tea

SNACK

Fruity Pudding (½ cup reduced-calorie vanilla pudding topped with ¼ cup fruit salad)

Optional Calories: 75

Day 7

BREAKFAST

1 serving Oatmeal with Dried Fruits (page 243)
1 cup Skim Milk
Coffee or Tea

LUNCH

Tuna-Bell Pepper Sandwich (2 ounces tuna with 4 green bell pepper rings, 2 lettuce leaves, and 2 teaspoons reduced-calorie mayonnaise on 2 slices reduced-calorie rye bread)
6 each Carrot and Celery Sticks
¼ small Cantaloupe
Coffee, Tea, or Mineral Water

DINNER

1 serving Beef Bourguignonne (page 136)
1 cup Cooked Noodles
2 Cooked Broccoli Spears
Spinach-Mushroom Salad (½ cup sliced mushrooms with 3 tomato slices, 2 tablespoons diced red onion, and 1 tablespoon French dressing on 1 cup torn spinach leaves)
½ cup Reduced-Calorie Orange-Flavored Gelatin
Coffee or Tea

SNACK

1 cup Strawberries, sliced, topped with ½ cup Plain Low-Fat Yogurt

Optional Calories: 98

Total Optional Calories for the Week: 491

MENU PLANNER #2

Day 1

BREAKFAST
2-inch wedge Honeydew Melon
½ Whole Wheat English Muffin, toasted
1 tablespoon Whipped Cream Cheese
¾ cup Skim Milk
Coffee or Tea

LUNCH
Shrimp Salad Pita (2 ounces tiny shrimp with 2 tablespoons chopped celery, 2 teaspoons reduced-calorie mayonnaise, 3 tomato slices, and ½ cup shredded lettuce in 1-ounce pita)
½ cup each Cauliflower and Broccoli Florets
1 small Pear
Coffee, Tea, or Mineral Water

DINNER
1 serving **Creamy Cheddar Chicken** (page 97)
½ cup Cooked Noodles
1 teaspoon Margarine
½ cup Cooked Chopped Spinach
1½ cups Tossed Salad with 1½ teaspoons Italian Dressing mixed with 2 teaspoons Red Wine Vinegar
½ cup Blueberries sprinkled with ½ teaspoon Confectioners' Sugar
Coffee or Tea

SNACK
1 serving **Apple-Spice Pudding** (page 334)

Optional Calories: 113

Day 2

BREAKFAST
½ medium Banana, sliced
¾ ounce Cold Cereal
¾ cup Skim Milk
Coffee or Tea

LUNCH
Turkey on Pumpernickel (3 ounces sliced turkey with 2 lettuce leaves, ½ cup bean sprouts, and 2 teaspoons reduced-calorie mayonnaise on 2 slices pumpernickel bread)
6 each Yellow Squash Sticks and Red Bell Pepper Strips
2 medium Plums
Coffee, Tea, or Mineral Water

DINNER
1 serving **Lamb Chops with Minted Horseradish Sauce** (page 155)
9 Cooked Asparagus Spears
Mushroom-Radish Salad (¼ cup each sliced mushrooms and radishes with 1½ teaspoons blue cheese dressing mixed with 2 tablespoons plain low-fat yogurt and ¼ teaspoon mustard on 4 lettuce leaves)
Coffee or Tea

SNACK
½ cup Orange Sections; 1 cup Skim Milk

Optional Calories: 80

Day 3

BREAKFAST
¾ cup Grapefruit Juice
1 Scrambled Egg
1 slice Multi-Grain Bread, toasted
1 teaspoon Margarine
¾ cup Skim Milk
Coffee or Tea

LUNCH
Ham and Swiss Cheese Sandwich (1 ounce each sliced ham and Swiss cheese with 3 tomato slices, ½ cup shredded lettuce, 2 green bell pepper rings, and 2 teaspoons mustard on 2 slices reduced-calorie wheat bread)
6 each Celery Sticks and Whole Mushrooms
1 small Apple
2 cups Plain Popcorn
Coffee, Tea, or Mineral Water

DINNER
2 ounces Baked Flounder Fillet sprinkled with Paprika
1 serving **Shredded Beets with Raisins** (page 209)
1½ cups Mixed Green Salad with 1½ teaspoons Buttermilk Dressing mixed with 2 tablespoons Plain Low-Fat Yogurt and ¼ teaspoon Mustard
Coffee or Tea

SNACK
½ cup Reduced-Calorie Chocolate Pudding; 2 Graham Crackers

Optional Calories: 15

Day 4

BREAKFAST
½ cup Blueberries
⅓ cup Cottage Cheese
1 slice Reduced-Calorie Wheat Bread, toasted
1 teaspoon Margarine
1 cup Skim Milk
Coffee or Tea

LUNCH
Tuna-Pasta Toss (2 ounces tuna with ½ cup *each* cooked spiral macaroni, broccoli florets, and sliced zucchini and 1½ teaspoons Italian dressing mixed with 2 teaspoons red wine vinegar)
1 cup Honeydew Chunks
Coffee, Tea, or Mineral Water

DINNER
2 ounces Sliced Poached Chicken
1 serving **Microwave Stuffed Onion** (page 221)
Mushroom-Asparagus Combo (½ cup *each* cooked sliced mushrooms and asparagus)
1-ounce Roll
Lettuce Wedge with ¾ teaspoon Olive Oil plus Red Wine Vinegar and Herbs
Coffee or Tea

SNACK
1 medium Plum; 1 serving Reduced-Calorie Vanilla Dairy Drink

Optional Calories: 20

Day 5

BREAKFAST
½ cup Orange Sections
¾ ounce Cold Cereal
¾ cup Skim Milk
Coffee or Tea

LUNCH
Spinach-Cheddar Salad (1 ounce sliced Cheddar cheese with 2 ounces rinsed drained canned chick-peas, 1 cup spinach leaves, 6 tomato wedges, ½ cup sliced cucumber, 6 red bell pepper strips, and 1½ teaspoons French dressing mixed with 2 teaspoons lemon juice and ¼ teaspoon mustard)
6 Melba Rounds
1 small Pear
Coffee, Tea, or Mineral Water

DINNER
1 serving **Sweet and Sour Meat Balls** (page 143)
¾ cup Cooked Rice
1 cup Cooked Cauliflower Florets sprinkled with 1 teaspoon Sesame Seed, toasted
Cherry Tomato–Carrot Salad (3 cherry tomatoes, cut into halves, with ½ cup sliced carrot and 1½ teaspoons Russian dressing mixed with 2 tablespoons plain low-fat yogurt and ¼ teaspoon mustard)
Coffee or Tea

SNACK
Banana Pudding (½ cup reduced-calorie vanilla pudding topped with ½ medium banana, sliced)

Optional Calories: 50

Day 6

BREAKFAST
1 cup Honeydew Balls
⅓ cup Cottage Cheese
1 slice Reduced-Calorie Wheat Bread
1 teaspoon Reduced-Calorie Margarine
1 cup Skim Milk
Coffee or Tea

LUNCH
1 serving **Chickado 'wiches** (page 94)
6 Carrot Sticks and ½ cup Broccoli Florets
2 medium Plums
Coffee, Tea, or Mineral Water

DINNER
2½ ounces Parslied Poached Shrimp
1 cup Cooked Fettuccine sprinkled with 1 teaspoon Grated Parmesan Cheese
9 Cooked Asparagus Spears
Yellow Squash and Cucumber Salad (½ cup each sliced yellow squash and cucumber with red wine vinegar and herbs on 4 lettuce leaves)
Coffee or Tea

SNACK
1 serving **Marshmallow-Popcorn Snack** (page 302); 1 cup Skim Milk

Optional Calories: 130

Day 7

BREAKFAST
½ cup Grapefruit Juice
1 Scrambled Egg
1 serving **Breakfast Puffs** (page 239)
½ cup Skim Milk
Coffee or Tea

LUNCH
Tuna Salad Sandwich (2 ounces tuna with 2 tablespoons chopped celery, 2 teaspoons reduced-calorie mayonnaise, and 2 each lettuce leaves and red onion slices on 2 slices reduced-calorie wheat bread)
6 each Celery Sticks and Zucchini Sticks
1 small Apple
Coffee, Tea, or Mineral Water

DINNER
1 serving **Bean Chowder** (page 164)
1-ounce slice Italian Bread
1½ cups Tossed Salad with Balsamic Vinegar and Herbs
½ cup Reduced-Calorie Butterscotch Pudding
Coffee or Tea

SNACK
1 Graham Cracker; 1 cup Honeydew Chunks

Optional Calories: 70

Total Optional Calories for the Week: 478

MENU PLANNER #3—
VEGETARIAN

Day 1

BREAKFAST
½ medium Banana, sliced
¾ ounce Cold Cereal
1 cup Skim Milk
Coffee or Tea

LUNCH
1 serving **Escarole and Vegetable Soup** (page 203)
Bean-Corn Salad (4 ounces rinsed drained canned black beans with ½ cup drained canned whole-kernel corn, ¼ cup diced red bell pepper, and 1½ teaspoons Italian dressing mixed with 2 teaspoons red wine vinegar on 4 lettuce leaves)
1-ounce Roll
20 small Grapes
Coffee, Tea, or Mineral Water

DINNER
Chick-Pea Pita Pizza (1-ounce whole wheat pita topped with ¼ cup tomato sauce, 3 ounces rinsed drained canned chick-peas, and ½ ounce shredded mozzarella cheese, grilled)
½ cup Broccoli Florets
1 serving **Parmesan and Mixed Green Salad** (page 40)
Coffee or Tea

SNACK
½ cup Orange Sections; ½ cup Reduced-Calorie Chocolate Pudding

Optional Calories: 8

Day 2

BREAKFAST
Peanut Butter-Raisin Toast (1 slice multi-grain bread, toasted and topped with 1 tablespoon peanut butter and 2 tablespoons dark raisins)
1 cup Skim Milk
Coffee or Tea

LUNCH
1 serving **Chick-Pea and Artichoke Salad** (page 191)
¾ ounce Breadsticks
1 small Apple
Coffee, Tea, or Mineral Water

DINNER
¾ cup Onion Bouillon with 1 tea-spoon Chopped Scallion
Oriental Tofu (6 ounces cubed tofu with ½ cup each sliced red bell pepper, pearl onions, and Chinese pea pods stir-fried in 1 teaspoon vegetable oil and 1 tablespoon reduced-sodium soy sauce)
½ cup Cooked Rice with ½ teaspoon Sesame Seed, toasted
Tea with Lemon Wedge

SNACK
Strawberry Yogurt (1 cup each strawberries, sliced, and plain low-fat yogurt with dash cinnamon)

Optional Calories: 30

Day 3

BREAKFAST
½ cup Orange Sections
Maple Oatmeal (1 cup cooked oatmeal drizzled with ½ teaspoon maple syrup)
1 cup Skim Milk
Coffee or Tea

LUNCH
Sliced Egg Pita Pocket (1 hard-cooked egg, sliced, with ¼ cup alfalfa sprouts, 3 tomato slices, and 2 teaspoons reduced-calorie mayonnaise in 1-ounce whole wheat pita)
6 *each* Carrot Sticks and Red Bell Pepper Strips
Coffee, Tea, or Mineral Water

DINNER
Feta Cheese Salad (2 ounces crumbled feta cheese with 2 cups torn lettuce, 4 tomato wedges, ½ cup sliced cucumber, and 1½ teaspoons Caesar dressing mixed with 2 teaspoons lemon juice and ¼ teaspoon mustard)
1 serving **Couscous Pilaf** (page 249)
Iced Tea with Mint Sprig

SNACK
3 Gingersnap Cookies; 1 serving Reduced-Calorie Chocolate Dairy Drink

Optional Calories: 100

Day 4

BREAKFAST
½ cup Orange Juice
1 serving **Blueberry Pancakes** (page 244)
1 cup Skim Milk
Coffee or Tea

LUNCH
Pasta-Bean Salad (4 ounces rinsed drained canned red kidney beans with ½ cup each cooked elbow macaroni, sliced zucchini, and sliced carrot and 1½ teaspoons Italian dressing mixed with 2 teaspoons red wine vinegar)
Coffee, Tea, or Mineral Water

DINNER
Tex-Mex Pintos (4 ounces rinsed drained canned pinto beans topped with ¼ cup each diced tomato and red onion and ½ ounce Monterey Jack cheese, melted)
1 Corn Tortilla, toasted and quartered
1½ cups Mixed Green Salad with 1½ teaspoons Buttermilk Dressing mixed with 2 tablespoons Plain Low-Fat Yogurt and ¼ teaspoon Mustard
1 cup Honeydew Chunks
Iced Tea with Lemon Slice

SNACK
¾ cup Applesauce; ¾ cup Skim Milk

Optional Calories: 40

Day 5

BREAKFAST
½ cup Grapefruit Juice
1 ounce Granola
1 cup Skim Milk
Coffee or Tea

LUNCH
Cottage Cheese Fruit Salad (⅔ cup cottage cheese topped with ½ cup each cantaloupe and pineapple chunks and 1 teaspoon shredded coconut, toasted)
6 each Red and Green Bell Pepper Strips
1 slice Multi-Grain Bread
1 teaspoon Margarine
Coffee, Tea, or Mineral Water

DINNER
Bean-Topped "Tater" (3-ounce baked potato, split and topped with 4 ounces rinsed drained canned red kidney beans and 1 teaspoon grated Parmesan cheese)
½ cup each Carrot Sticks and Cauliflower Florets
1 serving **Jicama Salad** (page 232)
Coffee or Tea

SNACK
Berry Yogurt (½ cup plain low-fat yogurt mixed with 1 teaspoon reduced-calorie strawberry spread); 2 Graham Crackers

Optional Calories: 88

Day 6

BREAKFAST
½ cup Orange Sections
½ Whole Wheat English Muffin, toasted
1 serving **Microwave Apple Butter** (page 285)
¾ cup Skim Milk
Coffee or Tea

LUNCH
Three-Bean Salad (2 ounces each rinsed drained canned red kidney beans and white kidney beans with ½ cup cooked sliced green beans, ¼ cup sliced red onion, and 1½ teaspoons Italian dressing mixed with 2 teaspoons red wine vinegar)
1 slice Reduced-Calorie Wheat Bread
½ cup Sliced Yellow Squash and 6 Celery Sticks
Coffee, Tea, or Mineral Water

DINNER
1 serving **Bean and Vegetable Soup with Pesto Topping** (page 166)
¾ ounce Breadsticks
Lettuce Wedge with 1½ teaspoons Thousand Island Dressing mixed with 2 tablespoons Plain Low-Fat Yogurt and ¼ teaspoon Mustard
1 cup Fruit Salad
Coffee or Tea

SNACK
1 serving Reduced-Calorie Hot Cocoa topped with 1 tablespoon Whipped Topping

Optional Calories: 43

Day 7

BREAKFAST
1 cup Cantaloupe Balls
1 serving **Scrambled Huevos Rancheros** (page 30)
1 cup Skim Milk
Coffee or Tea

LUNCH
1 serving **Lentils and Vegetables** (page 186)
1 slice Multi-Grain Bread
6 Cucumber Spears and 3 Cherry Tomatoes
Coffee, Tea, or Mineral Water

DINNER
Tofu Sauté (4½ ounces cubed tofu with ½ cup sliced celery, 6 red bell pepper strips, ¼ cup sliced scallions, and ½ teaspoon each minced garlic and minced pared gingerroot sautéed in 1 teaspoon vegetable oil)
1 cup Cooked Rice
1½ cups Mixed Green Salad with Balsamic Vinegar and Herbs
½ cup Strawberries
Tea with Cinnamon Stick Stirrer

SNACK
10 small Grapes; ½ cup Reduced-Calorie Butterscotch Pudding

Optional Calories: 15

Total Optional Calories for the Week: 324

MENU PLANNER #4— VEGETARIAN

Day 1

BREAKFAST
½ cup Orange Sections
1 serving **Blueberry-Corn Muffins** (page 257)
2 teaspoons Reduced-Calorie Grape Spread
1 cup Skim Milk
Coffee or Tea

LUNCH
Chick-Pea and Egg Salad (2 ounces rinsed drained canned chick-peas with 1 hard-cooked egg, cut into wedges, 3 cherry tomatoes, cut into halves, and 1½ teaspoons Italian dressing mixed with 2 teaspoons red wine vinegar on 4 lettuce leaves)
6 Melba Rounds
1 medium Plum
Coffee, Tea, or Mineral Water

DINNER
1 serving **Cream of Cucumber and Leek Soup** (page 201)
Ricotta-Vegetable Potato (6-ounce baked potato, split and topped with ½ cup each part-skim ricotta cheese, cooked broccoli florets, and cooked sliced yellow squash)
1½ cups Tossed Salad with 1½ teaspoons French Dressing mixed with 2 teaspoons Lemon Juice and ¼ teaspoon Mustard
Coffee or Tea

SNACK
1 small Pear; ½ cup Reduced-Calorie Chocolate Pudding

Optional Calories: 106

Day 2

BREAKFAST
½ cup Grapefruit Juice
Cheese Melt (1 slice reduced-calorie wheat bread, toasted and topped with 1 ounce Muenster cheese, melted)
1 cup Skim Milk
Coffee or Tea

LUNCH
Tropical Fruit Salad Platter (⅔ cup cottage cheese with ½ cup pineapple chunks and 1 teaspoon shredded coconut on 4 lettuce leaves)
1 Rice Cake
Honey-Yogurt Crunch (½ cup plain low-fat yogurt mixed with ½ teaspoon each wheat germ and honey)
Coffee, Tea, or Mineral Water

DINNER
Oriental Tofu with Pea Pods (6 ounces cubed tofu with ½ cup Chinese pea pods stir-fried in 2 teaspoons each vegetable oil and dry sherry and 1 teaspoon reduced-sodium soy sauce)
1 serving **Asian Noodle Salad** (page 272)
Tea

SNACK
Peach Shake (1 cup skim milk with ½ cup canned peach slices and 2 ice cubes, processed in blender)

Optional Calories: 35

Day 3

BREAKFAST
1 cup Strawberries, sliced
¾ ounce Cold Cereal
1 cup Skim Milk

LUNCH
Egg Salad Sandwich (1 hard-cooked egg, chopped, with 2 tablespoons chopped celery, 2 teaspoons reduced-calorie mayonnaise, ¼ teaspoon Dijon-style mustard, 2 lettuce leaves, and 3 tomato slices on 2 slices reduced-calorie wheat bread)
½ cup Cauliflower Florets and 6 Carrot Sticks
1 small Apple
Coffee, Tea, or Mineral Water

DINNER
Vegetarian Taco (3 ounces rinsed drained canned red kidney beans with ½ ounce shredded Cheddar cheese, ½ cup shredded lettuce, ¼ cup diced tomato, 1 tablespoon sour cream, and dash hot sauce in 1 taco shell)
½ cup Cooked Sliced Zucchini with ¼ cup Cooked Chopped Tomato
1 cup Cantaloupe Balls with Mint Sprig
1 cup Skim Milk
Coffee or Tea

SNACK
1 small Pear; 1 serving **Sugar-Spiced Pecans** (page 305)

Optional Calories: 88

BREAKFAST

½ cup Orange Juice
Egg-Stuffed Pita (1 egg, scrambled with 2 tablespoons chopped scallion, in 1-ounce whole wheat pita)
1 cup Skim Milk
Coffee or Tea

LUNCH

Peanut Butter and Apricot Spread Sandwich (1 tablespoon peanut butter with 2 teaspoons reduced-calorie apricot spread on 2 slices reduced-calorie wheat bread)
6 each Celery and Zucchini Sticks
1 medium Plum
Coffee, Tea, or Mineral Water

DINNER

1 serving Vegetarian Chili with Corn Muffin (page 259)
½ cup Cooked Broccoli Florets sprinkled with Grated Lemon Peel
Chick-Pea and Tomato Salad (4 ounces rinsed drained canned chick-peas with ½ cup diced tomato, ¼ cup sliced red onion, and 1½ teaspoons Italian dressing mixed with 2 teaspoons red wine vinegar on 2 lettuce leaves)
Coffee or Tea

SNACK

½ cup Strawberries; 1 serving Reduced-Calorie Vanilla Dairy Drink

Optional Calories: 61

BREAKFAST

Banana-Spiced Oatmeal (½ cup cooked oatmeal with ½ medium banana, sliced, and dash cinnamon)
¾ cup Skim Milk
Coffee or Tea

LUNCH

Vegetable Cottage Cheese (⅔ cup cottage cheese with ¼ cup each diced tomato, cucumber, and carrot and 2 tablespoons sliced radishes)
1 slice Reduced-Calorie Wheat Bread
Coffee, Tea, or Mineral Water

DINNER

1 serving Linguine with Vegetables (page 266)
Mozzarella Bread (1-ounce slice Italian bread topped with 1 ounce mozzarella cheese, melted)
1 cup Cooked Green Beans
1½ cups Tossed Salad with 1 teaspoon Olive Oil plus Red Wine Vinegar and Herbs
Coffee or Tea

SNACK

½ cup Orange Sections; 1 cup Skim Milk

Optional Calories: 30

BREAKFAST

½ cup Grapefruit Juice
1 Scrambled Egg
½ small Bagel, toasted
1 teaspoon Margarine
½ cup Skim Milk
Coffee or Tea

LUNCH

1 serving Fruit and Cheese Pizza (page 262)
6 each Carrot Sticks and Cucumber Spears
Coffee, Tea, or Mineral Water

DINNER

1 serving Creamy Gazpacho (page 202)
White Bean–Vegetable Toss (4 ounces rinsed drained canned white beans with 1 cup torn lettuce, 6 tomato wedges, ½ cup each sliced cucumber and broccoli florets, and 1½ teaspoons Thousand Island dressing mixed with 2 tablespoons plain low-fat yogurt and ¼ teaspoon mustard)
Coffee or Tea

SNACK

½ cup Fruit Salad; ¾ cup Skim Milk

Optional Calories: 55

BREAKFAST

1 cup Strawberries
1 serving Vegetable Pancakes (page 246)
1 cup Skim Milk
Coffee or Tea

LUNCH

Peanut Butter Crunchies (2 tablespoons peanut butter on 2 rice cakes)
½ cup Cauliflower Florets and 3 Cherry Tomatoes
1 small Apple
Coffee, Tea, or Mineral Water

DINNER

1 serving Black Bean Terrine (page 177)
1 cup Cooked Carrot Sticks
1½ cups Mixed Green Salad with 3 ounces Rinsed Drained Canned Chick-Peas and 1½ teaspoons Italian Dressing mixed with 2 teaspoons Red Wine Vinegar
2 medium Plums
Coffee or Tea

SNACK

1 slice Reduced-Calorie Wheat Bread with 2 teaspoons Reduced-Calorie Strawberry Spread; ¾ cup Skim Milk

Optional Calories: 116

Total Optional Calories for the Week: 491

MENU PLANNER #5—
SODIUM REDUCED

Day 1

BREAKFAST

½ cup Orange Juice
¾ ounce Cold Cereal
¾ cup Skim Milk
Coffee or Tea

LUNCH

Roast Beef and American Cheese on Rye (1 ounce each sliced roast beef and American cheese with 2 each lettuce leaves and tomato slices and 2 teaspoons reduced-calorie mayonnaise on 2 slices reduced-calorie rye bread)
6 each Cucumber Spears and Carrot Sticks
1 small Pear
Coffee, Tea, or Mineral Water

DINNER

1 serving **Parmesan Fillets** (page 73)
½ cup each Cooked Peas and Sliced Mushrooms
Cauliflower-Squash Combo (½ cup each cauliflower florets and sliced yellow squash with 1½ teaspoons buttermilk dressing mixed with 2 tablespoons plain low-fat yogurt and ¼ teaspoon mustard on 1 cup shredded lettuce)
½ cup Fruit Salad sprinkled with 1 teaspoon Shredded Coconut, toasted
Coffee or Tea

SNACK

Banana-Yogurt Crunch (½ cup plain low-fat yogurt mixed with ½ medium banana, sliced, and 1 teaspoon wheat germ)

Optional Calories: 20

Day 2

BREAKFAST

½ cup Grapefruit Sections
½ small Bagel
1 tablespoon Cream Cheese
½ cup Skim Milk
Coffee or Tea

LUNCH

Tuna Salad Platter (2 ounces tuna with 2 tablespoons chopped celery, 2 teaspoons reduced-calorie mayonnaise, 4 tomato wedges, ½ cup sliced cucumber, 3 red bell pepper rings, and 3 radish roses on 4 lettuce leaves)
¾ ounce Flatbreads
1 medium Kiwi Fruit
Coffee, Tea, or Mineral Water

DINNER

1 serving **Ground Lamb Lyonnaise** (page 153)
1 cup Cooked French-Style Green Beans
1½ cups Tossed Salad with ½ teaspoon Olive Oil plus Balsamic Vinegar and Herbs
1 serving **Figs with Pistachio Cream** (page 324)
Cappuccino (½ cup each hot espresso and hot skim milk with cinnamon stick stirrer)

SNACK

2 cups Plain Popcorn; 1 serving Reduced-Calorie Chocolate Dairy Drink

Optional Calories: 85

Day 3

BREAKFAST

1 cup Strawberries sprinkled with ½ teaspoon Confectioners' Sugar
½ cup Cooked Cereal
¾ cup Skim Milk
Coffee or Tea

LUNCH

Turkey-Vegetable Pita (2 ounces sliced turkey with ¼ cup alfalfa sprouts, 3 tomato slices, and 2 teaspoons reduced-calorie mayonnaise in 1-ounce whole wheat pita)
½ cup Broccoli Florets and 6 Zucchini Sticks
Coffee, Tea, or Mineral Water

DINNER

2 ounces Roast Veal
1 serving **Couscous Pilaf** (page 249)
6 Cooked Asparagus Spears
Romaine-Vegetable Toss (1 cup torn romaine lettuce with 3 cherry tomatoes, cut into halves, ¼ cup shredded carrot, and 1½ teaspoons Thousand Island dressing mixed with 2 tablespoons plain low-fat yogurt and ¼ teaspoon mustard)
½ cup Reduced-Calorie Butterscotch Pudding
Coffee or Tea

SNACK

1 medium Chocolate Chip Cookie (½ ounce); 1 cup Skim Milk

Optional Calories: 100

BREAKFAST

½ cup Grapefruit Sections
1 serving **Microwave Buttery Scrambled Eggs** (page 26)
½ small Bagel, toasted
1 teaspoon Reduced-Calorie Margarine
¾ cup Skim Milk
Coffee or Tea

LUNCH

Mozzarella-Pasta Salad (1 ounce cubed mozzarella cheese with ½ cup each cooked small shell macaroni and broccoli florets, 4 tomato wedges, ¼ cup sliced red onion, and 1½ teaspoons Italian dressing mixed with 2 teaspoons red wine vinegar)
1 medium Peach
Coffee, Tea, or Mineral Water

DINNER

1 serving **Poached Fillets Vinaigrette** (page 74)
½ cup Cooked Parslied Rice
½ cup Cooked Chopped Spinach
Red Cabbage Salad (½ cup each shredded red cabbage and carrot with 1½ teaspoons Russian dressing mixed with 2 tablespoons plain low-fat yogurt and ¼ teaspoon mustard on 4 lettuce leaves)
Coffee or Tea

SNACK

1 cup Cantaloupe Chunks; 1 cup Skim Milk

Optional Calories: 55

BREAKFAST

½ cup Orange Juice
1 ounce Swiss Cheese
6 Melba Rounds
½ cup Skim Milk
Coffee or Tea

LUNCH

Peanut Butter–Banana Sandwich (1 tablespoon peanut butter with ½ medium banana, sliced, on 2 slices reduced-calorie wheat bread)
6 each Celery and Carrot Sticks
1 small Pear
Coffee, Tea, or Mineral Water

DINNER

3 ounces Sliced Roast Turkey
3-ounce Baked Potato, split and topped with ¼ cup Plain Low-Fat Yogurt and 2 teaspoons Chopped Scallion
Minted Carrots (1 cup cooked sliced carrots with 1 teaspoon reduced-calorie margarine and ½ teaspoon chopped fresh mint)
1 serving **Asparagus and Strawberry Salad** (page 236)
Coffee or Tea

SNACK

10 small Grapes; 1 serving Reduced-Calorie Chocolate Dairy Drink

Optional Calories: 15

BREAKFAST

1 serving **Nutty Oatmeal with Raisins** (page 242)
1 cup Skim Milk
Coffee or Tea

LUNCH

Egg Salad Pita (1 hard-cooked egg, chopped, with 2 tablespoons chopped celery, 2 teaspoons reduced-calorie mayonnaise, ¼ teaspoon mustard, ¼ cup alfalfa sprouts, and 2 lettuce leaves in 1-ounce whole wheat pita)
½ cup Cauliflower Florets and 6 Red Bell Pepper Strips
1 medium Peach
Coffee, Tea, or Mineral Water

DINNER

3 ounces Broiled Flounder Fillet with 1½ teaspoons Tartar Sauce and Lemon Wedge
½ cup Cooked Sliced Zucchini with ¼ cup Cooked Pearl Onions
1-ounce Roll
1½ cups Tossed Salad with Tarragon Vinegar and Herbs
1 medium Kiwi Fruit
Coffee or Tea

SNACK

1 serving **Honey-Sesame Popcorn** (page 301); 1 cup Skim Milk

Optional Calories: 90

BREAKFAST

1 cup Cantaloupe Balls
⅓ cup Cottage Cheese
½ small Bagel
2 teaspoons Reduced-Calorie Margarine
½ cup Skim Milk
Coffee or Tea

LUNCH

Tuna and Tomato Sandwich (2 ounces tuna with 3 tomato slices, 2 lettuce leaves, and 2 teaspoons reduced-calorie mayonnaise on 2 slices reduced-calorie wheat bread)
½ cup Broccoli Florets and 6 Celery Sticks
20 small Grapes
Coffee, Tea, or Mineral Water

DINNER

1 serving **Pork Chops with Brandied Fruits** (page 146)
Caraway Noodles (½ cup cooked noodles sprinkled with ½ teaspoon caraway seed)
½ cup Cooked Shredded Red Cabbage
1½ cups Mixed Green Salad with Red Wine Vinegar and Herbs
Coffee or Tea

SNACK

½ cup Reduced-Calorie Cherry-Flavored Gelatin topped with ¼ cup Plain Low-Fat Yogurt; 1 cup Skim Milk

Optional Calories: 58

Total Optional Calories for the Week: 423

Day 1

BREAKFAST

Ricotta with Apricots (¼ cup part-skim ricotta cheese mixed with 4 dried apricot halves, chopped)
½ Raisin English Muffin, toasted
1 teaspoon Reduced-Calorie Margarine
¾ cup Skim Milk
Coffee or Tea

LUNCH

Spinach-Tuna Toss (1 ounce tuna with 1 cup torn spinach, ½ cup cubed red bell pepper, 6 tomato wedges, ¼ cup each sliced scallions and carrot, ½ ounce croutons, and 1½ teaspoons Italian dressing mixed with 2 teaspoons red wine vinegar)
2 Rice Cakes
1 cup Strawberries
Coffee, Tea, or Mineral Water

DINNER

1 serving Pork Medallions with Cran-Orange Sauce (page 148)
½ cup Cooked Rice
1 cup Cooked Cauliflower Florets with 2 teaspoons Diced Pimiento
Belgian Endive and Tomato Salad (1 cup Belgian endive leaves with 3 cherry tomatoes, cut into halves, and 1½ teaspoons Thousand Island dressing mixed with 2 tablespoons plain low-fat yogurt and ¼ teaspoon mustard)
Coffee or Tea

SNACK

Pineapple Pudding (½ cup reduced-calorie vanilla pudding topped with ¼ cup canned crushed pineapple and 1 tablespoon whipped topping)

Optional Calories: 83

Day 2

BREAKFAST

½ cup Grapefruit Juice
1 serving **Banana-Pecan Farina** (page 240)
½ cup Skim Milk
Coffee or Tea

LUNCH

Turkey-Mushroom Pita (2 ounces sliced turkey with ¼ cup each sliced mushrooms and shredded lettuce and 1½ teaspoons Russian dressing in 1-ounce pita)
6 each Cucumber Spears and Green Bell Pepper Strips
5 large Cherries
Coffee, Tea, or Mineral Water

DINNER

1 serving Fish Amandine (page 70)
½ cup Cooked Noodles
1 serving **Orange-Glazed Carrots and Onions** (page 211)
Two-Squash Salad (¼ cup each sliced yellow squash and zucchini with red wine vinegar and herbs on 4 lettuce leaves)
½ cup Reduced-Calorie Chocolate Pudding
Coffee or Tea

SNACK

½ cup Honeydew Chunks; ½ cup Skim Milk

Optional Calories: 170

Day 3

BREAKFAST

¾ cup Orange Sections
1 Scrambled Egg
½ English Muffin, toasted
1 cup Skim Milk
Coffee or Tea

LUNCH

Cheddar Bagel (1 ounce sliced Cheddar cheese with 2 each tomato slices and lettuce leaves and 1 teaspoon reduced-calorie mayonnaise on ½ small bagel)
6 Celery Sticks and ½ cup Cauliflower Florets
1 small Apple
Coffee, Tea, or Mineral Water

DINNER

3 ounces Sliced Poached Chicken with 1 serving **Raisin-Onion Sauce** (page 295)
3 ounces Parslied Boiled Red Potatoes
1 teaspoon Reduced-Calorie Margarine
½ cup Cooked Spinach
1½ cups Tossed Salad with 1½ teaspoons French Dressing mixed with 2 teaspoons Lemon Juice and ¼ teaspoon Mustard
Coffee or Tea

SNACK

Banana Shake (1 cup skim milk with ½ medium banana, ¼ teaspoon vanilla extract, and 2 ice cubes, processed in blender)

Optional Calories: 15

Day 4

BREAKFAST
3 medium Prunes, plumped
¾ ounce Cold Cereal
1 cup Skim Milk
Coffee or Tea

LUNCH
Roast Beef on a Roll (2 ounces sliced roast beef with ½ cup shredded lettuce, 3 tomato slices, ¼ cup sliced cucumber, and 1½ teaspoons Thousand Island dressing on 2-ounce roll)
6 Zucchini Sticks and 3 Radishes
1 small Pear
Coffee, Tea, or Mineral Water

DINNER
1 serving **Crustless Seafood Quiche** (page 57)
½ cup Cooked Barley with ¼ cup Cooked Sliced Mushrooms and 2 tablespoons Cooked Chopped Onion
Dilly Carrots (1 cup cooked carrots with ½ teaspoon chopped fresh dill)
1½ cups Mixed Green Salad with 1½ teaspoons Buttermilk Dressing mixed with 2 tablespoons Plain Low-Fat Yogurt and ¼ teaspoon Mustard
Coffee or Tea

SNACK
1 cup Strawberries topped with ¼ cup Plain Low-Fat Yogurt and dash Cinnamon

Optional Calories: 30

Day 5

BREAKFAST
2-inch wedge Honeydew Melon topped with ¼ cup Part-Skim Ricotta Cheese
½ Raisin English Muffin, toasted
1 teaspoon Reduced-Calorie Margarine
½ cup Skim Milk
Coffee or Tea

LUNCH
Tuna-Macaroni Salad (1¾ ounces tuna with ½ cup cooked elbow macaroni, 1 tablespoon each chopped celery and onion, and 2 tablespoons plain low-fat yogurt mixed with 2 teaspoons reduced-calorie mayonnaise on 2 lettuce leaves)
½ cup Broccoli Florets and 6 Cucumber Spears
10 large Cherries
Coffee, Tea, or Mineral Water

DINNER
1 serving **Chicken and Mushrooms in Parmesan Cream** (page 107)
½ cup Cooked Long Grain and Wild Rice
½ cup Cooked Cauliflower Florets
Bean Sprout Salad (½ cup bean sprouts with ¼ cup each sliced celery and carrot and ½ teaspoon olive oil plus balsamic vinegar and herbs on 1 cup torn lettuce)
Coffee or Tea

SNACK
½ medium Banana; ½ cup Reduced-Calorie Butterscotch Pudding

Optional Calories: 55

Day 6

BREAKFAST
½ cup Orange Sections
¾ ounce Cold Cereal
1 cup Skim Milk
Coffee or Tea

LUNCH
Peanut Butter and Apricot Sandwich (2 tablespoons peanut butter and 4 dried apricot halves, chopped, on 2 slices reduced-calorie wheat bread)
6 each Carrot and Celery Sticks
Coffee, Tea, or Mineral Water

DINNER
1 serving **Italian Clam Soup** (page 50)
1½ ounces Italian Bread
Parmesan Salad (2 ounces rinsed drained canned chick-peas with 1 cup torn lettuce, ½ cup chilled cooked artichoke hearts, and 2 teaspoons grated Parmesan cheese plus red wine vinegar and herbs)
Chocolate Pear (1 small pear, pared and poached, drizzled with 1 teaspoon chocolate syrup)
Coffee or Tea

SNACK
½ cup Canned Crushed Pineapple; 1 serving Reduced-Calorie Chocolate Dairy Drink

Optional Calories: 60

Day 7

BREAKFAST
½ cup Grapefruit Juice
1 serving **Mexican Eggs in Potato Shells** (page 31)
½ cup Skim Milk
Coffee or Tea

LUNCH
Tuna-Vegetable Pita (1¾ ounces tuna with 3 tomato slices, 2 lettuce leaves, ¼ cup sliced red onion, and 1 teaspoon reduced-calorie mayonnaise in 1-ounce pita)
6 each Green Bell Pepper Strips and Cucumber Spears
1 cup Honeydew Balls
Coffee, Tea, or Mineral Water

DINNER
3 ounces Broiled Lamb Chop
½ cup Cooked Chinese Pea Pods with 1½ ounces Water Chestnuts
Tomato-Mushroom Salad (4 tomato wedges with ½ cup sliced mushrooms and 1½ teaspoons French dressing mixed with 2 teaspoons lemon juice and ¼ teaspoon mustard on 4 lettuce leaves)
Coffee or Tea

SNACK
Cherry Yogurt (¾ cup plain low-fat yogurt mixed with 5 large cherries, pitted)

Optional Calories: 35

Total Optional Calories for the Week: 448

MENU PLANNER #7—
CHOLESTEROL REDUCED

Day 1

BREAKFAST
Raisin Oatmeal (½ cup cooked oatmeal with 2 tablespoons golden raisins and dash cinnamon)
¾ cup Skim Milk
Coffee or Tea

LUNCH
Turkey on Rye (2 ounces sliced turkey with ½ cup alfalfa sprouts, 2 lettuce leaves, and 2 teaspoons reduced-calorie mayonnaise on 2 slices reduced-calorie rye bread)
½ cup Broccoli Florets and 6 Carrot Sticks
1 small Apple
Coffee, Tea, or Mineral Water

DINNER
1 serving **Fisherman's Sausage** (page 71)
4½ ounces Cooked Small Red Potatoes
1 teaspoon Margarine
6 Cooked Asparagus Spears
1½ cups Tossed Salad with 1½ teaspoons Thousand Island Dressing mixed with 2 tablespoons Plain Low-Fat Yogurt and ¼ teaspoon Mustard
½ cup Fruit Salad
Coffee or Tea

SNACK
1 cup Honeydew Chunks; 1 serving Reduced-Calorie Chocolate Dairy Drink

Optional Calories: 10

Day 2

BREAKFAST
½ cup Orange Sections
¼ cup Egg Substitute, scrambled
1 slice Reduced-Calorie Wheat Bread, toasted
1 teaspoon Reduced-Calorie Apricot Spread
½ cup Skim Milk
Coffee or Tea

LUNCH
Tuna–Green Beans Vinaigrette (2 ounces tuna with 1 cup cooked sliced green beans, ¼ cup sliced red onion, and 1½ teaspoons Italian dressing mixed with 2 teaspoons red wine vinegar on 4 lettuce leaves)
¾ ounce Breadsticks
½ medium Banana, sliced
Coffee, Tea, or Mineral Water

DINNER
1 serving **Flaky Herb Chicken** (page 98)
1 serving **Spinach and Bacon Sauté** (page 223)
Lettuce Wedge with 3 Cherry Tomatoes, cut into halves, with Balsamic Vinegar and Herbs
1 small Nectarine, sliced and topped with ¼ cup Plain Low-Fat Yogurt and Dash Nutmeg
Coffee or Tea

SNACK
1 Graham Cracker; ¾ cup Skim Milk

Optional Calories: 133

Day 3

BREAKFAST
⅓ cup Pineapple Juice
Strawberry Farina (½ cup cooked farina topped with 2 teaspoons reduced-calorie strawberry spread)
1 cup Skim Milk
Coffee or Tea

LUNCH
Cheddar on a Roll (2 ounces low-fat Cheddar cheese with ½ cup shredded lettuce and 1 teaspoon reduced-calorie margarine on 1-ounce roll)
½ cup Cauliflower Florets and Zucchini Sticks
1 cup Strawberries
Coffee, Tea, or Mineral Water

DINNER
1 serving **Red Snapper with Tomato Sauce** (page 76)
1 cup Cooked Broccoli Florets
Pepper-Mushroom Salad (4 red bell pepper rings with ½ cup sliced mushrooms, ½ ounce croutons, and 1½ teaspoons Italian dressing mixed with 2 teaspoons red wine vinegar on 4 lettuce leaves)
Pudding Sundae (½ cup reduced-calorie vanilla pudding topped with 1 tablespoon whipped topping and 1 maraschino cherry)
Coffee or Tea

SNACK
2 medium Plums; 1 serving **Spiced Chick-Pea Snack** (page 304)

Optional Calories: 54

BREAKFAST

½ medium Banana, sliced
¾ ounce Cold Cereal
1 cup Skim Milk
Coffee or Tea

LUNCH

Salmon Salad Pita (2 ounces salmon with 2 tablespoons chopped celery, 1 tablespoon chopped onion, 2 teaspoons reduced-calorie mayonnaise, and ½ cup shredded lettuce in 1-ounce pita)
½ cup Sliced Zucchini and 6 Celery Sticks
1 small Orange
Coffee, Tea, or Mineral Water

DINNER

1 serving **Stewed Potatoes with Beans** (page 184)
½ cup Cooked Sliced Carrots
1½ cups Tossed Salad with 1½ teaspoons Russian Dressing mixed with 2 tablespoons Plain Low-Fat Yogurt and ¼ teaspoon Mustard
1 cup Honeydew Chunks
Coffee or Tea

SNACK

1 small Nectarine; ¾ cup Skim Milk

Optional Calories: 45

BREAKFAST

½ cup Fruit Salad
Monterey Muffin Melt (½ English muffin, toasted and topped with 1 ounce low-fat Monterey Jack cheese, melted)
Vanilla Yogurt Crunch (1 cup plain low-fat yogurt mixed with 1 teaspoon wheat germ and ¼ teaspoon vanilla extract)
Coffee or Tea

LUNCH

Peanut Butter and Grape Spread Sandwich (1 tablespoon peanut butter with 2 teaspoons reduced-calorie grape spread on 2 slices reduced-calorie wheat bread)
2 medium Plums
Coffee, Tea, or Mineral Water

DINNER

1 serving **Szechuan Chicken** (page 104)
½ cup Cooked Parslied Rice
1 teaspoon Margarine
1½ cups Mixed Green Salad with Red Wine Vinegar and Herbs
Tea

SNACK

1 cup Strawberries topped with 1 tablespoon Whipped Topping; 1 serving Reduced-Calorie Chocolate Dairy Drink

Optional Calories: 49

BREAKFAST

⅓ cup Pineapple Juice
½ cup Cooked Cereal sprinkled with 1 teaspoon Brown Sugar
1 cup Skim Milk
Coffee or Tea

LUNCH

1 serving **Minted Chicken and Rice Soup** (page 93)
1½ cups Tossed Salad with 1½ teaspoons French Dressing mixed with 2 teaspoons Lemon Juice and ¼ teaspoon Mustard
2-inch wedge Honeydew Melon
Coffee, Tea, or Mineral Water

DINNER

4 ounces Baked Sole Fillet
1 serving **Spanish Rice** (page 280)
Pepper-Radish Salad (6 red bell pepper strips with ¼ cup sliced radishes and 1½ teaspoons buttermilk dressing mixed with 2 tablespoons plain low-fat yogurt on 4 torn lettuce leaves)
Coffee or Tea

SNACK

1 Graham Cracker; ¾ cup Skim Milk

Optional Calories: 30

BREAKFAST

½ cup Orange Sections
¾ ounce Cold Cereal
¾ cup Skim Milk
Coffee or Tea

LUNCH

1 serving **Sweet and Sour Chicken Salad** (page 131)
1-ounce Roll
1 small Nectarine
Coffee, Tea, or Mineral Water

DINNER

1 serving **Quick Veal Stew** (page 139)
3 ounces Cooked Diced Potato with Dash Paprika
1½ cups Tossed Salad with 1½ teaspoons Thousand Island Dressing mixed with 2 tablespoons Plain Low-Fat Yogurt and ¼ teaspoon Mustard
Coffee or Tea

SNACK

2 cups Plain Popcorn; ½ cup Reduced-Calorie Hot Cocoa

Optional Calories: 75

Total Optional Calories for the Week: 396

MENU PLANNER #8 — CHOLESTEROL REDUCED

Day 1

BREAKFAST

Morning Peach Melba (¼ cup part-skim ricotta cheese topped with 1 medium peach, sliced, and 1 teaspoon reduced-calorie raspberry spread)
¾ cup Skim Milk
Coffee or Tea

LUNCH

Tuna Salad on a Roll (2 ounces tuna with 2 tablespoons chopped celery, 1 tablespoon chopped onion, 2 teaspoons reduced-calorie mayonnaise, ½ cup shredded lettuce, and 3 tomato slices on 1-ounce roll)
6 each Carrot Sticks and Cucumber Spears
Coffee, Tea, or Mineral Water

DINNER

3 ounces Baked Chicken
1 serving **Pasta Puttanesca** (page 267)
1 cup Cooked Whole Green Beans
Mushroom-Sprout Salad (½ cup each sliced mushrooms and alfalfa sprouts with 1½ teaspoons Thousand Island dressing mixed with 2 tablespoons plain low-fat yogurt and ¼ teaspoon mustard on 1 cup torn lettuce)
½ medium Pink Grapefruit sprinkled with ½ teaspoon Sugar
Coffee or Tea

SNACK

1 serving **Minted Three-Berry Ice** (page 320); 1 serving Reduced-Calorie Chocolate Dairy Drink

Optional Calories: 48

Day 2

BREAKFAST

¼ small Cantaloupe
1 ounce Granola
½ cup Plain Low-Fat Yogurt
Coffee or Tea

LUNCH

Turkey-Spinach Pita (2 ounces sliced turkey with 3 tomato slices, 2 spinach leaves, and 1 teaspoon reduced-calorie mayonnaise in 1-ounce whole wheat pita)
½ cup each Cauliflower Florets and Sliced Zucchini
Coffee, Tea, or Mineral Water

DINNER

1 serving **Fluke with Lemon Sauce** (page 75)
1 small ear Corn
1 teaspoon Reduced-Calorie Margarine
½ cup Cooked Brussels Sprouts
1½ cups Tossed Salad with ¼ ounce Croutons and 1½ teaspoons French Dressing mixed with 2 teaspoons Lemon Juice and ¼ teaspoon Mustard
1 serving **Bananas and Berries au Chocolat** (page 322)
Coffee or Tea

SNACK

1 small Nectarine; 1 cup Skim Milk

Optional Calories: 170

Day 3

BREAKFAST

1 cup Low-Calorie Cranberry Juice
1 ounce Low-Fat Monterey Jack Cheese
½ Whole Wheat English Muffin, toasted
1 teaspoon Reduced-Calorie Margarine
1 serving Reduced-Calorie Hot Cocoa

LUNCH

Tuna Salad Sandwich (2 ounces tuna with 2 tablespoons chopped celery, 2 teaspoons reduced-calorie mayonnaise, and 2 each lettuce leaves, tomato slices, and green bell pepper rings on 2 slices reduced-calorie rye bread)
½ cup Broccoli Florets and 6 Celery Sticks
1 small Orange
Coffee, Tea, or Mineral Water

DINNER

Tomato-Veal Bake (2 ounces baked veal cutlet with ½ cup tomato sauce)
½ cup cooked Ziti Macaroni
½ cup Cooked Sliced Zucchini
Cucumber-Carrot Toss (1 cup torn lettuce with ½ cup sliced cucumber and ¼ cup shredded carrot plus red wine vinegar and herbs)
Blueberry Pudding (½ cup each reduced-calorie vanilla pudding and blueberries)
Coffee or Tea

SNACK

1 serving **Santa Fe Peanuts** (page 303); 12 fluid ounces Light Beer

Optional Calories: 100

BREAKFAST
½ cup Blueberries
¼ cup Part-Skim Ricotta Cheese
1 slice Pumpernickel Bread
1 cup Skim Milk
Coffee or Tea

LUNCH
Tuna-Vegetable Toss (2 ounces tuna with 1½ cups torn lettuce, 4 tomato wedges, ½ cup each sliced cucumber and celery, ¼ cup each sliced carrot and radishes, and 1½ teaspoons French dressing mixed with 2 teaspoons lemon juice and ¼ teaspoon mustard)
1 serving Cranberry Cooler (page 311)

DINNER
1 serving Lemon Chicken with Mushrooms (page 113)
¼ cup each Cooked Cauliflower and Broccoli Florets
1½ cups Tossed Salad with 1½ teaspoons Italian Dressing
1 cup Cantaloupe Balls
Coffee or Tea

SNACK
3 Graham Crackers; 1 serving Reduced-Calorie Vanilla Dairy Drink

Optional Calories: 25

Total Optional Calories for the Week: 444

BREAKFAST
1 serving Cinnamon-Apple Farina (page 241)
1 cup Skim Milk
Coffee or Tea

LUNCH
Turkey Salad Sandwich (2 ounces diced turkey with 2 tablespoons chopped celery, 1 teaspoon reduced-calorie mayonnaise, and 2 each green bell pepper rings and lettuce leaves on 2 slices reduced-calorie wheat bread)
½ cup Reduced-Calorie Butterscotch Pudding
Coffee, Tea, or Mineral Water

DINNER
1 serving Escarole and Vegetable Soup (page 203)
3 ounces Baked Sole Fillet
3 ounces Cooked Sliced Red Potatoes
1 teaspoon Reduced-Calorie Margarine
6 Cooked Asparagus Spears
1½ cups Tossed Salad with Lemon Juice and Herbs
Honey Grapefruit (½ medium pink grapefruit drizzled with ½ teaspoon honey)
Coffee or Tea

SNACK
10 large Cherries; ¾ cup Skim Milk

Optional Calories: 50

BREAKFAST
½ cup Orange Juice
¼ cup Egg Substitute, scrambled
1 slice Reduced-Calorie Rye Bread, toasted, with 2 teaspoons Reduced-Calorie Raspberry Spread
1 cup Skim Milk
Coffee or Tea

LUNCH
Chick-Pea and Cheese Salad (2 ounces rinsed drained canned chick-peas with 1 ounce low-fat Cheddar cheese, shredded, 1 cup torn lettuce, 6 tomato wedges, ½ cup sliced cucumber, ¼ cup sliced celery, and 1 tablespoon sliced Caesar dressing)
¾ ounce Crispbreads
1 small Pear
Coffee, Tea, or Mineral Water

DINNER
3 ounces Sliced Poached Chicken
1 serving Southwestern Corn Bread "Stuffing" (page 253)
½ cup Cooked Cauliflower Florets
1½ cups Mixed Green Salad with Lemon Juice and Herbs
Coffee or Tea

SNACK
3 Graham Crackers; 1 cup Skim Milk

Optional Calories: 21

BREAKFAST
½ medium Banana, sliced
¾ ounce Cold Cereal
1 cup Skim Milk
Coffee or Tea

LUNCH
Turkey Sandwich (2 ounces sliced turkey with ½ cup each shredded lettuce and bean sprouts and 1 teaspoon reduced-calorie mayonnaise on 1-ounce roll)
1 Dill Pickle Spear and 6 Red Bell Pepper Strips
10 large Cherries
Coffee, Tea, or Mineral Water

DINNER
1 serving Swordfish Mediterranean (page 78)
Succotash (¼ cup each cooked green lima beans and drained canned whole-kernel corn)
Tomato-Broccoli Salad (3 cherry tomatoes, cut into halves, with ½ cup broccoli florets and 1½ teaspoons Italian dressing mixed with 2 teaspoons red wine vinegar on 2 lettuce leaves)
¼ small Cantaloupe
Coffee or Tea

SNACK
1 medium Peach; 1 serving Reduced-Calorie Chocolate Dairy Drink

Optional Calories: 30

Appendix

About Weighing and Measuring

- Always take time to measure and weigh ingredients carefully; this is vital to both recipe results and weight control. Don't try to judge amounts by eye.
- To weigh foods, use a scale.
- To measure liquids, use a standard glass or clear plastic measuring cup. Place it on a level surface and read markings at eye level. Fill the cup just to the appropriate marking. To measure less than ¼ cup, use standard measuring spoons.
- To measure dry ingredients, use metal or plastic measuring cups that come in sets of four: ¼ cup, ⅓ cup, ½ cup, and 1 cup. Spoon the ingredients into the cup, then level with the straight edge of a knife or metal spatula. To measure less than ¼ cup, use standard measuring spoons and, unless otherwise directed, level as for measuring cup.
- A dash is about ¹⁄₁₆ of a teaspoon (½ of a ⅛-teaspoon measure or ¼ of a ¼-teaspoon measure).
- In any recipe for more than one serving it is important to mix ingredients well and to divide evenly so that each portion will be the same size.
- Weights in recipes are given in pounds and fractions of a pound. See below for ounce equivalents.

1 pound = 16 ounces	½ pound = 8 ounces
¾ pound = 12 ounces	¼ pound = 4 ounces

Pan Substitutions

It's best to use the pan size that's recommended in a recipe; however, if your kitchen isn't equipped with that particular pan, chances are a substitution will work just as well. The pan size is determined by the volume of food it holds. When substituting, use a pan as close to the recommended size as possible. Food cooked in too small a pan may boil over; food cooked in too large a pan may dry out or burn. To determine the dimensions of a baking pan, measure across the top, between the inside edges. To determine the volume, measure the amount of water the pan holds when completely filled.

When you use a pan that is a different size from the one recommended, it may be necessary to adjust the suggested cooking time. Depending on the size of the pan and the depth of the food in it, you may need to add or subtract 5 to 10 minutes. If you substitute glass or glass-ceramic for metal, the oven temperature should be reduced by 25°F.

The following chart provides some common pan substitutions.

Recommended Size	Approximate Volume	Possible Substitutions
8 x 1½-inch round baking pan	1½ quarts	10 x 6 x 2-inch baking dish 9 x 1½-inch round baking pan 8 x 4 x 2-inch loaf pan 9-inch pie plate
8 x 8 x 2-inch baking pan	2 quarts	11 x 7 x 1½-inch baking pan 12 x 7½ x 2-inch baking pan 9 x 5 x 3-inch loaf pan two 8 x 1½-inch round baking pans
13 x 9 x 2-inch baking pan	3 quarts	14 x 11 x 2-inch baking dish two 9 x 1½-inch round baking pans two 8 x 1½-inch round baking pans

Dry and Liquid Measure Equivalents

Teaspoons	Tablespoons	Cups	Fluid Ounces
3 teaspoons	1 tablespoon		½ fluid ounce
6 teaspoons	2 tablespoons	⅛ cup	1 fluid ounce
8 teaspoons	2 tablespoons plus 2 teaspoons	⅙ cup	
12 teaspoons	4 tablespoons	¼ cup	2 fluid ounces
15 teaspoons	5 tablespoons	⅓ cup less 1 teaspoon	
16 teaspoons	5 tablespoons plus 1 teaspoon	⅓ cup	
18 teaspoons	6 tablespoons	⅓ cup plus 2 teaspoons	3 fluid ounces
24 teaspoons	8 tablespoons	½ cup	4 fluid ounces
30 teaspoons	10 tablespoons	½ cup plus 2 tablespoons	5 fluid ounces
32 teaspoons	10 tablespoons plus 2 teaspoons	⅔ cup	
36 teaspoons	12 tablespoons	¾ cup	6 fluid ounces
42 teaspoons	14 tablespoons	1 cup less 2 tablespoons	7 fluid ounces
45 teaspoons	15 tablespoons	1 cup less 1 tablespoon	
48 teaspoons	16 tablespoons	1 cup	8 fluid ounces

Note: Measurements of less than ⅛ teaspoon are considered a dash or a pinch.

Metric Conversions

If you are converting the recipes in this book to metric measurements, use the following chart as a guide.

Volume

¼ teaspoon	1 milliliter
½ teaspoon	2 milliliters
1 teaspoon	5 milliliters
1 tablespoon	15 milliliters
2 tablespoons	30 milliliters
3 tablespoons	45 milliliters
¼ cup	50 milliliters
⅓ cup	75 milliliters
½ cup	125 milliliters
⅔ cup	150 milliliters
¾ cup	175 milliliters
1 cup	250 milliliters
1 quart	1 liter

Weight

1 ounce	30 grams
¼ pound	120 grams
½ pound	240 grams
¾ pound	360 grams
1 pound	480 grams

Length

1 inch	25 millimeters
1 inch	2.5 centimeters

Oven Temperatures

250°F	120°C
275°F	140°C
300°F	150°C
325°F	160°C
350°F	180°C
375°F	190°C
400°F	200°C
425°F	220°C
450°F	230°C
475°F	250°C
500°F	260°C
525°F	270°C

Index